ZEW Economic Studies

Publication Series of the Centre for European Economic Research (ZEW), Mannheim, Germany

Friedrich Heinemann • Philipp Mohl
Steffen Osterloh

Reform Options for the EU Own Resources System

Physica-Verlag
A Springer Company

ZEW
Zentrum für Europäische
Wirtschaftsforschung GmbH

Series Editor
Prof. Dr. Dr. h.c. mult. Wolfang Franz

Authors
Dr. Friedrich Heinemann
Philipp Mohl
Steffen Osterloh

Centre for European Economic Research (ZEW)
L7, 1
68161 Mannheim
Germany

heinemann@zew.de
mohl@zew.de
osterloh@zew.de

ISBN 978-3-7908-2065-2 e-ISBN 978-3-7908-2066-9

DOI: 10.1007/978-3-7908-2066-9

Library of Congress Control Number: 2008929499

Cover design: WMXDesign GmbH, Heidelberg

Printed on acid-free paper

9 8 7 6 5 4 3 2 1

springer.com

Preface

The general review of the European Union's budget scheduled for the years 2008 and 2009 offers a unique opportunity for reflections. Explicitly this review is "without taboos" so that also substantive changes can and should be debated.

Without doubt much better budgetary systems can be imagined compared to the status quo of the EU budget which is the outcome of a path-dependent process and where many details are only understandable by taking account of the historical context of past decisions. However, even if much better systems could be designed in theory, each reform suggestion, in the end, must pass the reality check of finding unanimous support from all 27 member countries. This restriction heavily limits the universe of available reform options.

Faced with that difficulty the ZEW project team embarked on the adventure to think about possible reform options for the future EU own resource system. This volume documents the conclusions. At first sight our reform suggestion may appear to be of a rather piecemeal nature since we recommend a reform model with strong ties to the status quo. Nevertheless, we are convinced that our seemingly minor changes will set the budget on a path towards a more rational European budget which, in the end, will create leeway for financing European policies with a true European value added.

We gratefully acknowledge financial support from the German Federal Ministry of Finance in conducting this study.

Mannheim, April 2008

Friedrich Heinemann, Philipp Mohl and Steffen Osterloh

Table of Contents

1 Introduction

The agreement on the EU financial framework for the years 2007-2013 has been received with mixed feelings both in the political and the academic debate. On the one hand, the very fact that the enlarged Union is able to reach a consensus on a highly contentious issue like the budget demonstrates that the financial constitution functions and safeguards the capability to act. On the other hand, the agreement does not include any far-reaching reforms neither on the expenditure side nor on the revenue side although the need for reforms is hardly debatable for either side of the budget. Furthermore, an inflation of special provisions has occurred which was obviously necessary to buy consensus from all involved parties. This has come at the cost of an increasing intransparency of the system which stands in sharp contrast to the aim of making the system more comprehensible for European voters and taxpayers.

Since the heads of states and governments themselves had to acknowledge the limits of the budgetary settlement, they agreed on "a comprehensive reassessment of the financial framework, covering both revenue and expenditure" which is to take place in the years 2008/2009 (European Council, 2005). This review will offer an opportunity which has not been given in earlier negotiations: the chance for fundamental reflections on reform options without the urgent pressure to instantly arrive at a final decision. In this sense the review can be seen as a chance to develop options which will be available at the next settlement which is due towards the end of the current financial framework.

This report aims at contributing to this review with a clear focus on the revenue side of the budget. Key questions addressed in this study refer to the preferable types of own resources, fundamental alternatives to the existing sources and the justification and specification of an appropriate correction mechanism. Although this report's analytical work is thus clearly targeted at the revenue side, it is nevertheless based on the understanding that budgetary reform must simultaneously relate to both sides of the budget. The suitability of certain solutions on the revenue side heavily depends on the achievable changes on the expenditure side.

Even though our work benefits from the preceding literature dealing with possible revenue side reforms, such as the Commission's own resource reports, it nevertheless advances this literature in some important respects. First, we base our analysis on a comprehensive study of the incentives faced by all budgetary players. As the literature on budgetary institutions for national states has clarified, institutionally determined incentives are crucial for the efficiency of budgetary policy. In particular, institutional safeguards against the so-called "common pool problem" are important. The common pool problem is linked to the fact that a jurisdiction's overall revenue is used to finance programmes for the benefit of particular constituencies. Up to now this problem has been widely ignored in the reform literature on the EU own resources system, even though its relevance for budgetary policy in general is an established fact in the literature. This perspective leads us to an important conclusion. In particular, the expectation that the mere establishment of a new tax-based own resource would advance fiscal discipline is shown to be too simplistic. Secondly, we take the distribution issue into account as an important restriction to any politically realistic reform. It may be regrettable but the "juste retour" thinking cannot be neglected and limits the set of available reform options. Any reform which would involve a substantial divergence in distributive effects from important reference points (which are either the status quo's distribution or a burden sharing corresponding to countries' relative wealth) will hardly reach a consensus.

We come to the conclusion that even when taking these severe restrictions into account, the own resource system can be improved. Our reform model, based on a complete elimination of the VAT resource and a generalised (with respect to the benefiting countries) but limited (with respect to the included types of expenditures) correction mechanism, not only sets the incentives right. It also creates a distributive outcome with a logical correspondence to relative wealth and does not diverge too far from the status quo.

2 Criteria for a Fair and Efficient Own Resources System

Both the evaluation of the own resource system's status quo and the reform suggestions should be based on well-defined assessment criteria. The explicit formulation of such criteria is indeed a common feature of many contributions to the literature on the own resource system (European Commission, 1998, 2004a; Caesar, 1990; Cattoir, 2004; Begg & Grimwade, 1998; Walthes, 1996; Henke, 1997; Heinemann, 2003).

However, with regard to these criteria lists alone, caution is required. The manner in which assessment criteria are defined and (explicitly or implicitly) weighted predetermines analytical results. Hence, the definition of criteria is a degree of freedom to influence subsequent recommendations. This problem is aggravated by the fact that an ad hoc approach often characterises the foundation of criteria lists: Plausible and appealing dimensions for assessment benchmarks are formulated without paying too much attention to their link to well-established theories.

Obviously, a certain degree of subjectivity in the definition of criteria is unavoidable since their choice and specification is also influenced by assumptions and value judgements, for example, with regard to the role of the state in the economy, the future model of the European Union or the importance of budgetary restrictions for politicians and bureaucrats. Nevertheless, these assumptions should be explicated as far as possible.

In the following, we exemplify by means of the Commission's own resources report of 2004, how problematic and incomplete some of the criteria lists are. We, then, proceed to specify our own list of assessment criteria. Although we are aware of the fact that our list is also influenced by subjective assumptions and value judgements, we attempt to be explicit about our assumptions and the link to theory. These links to the literature strands of fiscal federalism and public choice theories and other theoretical concepts are further developed in the appendix (see section 8.1).

Box 1. Assessment criteria of the own resources report 2004

Visibility and simplicity

Contents: The financing system should create a direct and visible link between the citizens and the EU budget. The system should be comprehensible for the citizens.

Main argument: Citizens should have a clear perception of the costs of the EU budget which would also make the European Parliament more accountable for the cost dimension of EU policy measures.

Financial autonomy

Contents: The EU budget should be financed from an autonomous manner. A significant dependence of the budget on national budgets should be avoided.

Main argument: The link between national budgets and the EU budget causes member states to follow "ill-defined concepts of national benefit" with regard to the financing of the budget.

Efficient allocation of economic resources

Contents: Own resources should impose as few economic distortions on relative prices or revenue collection incentives as possible. The system should contribute to internalising externalities arising, e.g., from pollution.

Main argument: Own resource system should not distort the functioning of the internal market.

Sufficiency and stability

Contents: The resources must be sufficient to finance the EU budget in the long run. Individual financing sources should, therefore, be significant in relation to the EU budget.

Main argument: The EU budget needs a stable and reliable financing source.

Cost-effectiveness

Contents: Administrative costs of any own resource should be low relative to its yield.

Main argument: Standard desideratum.

Equity

Contents: The budgetary burden – defined as gross contributions – should be distributed justly shared among both member states and citizens. The own resources report focusses on member states' equity and regards GNI as the appropriate benchmark.

Main argument: Fairness considerations.

Source: European Commission (2004a).

The criterion "visibility and simplicity" exclusively focusses on the link between citizens and the budget. Without a doubt, cost transparency on the side of citizens-taxpayers is a helpful element in guaranteeing incentives for balancing costs and benefits of public activities. However, this element is by no means a sufficient condition for efficient budgetary outcomes. As we will analyse in detail (see section 3.5), budgetary decision processes are confronted with many other problems which are virulent even if there is a clear tax link between citizens and the budget: Information problems on the side of voters, bureaucratic self-interests, lobby power and many other phenomena can impair budgetary efficiency and are not simply solved by a direct tax paid by citizens to the budget in question. Problems are aggravated if there is a discrepancy between the regional or sectoral concentration of those who benefit from a budget and those who pay for it (the "common pool problem") – a problem highly relevant in the context of the EU budget. A full analysis of the overall system's incentives is necessary to judge which improvements would optimise the budgetary outcomes.

The criterion "financial autonomy" is probably the clearest example that reflects the self-interest of the Commission's criteria list. It is obvious that autonomy in raising EU revenues is in the interest of the European bureaucracy. It is, however, much less obvious whether revenue autonomy of the EU level is really desirable without further conditions. The authors of the 2004 own resources report argue that today's own resources system with its de facto national contributions was responsible for the "narrow focus on national interest". This argument is hardly convincing. The net balance thinking of member states which indeed is an obstacle to the rational evolution of the system is not caused by the revenue side of the budget in the first place. It is rather a consequence of current spending priorities where the location of recipients is clearly identifiable. Simply transforming the revenue side of such a system towards financial autonomy would not reduce the member states' interests to fight for receipts from structural or agricultural transfer policies to be as high as possible. A further shortcoming of the report's argumentation in this regard is that it ignores the possibility that financial dependence on member states may have its merits with respect to budgetary discipline. Institutions such as the Stability and Growth Pact or constitutional debt or spending limits as they exist in many states indicate that unrestricted "financial autonomy" can be problematic. This kind of reasoning convincingly motivated, for example, by public choice theory (see section 8.1.3) is largely absent in the own resources report.

The "efficient allocation" criterion of the own resources report is also applied in a fairly restricted fashion and is only related to immediate distortions and incentives resulting from the specification of own resources. The insights are not unreasonable. Nevertheless, in a wider perspective, the efficient allocation criterion should be based on fiscal federalism insights and this theory's messages about the conditions for an efficient public goods provision (see section 8.1.2). In this wider perspective, the key question is whether marginal benefits from the provision of public goods match marginal costs in a federation and whether the resulting public goods provision reflects the true (and possibly heterogeneous) preferences of the citizens.

In this general formulation the criterion of "sufficiency" is also prone to misunderstandings. On the one hand, it is desirable that revenue sources' yields stand in a reasonable relation to the targeted budget size – also from the point of view of administrative cost-effectiveness. On the other hand, however, the perceived scarcity of resources is a desirable feature of any disciplining budgetary system. Frequent experiences in the field of budgetary policy show that the size of available revenues determines spending and not the other way round. Therefore, revenue reforms should avoid any movement towards a softer budget constraint. The national experience of recent years with serious budgetary restrictions has demonstrated how helpful revenue constraints are for boosting efficiency of public spending. If one assumes (quite realistically with a look at current spending priorities) that significant shares of EU expenditure are questionable with regard to the resulting European value added, "scarcity" of own resources would be no disadvantage. A new own resource giving substantial revenue leeway to the budget would risk, for example, a possible abatement of the beneficial budgetary reform pressure on the Common Agricultural Policies. Therefore, the sufficiency criterion should be applied with caution and should be understood as a mere screening criterion to exclude revenue sources with trivial yield in the view of the EU budget's dimension.

The "stability" criterion is hardly controversial. Given that EU spending priorities follow long-run objectives and given the absence of debt facilities, EU own resources should not be characterised by volatility. Not questionable is also the fact that the own resources should be characterised by a "cost-effectiveness" of administration.

Finally, fairness considerations do indeed deserve considerable large attention because an EU budgetary system which is perceived to be unfair puts the support for European integration at risk. However, also with respect to this criterion, the subtleties of specification are also crucial. In the Commission's own resources report the authors limit these considerations to the gross contributions ("equity in gross contribution"*)*. It is hardly possible to judge on fairness perceptions in an objective way. However, the implied isolated view at the own resources side of the budget hardly reflects fairness perceptions as they are politically relevant. We will demonstrate in section 3.6 that the own resources distributive patterns stand in a close logical relation to the distributive pattern of the expenditure side. It is neither logically convincing nor politically realistic to neglect this by limiting fairness considerations to the issue of gross contributions.

In summary, a criteria list as the one used by the authors of the Commission own resources report is open for improvement:

- It widely ignores the fact that the efficiency of budgetary outcomes cannot be pinned down to isolated aspects, such as revenue transparency, but must be safeguarded by well-balanced institutional constraints and incentives for all players in the "budgetary game".
- The criteria do not exploit the differentiated insights of the theory of fiscal federalism with respect to conditions for an efficient public goods production in a multi-layer system.

- The list and its motivation largely ignore political-economic considerations and problems associated, for example, with the budget-maximising motivations of bureaucrats or the fundamental common pool problems virulent in practically all budgetary contexts. With regard to political-economic aspects, the Commission approach is characterised by a subtle asymmetry: While "a narrow focus on national self-interest" is said to characterise national approaches to the EU budget, European actors are implicitly assumed to be European welfare maximisers. Here, a more balanced view is desirable.
- The list suffers from selective interpretations for which the equity interpretation is a prominent example.

Given these problems, we prefer to base our analysis of the status quo and reform options on an improved list of guiding criteria. Theoretical reference points are the following (for details, see section 8.1).

The Theory of Fiscal Federalism

This theory has developed a set of criteria such as preference homogeneity, spillovers or economies of scale in public goods production in order to decide on the optimum assignment of competencies in a multi-layer federal system. Corner stones are the decentralisation theorem by Wallace Oates (1972) and the principle of fiscal equivalence (Olson, 1969). The decentralisation theorem stresses the merits of lower level competencies in reflecting different public goods preferences, whereas the principle of fiscal equivalence demands the identity of public good's users and payers in order to guarantee an efficient public goods production. The case for centralisation is supported by substantial externalities of decentralised competencies or economies of scale in the provision of public services. With regard to the debate on revenues this theory has at least two messages: First, a precondition for efficient public goods production is the correct simultaneous assignment of both revenue and spending competencies. Financing national or regional public goods by European resources contradicts the equivalence principle and fosters inefficiencies. Secondly, if there are substantial heterogeneities with regard to distributive and tax preferences, the own resources system should offer degrees of freedom to reflect this preference divergence.

Public Choice Approaches

Even if one does not accept the idea that politicians and bureaucrats are mere maximisers of narrow self-interest, any realistic analysis will take into account that in addition to general welfare motivations other aspects such as budget maximisation are relevant drivers of bureaucrats' behaviour at all federal levels. Furthermore, politicians are realistically modelled to pay close attention to re-election chances which are not necessarily maximised by following long-run strategies to foster welfare. As a consequence of this balanced view, budgetary restrictions are an important element at the national and European level alike. In particular, the common pool problem associated with the financing of regional spending projects from a common pool of public revenues must be addressed.

Further theoretical considerations are related to the compatibility of an own resources system with a stable integration process (see section 8.1.4) and the merits of general taxation principles (see section 8.1.5). On that basis we summarise our assessment criteria for a rational own resources system as depicted in Box 2 (for further details and refinements, see section 8.1).

Box 2. Assessment criteria for a rational own resources system

Fostering efficient public goods provision

Theoretical basis: Theory of fiscal federalism

Desiderata:

- Allowing for heterogeneous tax preferences
- Internalisation of externalities
- Identity of users and payers of public goods
- Subsidiarity principle (based on decentralisation theorem)
- Respecting national federal systems

Constraining narrow self-interest and creating budgetary discipline

Theoretical basis: Public choice theory

Desiderata:

- Robust budgetary institutions counterbalancing narrow self-interest of bureaucrats, politicians or lobby power
- Solutions to the "common pool" problem of budgetary policy

Integration compatibility

Theoretical basis: Integration theory

Desiderata:

- Low transaction costs in the settlement of political conflicts
- Fairness according to generally accepted fairness judgements
- Transparency

General principles of taxation

Theoretical basis: Tax theory, welfare economics

Desiderata:

- Neutrality
- Stability
- Cost-effectiveness of administration
- Reliability

Fostering Efficient Public Good Provision

The appropriate assignment of political competencies to the different levels in a federation is crucial for the resulting efficiency of public goods provision. Nevertheless, the manner of financing the different government budgets in a federation offers additional handles to set efficiency-inducing incentives. The case for a high degree of revenue autonomy of the European level is weakened if tax preferences are heterogeneous among member countries or if EU spending priorities cannot be classified as European public goods.

Constraining Narrow Self-Interest and Creating Budgetary Discipline

The Community's revenue system should contribute to an institutional environment conducive for budgetary discipline and helpful in overcoming bureaucratic or political overspending incentives. This criterion can hardly be used in favour of or against a specific revenue source but must be applied to the overall budgetary system, its function, interdependencies and incentives for all relevant actors.

Integration Compatibility

Conflicts of interest will always be a fact of life in European budgetary politics as it continues to be the case in federal countries. Budgetary institutions and the revenue system should contribute to efficient and low transaction costs in the settlement of conflicts. The institution of the multi-annual financial framework is a good example for an institutional innovation which has significantly reduced transaction costs by relieving the annual budgetary process of distribution fights.

Since the political support of citizens is crucial for the long-run success of European integration, restrictions with regard to the perceived fairness and transparency of the budgetary system must be respected.

General Principles of Taxation

Once it comes to the scrutiny of single revenue items, general principles of taxation become helpful. If there is a choice between different revenue types which have similar desirable effects within the overall budgetary system, this choice will clearly be guided by criteria such as neutrality, cost-effectiveness, stability or reliability.

Compared to the European Commission's list, our assessment criteria clearly pay more attention to the incentives set by the own resources system within the context of the budgetary system as a whole. We are convinced that this holistic approach is the appropriate starting point to reflect the desirable evolution of the own resources system. In the following, these criteria will guide our analysis both in the assessment of the status quo and in the derivation of reform proposals.

3 Assessing the Status Quo

3.1 Introduction

This section is devoted to an analysis of the status quo of the EU system of own resources within the context of the overall budgetary system of the EU. Such a status quo analysis is indispensable for defining priorities for reform. In order to do justice to the current own resources system, it is necessary to look at it within its overall context. Many characteristics of the revenue side are hard to understand by themselves because they reflect adjustments deemed necessary with respect, for example, to spending side developments. Furthermore, it is essential to understand how the current own resources system, its instruments and definitions interact with the other budgetary institutions in the overall institutional context. Finally, it is important to develop an understanding of how the relevant players in EU budgetary policy may react to the incentives set by the design of the own resources system. This broad analytical perspective explains the section's structure. Before looking at the details of the own resources system and the single items, we start by summarising key institutional features of the system and identifying incentives of major players within that system. Furthermore, we briefly look into its historical evolution and analyse the extent and sources of redistribution arising before proceeding to the details of the own resources system. These analytical elements allow us to draw comprehensive conclusions about the strong and weak features of the system.

3.2 Key Institutional Features of the System

This section briefly presents the key institutional aspects of the EU budgetary system (for a more detailed description, see European Commission, 2002). Although this study concentrates on the analysis of the revenue side of the EU budget, a good understanding of the expenditure side is necessary for a profound analysis of the institutional set-up and the resulting budgetary incentives.

To begin with, the EU is almost entirely financed by the so-called own resources, which are collected by the member states but to which the EU is legally entitled. Generally, expenditures that are decided by the European Council have to be financed. Nevertheless, the power of the EU with regard to fiscal policy is limited (Art. 268-280 Treaty establishing the European Community, TEC). The European Union is not allowed to open new sources of money. Instead, the introduction of new own resources would require both an unanimous decision of the members of the European Council and the approval of the national parliaments according to their legal norms (Art. 269(2) TEC). This hints at the intergovernmental nature of the Union's budgetary system implying that the member states are de facto still the main actors bearing the financial responsibility for the European Union. In this respect, labelling the EU financial resources as "EU own resources" is rather misleading because even though the EU is legally entitled to the "EU own-resources", it ignores the dependence on the member states.

Furthermore, since the Treaty of Rome the EU has operated under the following budgetary principles (Begg & Grimwade, 1998):

- unity, i.e. all revenues and expenditures must be included in a single budget;[1]
- annuality, i.e. revenues and expenditures must be drawn up and adopted on an annual basis;
- equilibrium, i.e. revenue must always equal expenditure (the balanced budget rule);
- universality, i.e. total revenue must cover total payment appropriations and all revenue and expenditure must be entered in full without any adjustment against each other;
- specification, i.e. each expenditure item must have a specific objective;
- transparency (since 2002), i.e. the European Commission has to publish the adopted budget and consolidated financial statements and financial management reports immediately.

The principle of equilibrium in particular is important for the understanding of the revenue and expenditure policy of the EU. From this principle the interdependence between revenue and expenditure side of the budget is derived. It is not possible to reduce the own resources independently from the expenditure side. Furthermore, the budget has to be balanced according to Art. 268 TEC. Consequently, the European institutions are generally not allowed to borrow for budgetary purposes. There are only few exceptions to this, for example, credits to non-European countries as well as the limited right to borrow for the European Investment Bank.

---

1 One exception to this principle is that the spending for the European Development Fund (EDF) (22.7 billion EUR) is not included in the final Financial Perspective (see section 3.4). The reason for this is that the EDF is not funded from the European budget but through separate contributions by the member states. In its original 2004 proposal, the Commission proposed the 'budgetisation' of the EDF and, therefore, included it into the financial framework. However, this proposal was not accepted by the member states, which means that the EDF will continue to be financed outside the EU budget.

3.2.1 The Budgetary Process in Brief

The preparation of the budget is divided into two parts:

- The multi-annual guidelines and ceilings of the EU budget are regulated within the "Financial Perspective" (FP).
- The precise annual amounts of revenue and expenditure are regulated in the annual budget procedure.

The introduction of the multi-annual budget plan dates back to the experiences of the late 1970s and early 1980s. At that time, budgetary negotiations were characterised by heavy confrontations between the European Parliament and the European Council, which even ended up with entire draft budgets being rejected by the European Parliament. Furthermore, the rise in spending on the agricultural policy and the introduction of the UK rebate led to a lack of sufficient resources. In order to counteract these developments, the European Council decided to adopt the EU budget via multi-annual Financial Perspectives (for more details, see Lindner, 2003). Within these packages, the overall ceiling of the budget relative to the GNI of the EU member states and the general levels of expenditure for each main budgetary category are defined.

The Financial Perspective combines intergovernmental and supranational elements. Basically, it is implemented in three steps, this sequence being crucial for the relative negotiation power of the budgetary institutions. In a first step, the European Commission initiates the bargaining process on the Financial Perspective. The Commission serves as an agenda-setter preparing the strategic goals and the financial focus of the EU. This first step of the process is completed with the Commission's proposal of a multi-annual Financial Perspective.

In a second step, the members of the European Council enter the bargaining process. The bargaining is restricted by the requirement of unanimity of the member states in the Council. Furthermore, the members have to take into account that they need the approval of the European Parliament and the Commission. Against the background of this strategic constellation, the European Council determines a Financial Perspective.

In the third step of the bargaining process, the European Parliament (EP) enters the negotiations. This is necessary because the legal codification of the political agreement of the member states requires three legal instruments:

- The term "Financial Perspective" is not legally codified. Art. 272 TEC only regulates the annual budget procedure. As a result, in order to enforce the Financial Perspective, an Inter-Institutional Agreement is necessary to commit the European Parliament and the European Commission to the targets of the Financial Perspective (Monar, 1994). One important feature of the Financial Perspective binds the three parties to the ceilings of the Financial Perspective.
- As the pattern of the financing of the European Union is not legally codified, the Financial Perspective has to be determined within an own resources decision (Art. 269 TEC). This decision has to be unanimously adopted in the European Council and must be ratified by the national parliaments. In this manner, the responsibility for the financing of the EU is transferred to the national level.

- The final implementation requires the adoption of numerous regulations which serve as a legal basis of the expenditure programmes of the EU policies. In most cases, these regulations are implemented under the codecision procedure. Almost 90 % of the expenditure programmes expire so that they require a new legal basis at the beginning of each Financial Perspective.

In the third step, the Members of Parliament (MEP) can postulate changes in the agreement of the European Council. The EP can hardly re-negotiate single items of the Council's agreement. However, it can threaten not to agree to the compromise within the final Inter-Institutional Agreement. Thus, it often succeeds in introducing several (albeit limited) modifications (Becker, 2000, 2005a, 2005b). If the EP rejected the agreement, the EU budget would operate on the basis of the annual budget procedure according to Art. 272 TEC. This would imply less planning reliability concerning the distribution of EU expenditure.

While the member states have a strong interest in preventing a re-negotiation of the compromise, the MEP aim at asserting their claims. Nevertheless, at this stage the EP, the Commission and the Council do not have an interest in a breakdown of the Financial Perspective because this might lead to delayed start-up of the EU policies leading to a reduced level of EU policies. Hence, the "semi-voluntary character" (Enderlein, Lindner, Calvo-Gonzalez & Ritter, 2005: 16) of the Financial Perspective obliges actors to cooperate.

Summing up, due to the fact that the Financial Perspective is not established by law, the FP is not automatically renewed and its existence hinges on the ability of the member states and subsequently of the Commission and the European Parliament to agree on a new multi-annual budget plan. One feature of the use of the unanimity rule is that the overall policy impact must be allocative rather than redistributive: Everyone must win, otherwise an individual member would exercise a veto (Mueller, 2003). Generally, the overall influence of the EP to enforce modifications is limited because the costs of a failure of the implementation of a Financial Perspective are high. Although the Commission and the EP as signatories of the Inter-Institutional Agreement have a veto power over the ceilings of the Financial Perspective, they rarely exercise it. The negotiations on the most recent Financial Perspective showed that the EP had only a marginal impact on the allocation of the total amount of the EU budget (see Becker, 2006).

Apart from the multi-annual perspective, the precise amounts of revenue and expenditure are agreed upon within the annual budget procedure. Without going into great detail, the annual budget procedure is set out in Art. 272 of the TEC. It is passed within an Inter-Institutional Agreement between the Council, the EP and the Commission.[2] The Council has the final say on compulsory expenditure, i.e. expenditure that is necessary under the treaties. This is mostly expenditure on the Common Agricultural Policy (CAP) and the small amount of expenditure arising from international agreements. In combination, the Council and the EP have the final say on non-compulsory expenditure, which includes the annual expenditure on economic and social cohesion and most expenditure on other internal policies,

---

2 For a more detailed explanation of the inter-institutional annual budget cycle, see, among others, Hix (2005: 280).

such as research, education and financial support for the European level interest groups. In contrast to the requirement of unanimity in the Council for the multi-annual package deals, the annual budget is adopted by qualified majority voting in the Council and by an absolute majority of all MEP.

Assessing this EU financial framework, the big advantages of the Financial Perspective are the planning stability and a reduction of conflict by agreeing on a binding 7-year budget perspective. In that respect, the introduction of the Financial Perspective can be seen as an attempt to restrict the scope for political choice during the annual budgetary procedure (Enderlein et al., 2005). Furthermore, the link of expenditure and revenue side within the Financial Perspective has made it impossible for expenditure-led budgets to exceed existing resources (Shackleton, 1990). Hence, the balanced budget rule, i.e. EU expenditures must not exceed EU revenues, is a significant institutional constraint for the EU budget.

One disadvantage of the Financial Perspective is that it limits the flexibility of budgetary actors and introduces a strong status-quo bias. Even though the Financial Perspective is not automatically renewed at the end of the 7-year period, the use of veto power and the bargaining dynamics lead to a largely incremental revision of the ceilings (Hix, 2005), thus, respecting the key spending of member states, such as the rebate for the United Kingdom or regional spending for the countries benefiting from the Cohesion Fund while hardly changing CAP spending at all. Furthermore, the annual expenditure ceilings from regional spending have the status of spending targets and, thus, commit annual budgetary decisions over a period of 7 years. Additionally, one might criticise that the negotiations of the FP are mainly driven by the goal of maximising the national budgetary gains. Finally, taking into account that re-negotiations in the European Council take place in conjunction with other political issues, bargaining among member states combines budgetary issues with non-budgetary issues.

3.2.2 Discussion of Institutional Reforms to Be Implemented

Possible reforms of the institutional set-up of the EU budgetary policy have recently been debated controversially. The future of the EU financial constitution was discussed in the EU Constitutional Convention. Summarising the relevant contents of the Treaty establishing a Constitution for Europe, the proposed Constitution would:

- Abolish the distinction between compulsory and non-compulsory expenditure, and, thus, slightly increase the EP's influence over the annual budget;
- Codify the multi-annual Financial Perspective and the annual budget preparation in the EU Treaty (Art. I-55 TEC): The Financial Perspective should be decided under the unanimity rule by the European Council upon approval by the European Parliament;
- Enable the possibility to introduce majority voting with regard to the implementation of the Financial Perspective after an unanimous decision of the European Council;

- Codify that the annual budget plans have to take the ceilings determined in the Financial Perspective into account;
- Regulate statutorily that there is no right to borrow for the European Union (Art. I-54 (4-5) TEC);
- Codify that the EU budget is completely financed by own resources: This system could only be changed after an unanimous decision in the European Council, consultation of the European Parliament and approval of the member states according to their legal norms.

According to the presidency conclusions of the summit of the European Council in Brussels in June 2007 (European Council, 2007), the substance of the decision of the Constitutional Treaty with regard to the financial framework is planned to be part of the coming amendment to the TEC. Apart from the Constitution, the European Parliament (2004) proposed to synchronise the time frame with the term of office of the European Parliament. This would shorten the time frame from 7 to 5 years and, thus, (slightly) reduce the high degree of pre-commitment that the current 7-year cycle entails. Moreover, the European Parliament (2005) and the Sapir report (2004) proposed to increase the flexibility of the expenditure headings. The ceilings imposed on specific expenditure headings for the fairly long time period of a FP may be regarded as questionable because a potentially useful degree of flexibility is lost.

3.3 The Financing of the EU Budget

3.3.1 Explaining the System's Evolution

The history of the system of EU own resources began with the foundation of the European Economic Community (EEC) in the Treaty of Rome in 1957. On this occasion, member countries agreed to finance the new tasks through national contributions which were fixed according to an allocation formula reflecting the relative size of the member states. However, at this early stage Art. 201 of the Treaty demanded the review of the introduction of a system of own resources at a later date.

This was the basis for the first own resources decision in April 1970, which finally assigned the customs duties and agricultural levies to the EU budget. Moreover, the introduction of a third revenue source which was based on a harmonised assessment base of VAT revenue was agreed upon, which was gradually implemented until 1980. These decisions fundamentally explain the current status quo of the revenue side of the EU budget. The development of the single items are summarised in Table 1.[3] The quantitative impact of this development on the composition of the system of own resources can be seen in Fig. 1.

3 A detailed historical overview can be found in Euler (2005) and Raddatz (2005).

Table 1. History of the system of own resources

	Traditional own resources (TOR)	VAT resources	GNP/GNI resources	Abatements	Reasons
1971-1985 First own resources decision (1970)	Introduction; 10% of the revenues refunded as collection costs via the expenditure side	Introduction; Should cover the difference between revenues from TOR and the overall expenditures, therefore, rate variable (fixed at the annual budgetary procedure); maximum rate initially limited to 1% of the harmonised VAT base	–	–	Proceeding integration of the European Community (EC) and request to reduce dependency from the member states put pressure on the enforcement of Art. 201 of the Treaty of Rome
1986-1988 Second own resources decision (1985)		VAT rate increased to 1.4% of the harmonised VAT base	–	Flat rate reduction for UK for 1985; Introduction of UK correction mechanism in 1986; German share of correction reduced by 1/3	UK's demand for reduction of net contributions due to low backflows (low share of agriculture) and high payments (high own resources and consumption rate); Financial crisis (declining VAT revenues)
1988-1994 Third own resources decision (Delors I, 1988)		Introduction of the capping of the harmonised VAT base at 55% of the national GNP for countries with GNP per head of less than 90% of the average	Introduction; Replaces VAT as residual; new ceiling for overall expenditure set at 1.15% of EU GNP	UK mechanism technically adjusted	Again insufficient revenues (decline of TOR revenues, increase in spending for agricultural policy and for enlargement); Complaints by poorer member states with higher consumption rate about regressive character of VAT resource

Table 1. History of the system of own resources (continuous)

	TOR	VAT resource	GNP/GNI resource	Abatements	Reasons
1995-2002 Fourth own resources decision (Delors II, 1992)		Maximum rate reduced to 1% of the harmonised VAT base (until 1999); reduction of base cap to 50% (for four countries from 1995 on, for the others from 1999)			Further integration called for another increase in the funds; poorer countries still critical about regressive effect of VAT resource
2002-2006 Fifth own resources decision (Agenda 2000, 2000)	Allowance for collection increased to 25% of revenues	Reduction of rate of call to 0.75% in 2002 and 2003 and to 0.5% from 2004 on		Reduction of contribution to UK rebate for four countries to ¼ of normal share; Technical adjustments	Complaints by several net contributors about excessive net burdens; Foreseeable accession of CEE-countries
2007 Financial framework 2007-2013 (2005)		Reduction of rate of call to 0.3%; Reduction for individual countries (AT: 0.225%; DE: 0.15%; NL, SE: 0.1%)		UK correction reduced by costs due to enlargement by up to 10.5 bn EUR; Yearly flat rate reduction for NL (605 m EUR) and SE (150 m EUR)	

Fig. 1. Development of own resources

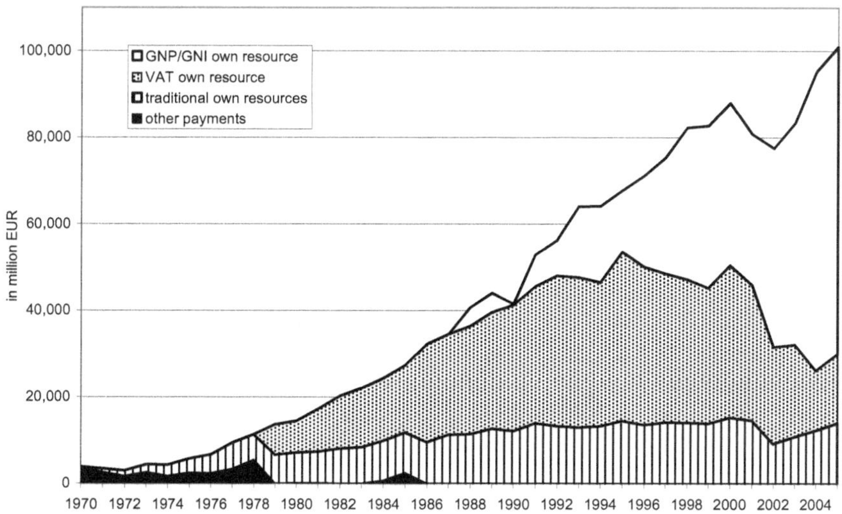

Source: European Commission (2006a).

The system's evolution is described at length in section 8.2. The following conclusions can be drawn from the development of the different resource items.

(1) Changes Mainly due to Changes on the Expenditure Side

It is remarkable that major changes of the structure of the system mainly occurred as a response to changes on the expenditure side. This holds for the repeated increases of the rate of call of the VAT resource in the first years and the introduction of the fourth resource. In all these cases, the adjustments were necessary because developments such as new political tasks or enlargements of the Union led to increased spending which, in turn, caused financial strain.

Moreover, the initial reason for the UK rebate as well as all other rebates subsequently decided was due to excessive net payments by the respective countries, caused by relatively low backflows from the expenditure side.

(2) Trend Towards GNI-Based System

Ever since its introduction a constant increase of the fourth resource's quantitative importance at the expense of the VAT resource has been observed. The reasons for this may be seen in the accession of countries with high consumption ratios (e.g., Spain) which had an incentive for opposing against this disadvantageous item. However, the opposition of countries benefiting from a strong VAT resource (especially Italy) averted its complete abolition. The declining share in the total revenue was caused by frequent cuts in the rate of call and the reduction of the capped VAT base as well as by the introduction of the fourth resource. Moreover, this development obviously reflects the member states' agreement that the allocation of the revenues based on the national Gross National Income (GNI) shares corresponds to distributive fairness.

(3) Inflation of Rebates

As can be seen from the historical development, the number of exception rules which favour single countries has significantly increased since the introduction of the UK rebate at the Fontainebleau Council in 1984. After this opening of Pandora's box, any rebate introduced has shown a remarkable durability even though the main reasons for its introduction (in the case of the UK rebate) lost their significance.[4] Instead, the one-sided exception for one country (UK rebate) was offset by granting rebates for other countries (Germany was granted a reduction of the correction payments), thus, increasing the demands of third countries (extension of the reduction of correction payments to other countries). In the negotiations on the Financial Perspective 2007-2013, long discussions were necessary to wrest at least a cut in the rebate from the UK to prevent it from benefiting from the Eastern enlargement of the Union. Against this background the persistence of all discretionary rebates significantly shaped the current status quo resulting in a significant quantitative importance of exception rules on both the revenue and the expenditure side.

3.3.2 The Current Financing of the EU

The agreement on the Financial Framework 2007-2013 has in principle confirmed the following types of own resources (European Parliament, 2006c):

- "Traditional own resources" (TOR) consisting of
  - Agricultural duties and levies (budget share 2006: 0.9 %), and
  - Customs duties (12.9 %);
- VAT resources (16.0 %);
- GNI resources (64.2 %).

The remaining part of the EU budget is financed by the budget surplus from the preceding year (2.2%) and further miscellaneous receipts (2.2%).

Traditional Own Resources

The traditional own resources comprise revenues which accrue as a consequence of the common agricultural and trade policy of the EU. Revenues arising from the

4 Initially, the introduction of the UK rebate was justified by the fact that the UK was a relatively poor country with only a minor interest in agricultural policy given the high importance of CAP in the EC. Due to the constantly declining share of CAP spending in the total EU budget and due to increased prosperity of the UK, these arguments lost much of their justification.

CAP consist of agricultural duties and sugar levies. Agricultural duties are raised on agricultural goods imported from non-member countries; sugar levies are raised from producers of sugar in order to avoid an overproduction. The revenue from the current trade policy is equivalent to common tariff duties and other duties established by the European Communities (European Commission, 2002).

The EU has the autonomy to collect the revenues from the traditional own resources from the member states. These are completely paid to the EU after a deduction of currently 25% which is retained by the respective country as a compensation for collection costs.

VAT-Based Own Resources

The VAT resource is paid by the member states on the basis of a harmonised base. This harmonised base is calculated by adjusting the annual national VAT revenue for sales, which differ from the harmonised base, and dividing it by the average weighted VAT rate in this country. To avoid an excessive burden for those countries with an unusual high share of the VAT revenue compared to GNI, the base is capped, currently at a level of 50% of the country's GNI.

Before the changes of the new Financial Perspective took effect, the calculation of the national VAT contributions was even more complicated as the reductions, due to the UK rebate, were incorporated in different rates of call. This led to a split rate for different countries: From the maximum rate, which was finally fixed at 0.5%, a frozen rate was subtracted which accounted for the amount of financing of the UK rebate. The rest was defined as the uniform rate. The different countries had to pay VAT contributions in the amount of this uniform rate plus a markup according to their obligations regarding the financing of the UK rebate.

Since the new Financial Perspective 2007-2013, the markup for the UK rebate is directly paid via higher GNI contribution. Therefore, a uniform rate of call of 0.3% is fixed. Exceptions are made for the four biggest net contributors: For the period 2007-2013 their rates are exclusively restricted to 0.225% (Austria), 0.15% (Germany) and 0.10% (the Netherlands and Sweden). These changes lead to lower rates of call for all countries apart from the UK and, hence, a further shift of revenues to the GNI resource. Thus, the decrease in significance of the VAT-based contributions will continue in the years to come.

GNI-Based Own Resources

The GNI resource ("fourth resource") was introduced in 1988 in order to top up revenues of the three "old" resources to the level of expenditure demanded by the Financial Perspective. It is determined by splitting the amount which has not been contributed by the other three resources among the member states according to their shares of EU-wide GNI. This leads to a uniform rate of call among the countries in every year, which varies on an annual basis, depending on the respective amount to be covered.

UK Correction

As shown in more detail in section 8.2, the UK correction mechanism was introduced at the Fontainebleau Council in 1984 and has been adjusted several times since then. At the time, the introduction was justified by UK's disproportionally high net burden compared to the UK's actual welfare due to its relatively small agricultural sector. This led to a comparatively low reception of payments from the agricultural funds but to high payments of levies for the imported goods. Furthermore, the UK showed a fairly high consumption rate, which led to relatively high payments according to the VAT resource.

In the course of time, the calculation of the correction amount has been changed several times increasing the complexity of the correction mechanism while leaving the general principle of the mechanism unchanged.[5] These changes were mainly due to changes in the composition of the budget (introduction of the fourth resource, capping of VAT base) as well as the Eastern enlargement in order to limit the amount of correction for the UK. The latest changes occurred with the introduction of the Financial Perspective 2007-2013 (see European Commission, 2004d). This was the first time that the modification of the rebate led to a significant reduction of the amount of correction. The rebate was restricted in order to oblige the UK to participate in the financing of the Eastern enlargement process. The maximum amount of increased UK spending due to these changes was capped at 10.5 billion EUR.

The corrected amount is financed by all EU members apart from the UK. It is shared according to the national share of EU-wide GNI less the British share. For the four biggest net contributors (DE, NL, AT, SE), the contributions are restricted to ¼ of the calculated payments, the remaining financial burden is borne by all other countries. The respective national shares of the UK rebate payments are contributed via increased GNI resource payments.

The Refinancing of the Financial Burden in the EU Member States

As mentioned in section 3.2.1, the financing of the European Union is not codified in detail in the Treaty. Instead, the Financial Perspectives' consequences for national contributions are to be implemented through own resources decisions (Art. 269 TEC). These decisions are ultimately adopted under unanimity in the European Council and under the agreement of the national Parliaments according to their respective legal norms. Accordingly, there are no EU regulations specifying *how* the EU contributions are to be refinanced at the national level, i.e.

---

5 The initial correction mechanism was calculated as follows: First, the difference between the British share of contributions according to the VAT resources and its share of attributable received payments was calculated. This difference was multiplied with the overall EU-wide attributable expenditures indicating the British net position. From this net position, two thirds were finally refunded as a correction and subtracted from the British VAT resource contributions.

- the EU member states are free to choose how to refinance the EU contributions at the national level – at least with respect to GNI and VAT own resources, which currently constitute more than 80% of the current revenue;
- the EU member states are free to choose *how to share* the burden intra-nationally, i.e. they are free to decide if the regions should contribute to the funding of the EU.

The free choice of the financial resources to refinance the EU contributions enables the EU member states to take into account their tax preferences, i.e. national tax policy is not restricted by the EU system of own resources. This feature is the more advantageous the more diverse taxation systems and taxation preferences are among EU countries. The freedom to choose how to refinance contributions to the European budget is a greater advantage if member countries still differ with regard to their tax system preferences (for a more detailed analysis, see our background analysis in section 4.2).

Concerning the regional involvement in refinancing own resources' payments, there is hardly any public information on how the regional level is participating in national EU contributions.[6] Therefore, we consulted several national experts and collected information for Austria, Belgium, Denmark, Germany, Italy, Poland, Spain, the Netherlands and the United Kingdom.

The results are very clear cut: In all countries, the EU contributions are paid exclusively at the national level, i.e. neither the federal states nor the municipalities are involved in financing the EU. To our knowledge there is only one exception to this approach: In Austria, both the federal states and the municipalities have to bear part of the costs of the Austrian EU contributions. According to § 9 Abs. 3 Z 1 lit a Finanzausgleichsgesetz 2005, the amount of the federal level is calculated by summing up the Austrian share of the GNI and VAT contributions to the EU and by adding a fix amount representing the country's payments of TOR (totalling 781 m EUR in 2005). The federal states are charged a share of 16.835% of this amount resulting in 478 m EUR in 2005. This is equal to a share of 19.6% of the total Austrian EU contributions paid in 2005 (2.444 billion EUR). The share of the municipalities is calculated by taking 16.6% of the annual total tax revenues of income-related taxes in Austria (corporate tax, wage tax, tax on income etc.). This amount totalled 87 m EUR in 2005, which is equal to a share of 3.6 % of the total Austrian EU contribution in 2005. As a consequence, the federal level in Austria "only" finances 76.8% of the EU contributions, whereas the federal states level (19.6%) and the municipalities (3.6%) share the burden of the EU contribution.

3.4 The Financial Perspective 2007-2013

As mentioned above, the EU budget financing stands in a close logical context to the expenditure side. Thus, this section briefly presents the main aspects of the

---

6 One exception for Germany is the report by the Sachverständigenkommission (1981) defining how to distribute the VAT.

spending side of the EU budget. As the expenditures have been implemented within the Financial Perspectives (for the institutional set-up, see section 3.2.1) since 1988, this section focusses on the key features of the latest, the fourth, Financial Perspective ranging from 2007-2013.

The Level of the EU Budget

When the European Commission opened the bargaining process on the Financial Perspective in July 2004, it proposed that the total commitment appropriations should amount to 1,025 billion EUR (2004 prices, equivalent to 1.24% of GNI, see European Commission, 2004a). However, the final amount has decreased continuously in the course of the bargaining process (for details, see section 3.5.3). Finally, in the Inter-Institutional Agreement it was agreed to spend 864 billion EUR (1.048% of GNI) between 2007 and 2013 (see Table 2).

Table 2. The Financial Perspective 2007-2013 (in billion EUR, 2004 prices)

		2007	2008	2009	2010	2011	2012	2013	TOT.
1	Sustainable growth	51.3	52.4	53.6	54.3	55.4	56.9	58.3	382.1
1a	Competitiveness for growth & employment	8.4	9.1	9.8	10.4	11.3	12.2	13.0	74.1
1b	Cohesion for growth and employment	42.9	43.3	43.9	43.9	44.1	44.7	45.3	308.0
2	Conservation and management of natural resources	55.0	54.3	53.7	53.0	52.4	51.8	51.2	371.3
	of which: Agriculture – market support measures and direct payments	43.1	42.7	42.3	41.9	41.5	41.0	40.6	293.1
3	Citizenship, freedom, security and justice	1.2	1.3	1.4	1.5	1.6	1.8	2.0	10.8
3a	Freedom, security and justice	0.6	0.7	0.8	0.9	1.1	1.2	1.4	6.6
3b	Citizenship	0.6	0.6	0.6	0.6	0.6	0.6	0.6	4.1
4	EU as global partner	6.2	6.5	6.7	7.0	7.3	7.7	8.0	49.5
5	Administration	6.6	6.8	7.0	7.1	7.3	7.4	7.6	49.8
6	Compensation	0.4	0.2	0.2					0.8
Total committment appropriations		120.7	121.5	122.6	123.0	124.0	125.5	127.1	864.3
% of GNI		1.10	1.08	1.07	1.04	1.03	1.02	1.01	1.048

Source: European Parliament, European Council and European Commission (2006).

Nevertheless, one has to consider that the de facto level of the EU budget is even higher since not all spending categories are included in the Financial Perspective. Adding off-budget items, flexibility and emergency cash reserves would increase the budget by 36 billion EUR[7] to 900.4 billion EUR (see Becker, 2007: 9).

The peculiar metrics used in defining the future size of the EU budget are hardly ever debated: Contrary to usual practices at the national level, the planned budget size is defined in terms % of GNI or in amounts of real EUR. At the national level, definitions of the nominal size of the budget are prevalent. This EU practice is not unimportant with respect to its psychological impact and the resulting definition of natural reference points in negotiations. We will return to this aspect in section 6.4.

The Allocation of Expenditures

In the latest Financial Perspective, many facets of the budget have acquired new labels compared to the previous FP. Nevertheless, it is striking how little was changed in the 2007 budget compared to the previous ones (for a detailed comparison, see Begg, 2007). The major part of the budget is spent for cohesion (EUR 308 billion (35.6%)) and agricultural policy (293 billion EUR (33.9%)) totalling around 70% (600 billion EUR) of the EU budget (see Fig. 2). Concerning cohesion policy one has to take into account that in the future the co-financing share to which the poorer member states will have to contribute out of their national budgets will be reduced by 10 percentage points while even private investment costs and VAT will be included into this co-financing share (see Becker, 2006, for a more detailed analysis). Moreover, the period during which cohesion allocations must be spent was extended from 2 to 3 years. This is a big advantage for those countries with smaller or slower working bureaucracies.

Increase of Special Regulations/Provisions

The Financial Perspective 2007-2013 is characterised by a sharp increase in special regulations for single regions and/or countries. While the Agenda 2000 included 13 special regulations totalling 5.6 billion EUR (Becker, 2006), the new FP incorporates special regulations of around 12 billion EUR (for a more detailed analysis of the distribution of these expenditures, see section 3.6). These regulations include special payments for single regions such as Prague, Northern Ireland and Corsica, as well as poor regions in Eastern Germany and Bavaria.

7 The total amount of 36 billion EUR results from the following expenditure categories: European Development Fund 22.7 billion EUR, solidarity fund for catastrophe reserves 7 billion EUR, catastrophe reserve for countries outside the EU 1.4 billion EUR, globalisation fund for losers of the globalisation 3.5 billion EUR, flexibility reserve 1.4 billion EUR.

Fig. 2. Allocation of expenditures of the Financial Perspective 2007-2013

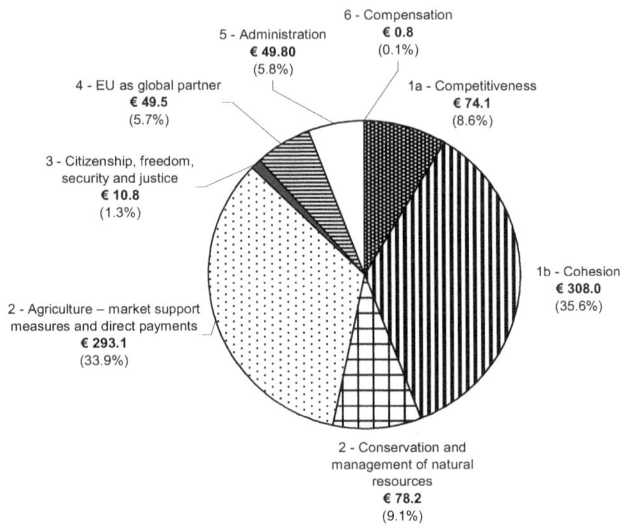

Source: European Parliament, European Council and European Commission (2006).

3.5 Incentives of Important Actors in the System

3.5.1 The Role of Incentives

In order to judge to which extent the institutional framework described above safeguards an efficient budgetary policy and successfully limits narrow self-interest of actors, an analysis of incentives within that system is helpful. A key challenge in the design of any rational budgetary system in this respect is to create institutions which induce decision makers to give equal weights to both the benefits and the costs of public spending. Only if the budgetary authorities pay an equal amount of attention to the costs in form of the fiscal burden on taxpayers as to the benefits associated with spending, an efficient outcome can be expected.

In theory, there would be no fundamental incentive problem if:

- The budget is exclusively devoted to the supply of public goods benefiting the whole jurisdiction and –
- The jurisdiction's taxpayers bear the revenue burden.

If these two conditions were fulfilled, the principle of fiscal equivalence (Olson, 1969) would hold so that there would be a full overlap of those who benefit and those who finance public services. Marginal costs and benefits would be equalised in the calculus of budgetary authorities resulting in an efficient public goods production.

Obviously, no budgetary system in the real world would be able to fulfil these textbook conditions entirely, and it would be completely unrealistic to demand a full match for the EU budget. In practice, public budgets regularly finance a broad range of goods, ranging from classical private goods over regional to general public goods. In addition, the EU budget is characterised by a substantial budgetary share for transfers benefiting certain sectors (agriculture), individuals (farmers) or regions (in the context of cohesion policy). Thus, the EU budget does not only serve the purpose of providing European public goods but, instead, constitutes a transfer mechanism channelling funds between EU member countries.

While there may be good arguments in favour of this expenditure focus (such as "solidarity") one should, nevertheless, have a clear understanding of the incentives of budgetary actors within that system. Understanding these incentives is important not only in the light of our assessment criteria (particularly the criteria of "fostering efficient public goods provision" and "constraining narrow self-interest and creating budgetary discipline", see Box 2). Furthermore, it helps to understand the system's status quo bias. The fact that fundamental changes to the system are obviously extremely difficult to achieve must have its roots in the incentives of important institutional actors. Hence, a better understanding of these incentives must be part of any reform reflections.

3.5.2 The Common Pool Problem in General

Misguided budgetary incentives typically become virulent if a budget will, at least partially, also finance projects from which only a regional (or sectoral) subsection of voters benefits. On that condition the so-called "common pool" problem arises that is characterised by an asymmetry of perceived spending benefits and costs: From the regional perspective a regional spending project is characterised by highly salient benefits whereas the common pool financing (the project is financed by the jurisdiction's total revenues) renders the cost side of the project less salient.

These problems are acute in any budgetary system with regionally anchored representatives who have a say in budgetary decision-making (see Shepsle & Weingast, 1982). The representatives will always tend to support so-called "pork barrel" projects. In the context of U.S. financial policy this term is used for projects which are financed by nationwide tax revenues while benefits concentrate on one electoral district only. Local politicians hope that these projects help to increase their popularity and chances for re-election. The representatives from all electoral districts have a high incentive to support projects that benefit their own electors in particular as, in case of success, the representatives gain an electoral advantage.

Why would the other veto players agree to the request of only one regional representative? They do so because they have similar regional interests for their electoral districts. The incentives described above, therefore, apply to all regional representatives. This can lead to a prisoner's dilemma-like situation: All regional representatives and the taxpayers they are representing could increase their welfare if they abandoned the inefficient expansion of regional public goods. However, this efficient allocation is not a Nash equilibrium. Regional representatives would have an advantage enforcing regional projects in isolation. Schwartz (1994) explains the incentives of regional representatives with parochialism as their electors only evaluate them on the basis of regional welfare increases. One single representative cannot prevent the other representatives from following their regional interests. He is, therefore, left with the strategy of receiving the acceptance of his electors, i.e. of focussing on the interests of his electoral district. Hence, the source of the inefficiency is a coordination problem: If all representatives abandoned regional benefits, the welfare of all would be increased. However, with an increasing number of actors, the difficulty of coordinating themselves increases as well.

Nowadays, the common pool problem is a standard approach to understand incentive problems in national budgetary decisions (see, among others, von Hagen, 1992; Hallerberg & von Hagen, 1999), and there are principle solutions to solve it as well (see Box 3). Surprisingly, it has not yet been systematically applied to the incentives in EU budgetary decisions (exceptions concern a brief excurse in Mueller, 2003, and Heinemann, 2006).

This neglect in the EU context is dissatisfying given the fact that the common pool problem in principle becomes more serious the larger a federation becomes. EU spending is financed by a European common pool of public revenues so that the potential for disincentives is far more substantial than it would be the case at national or regional level.

Box 3. Principle solutions to the common pool problem

In academia, one principle solution to the common pool problem is the centralisation of the budgetary process to ensure that policy makers internalise the common pool externality. Reviewing the budget processes in Europe, the US, Latin America and Asia reveals that centralisation basically follows two approaches: The first is centralisation based on delegation, the second is centralisation based on contracts (see von Hagen, 2005).

The delegation solution implies that the rules of the executive planning stage of the budget process are given to a central agent who is responsible for the determination of the central parameters of the budget. This agent enforces that these parameters are binding by using selective punishments for defecting spending ministers. Usually, this agent is the finance minister who can internalise the common pool externality by having the most comprehensive view of the budget among all the members of the executive. The delegation approach lends large agenda-setting powers to the executive at the legislative approval stage. Moreover, centralisation puts tight limits on any changes in the budget law during the fiscal year and limits the use of supplementary budgets. At the implementation stage, centralisation requires the central agent to control and monitor the flow of expenditures during the year in order to prevent spending departments from overspending.

In contrast, the contract approach focusses on binding budgetary agreements on a set of fiscal targets negotiated among all members of the executive at the beginning of the executive planning stage. As a consequence, the bargaining process helps internalising the common pool externality. Generally, the targets are often derived from coalition agreements among the ruling parties or medium-term fiscal programmes. The task of the finance ministry is to evaluate the consistency of the individual departments' spending plans within these limits. Hence, the finance minister has information advantages but no extra strategic powers. At the implementation stage, the contract approach is similar to the delegation approach by demanding strong monitoring and control powers of the finance minister. At the legislative stage, the contract approach places more weight on the role of the legislature monitoring the faithful implementation of the fiscal targets and less on controlling parliamentary amendments.

Furthermore, Hallerberg & von Hagen (1999) derive the link between the most appropriate form of centralisation and the electoral rules as well as the type of government. Summing up, they conclude that delegation is appropriate for single-party governments whereas the contract approach is appropriate for multi-party coalition governments.

Additionally, the electoral rule has an impact on the evolution of the type of government. Elections based on the plurality rule promote the emergence of two-party systems and one-party majority governments (Duverger, 1954). In contrast, proportional representation is consistently characterised by multi-party coalition governments (Lijphart, 1984, 1994). This suggests that countries are more likely to opt for the contract approach if their elections are based on proportional representation (and low thresholds) whereas they are more likely to opt for delegation if their elections are based on plurality rule.

Hallerberg & von Hagen (1999) test and confirm these hypotheses for the European Union states. Thus, different electoral rules demand different institutional solutions to the common pool problem.

3.5.3 The Relevance of the Common Pool Problem in the EU Budget Process

In this section we analyse the institutional set-up, i.e. the intergovernmental and supranational decision makers involved in EU budget policies, in order to find out how relevant the common pool problem is under the current institutional regime.

The European Council

In their agreement on the Financial Framework, the Heads of State or Governments determine the level and the structure of the European budget by consensus. Due to the Inter-Institutional Agreement (see section 3.2.1) the ceilings of the Financial Perspective are binding for the Commission, the Council and the Parliament.

The European Council clearly represents the intergovernmental perspective of decision-making so that the preferences of the members of the European Council are strongly influenced by the national perspective. This is demonstrated again in the bargaining on the Financial Perspective including the observed member countries' preoccupation with national net balances (Begg & Heinemann, 2006). The long list of exceptional provisions on the expenditure side of the December 2005 agreement (Becker, 2005b, 2006; see also section 3.4) constitutes a "pork barrel list" in the terminology of the common pool literature.

From the point of view of a member state, this engagement for special provisions is completely understandable and rational if one considers the low marginal costs of any budgetary expansion from the national perspective. As an indicator for the asymmetry between costs and benefits, Table 3 displays the national shares of EU own resources in 2005 ignoring any co-financing share of EU spending. If the EU spent an additional 100 EUR say for a locally focussed project in Germany, Germany would have to bear EUR 21.50 of the costs, i.e. 78.50 EUR are paid by the other members of the European Union. While the "Big 5" (Germany, France, Italy, UK and Spain) have to pay at least 11% of the costs, the smaller member states have even higher incentives to fight for additional spending projects benefiting their constituencies. The Netherlands, for example, have to pay only 5% of the costs. The seven "smallest" countries (Hungary up to Malta, right column of Table 3) have to bear less than 1% of the costs. This asymmetry between costs and benefits and the intergovernmental feature of the European Council render the common pool problem highly virulent in the case of the European Council.

The Council of Ministers

In the Council of Ministers, representatives of national governments make detailed policy decisions on the basis of legislative initiatives from the supranational European Commission. Voting rules vary depending on the policy area.

When thinking about decisions on EU spending, the representatives do not fully internalise the total costs of the EU projects because the total costs are divided by all EU member states according to the shares displayed in Table 3. Furthermore, – in contrast to the Heads of State or Governments in the European Council – "spending ministers" are not made responsible for an increasing European tax burden. Instead, they are typically evaluated according to the performance of their own department. For example, higher spending for agriculture is regularly perceived to be a political success for the agricultural minister. Thus, assuming that the Council of Ministers could decide independently from the European Council, the common pool problem is even aggravated because the immediate budgetary interest to limit the national contributions to the EU budget is less present in the case of the members of the Council of Ministers compared to the calculus of the Heads of State or Governments in the European Council.

As the final decision on spending limits is made by the European Council, the power of the spending ministers is limited. Nevertheless, to the extent that decisions of the Council of Minister influence spending levels, this is definitely in conflict with the budgetary discipline criterion.

Table 3. Share of EU own resources (2005)

Country	Share in %	Country	Share in %
Germany	20.1	Ireland	1.5
France	17.9	Poland	2.4
Italy	14.1	Czech Republic	1.0
UK	11.1	Hungary	0.8
Spain	9.7	Slovak Republic	0.4
The Netherlands	5.1	Slovenia	0.3
Belgium	3.1	Latvia	0.2
Sweden	2.7	Lithuania	0.2
Austria	2.3	Luxembourg	0.2
Denmark	1.9	Cyprus	0.1
Greece	1.8	Estonia	0.1
Finland	1.6	Malta	< 0.1
Portugal	1.6		

Source: Own calculations.

The European Parliament

The directly elected European Parliament provides a link between the supranational decision-making process and the citizens. As in any other parliamentary democracy, there is the traditional problem of "pork barrel fights". The MEP have strong incentives to fight for additional spending for their own constituency in order to increase their popularity. As the total costs of spending are paid by all constituencies, the payments of the voters of their individual constituency will increase only marginally if they lobby successfully.

Furthermore, in contrast to national parliamentary systems there is a difference for the EP: The chance of standing as a candidate and of being reselected is not determined by the party group in the EP but by the national party leadership (Norris & Franklin, 1997). Consequently, to secure reselection and re-election they must cater to national party interest. In this context Turnovec, Mercik and Mazurkiewicz (2007) show that the national dimension is indeed relevant when analysing the decision-making in the European Parliament. In contrast, Hix and Noury (2007) and Noury (2002) conclude that MEP primarily vote along transnational party lines and that voting along national lines is very low in the European Parliament. Nevertheless, in addition to the focus on their own constituency, the MEP might also fight for national pork barrels. These aspects clearly show the existence of the common pool problem in the case of the European Parliament.

The parliamentary common pool problem increases with the number of seats since an increasing number of seats implies falling marginal costs of pork barrels from the perspective of the individual constituency. Hence, the enormous size of the European Parliament is problematic in this regard and makes it particularly vulnerable to common pool disincentives (see Table 4).

Against this background, it is not surprising that the members of the EP have (recently) preferred higher EU expenditures in the bargaining on the FP (see section 3.2). Due to the weak decision-making power of the European Parliament in the current EU budgetary process (see section 3.2), its influence on the level of spending is minor so that the status quo's institutions limit the negative impact of EP spending incentives.

Table 4. Comparison of the number of seats in selected national parliaments and in the EP (June 2007)

Parliament	Number of seats
European Parliament	785
United Kingdom – House of Commons	646
Italy – Camera dei Deputati	630
Germany – Bundestag	614
France – Assemblée Nationale	577
Poland – Sejm	460
Russia – Duma	450
United States – House of Representatives	435
Sweden – Riksdag	349
Greece – Parliament	300
Portugal – Assemblá da República	230
Switzerland – Nationalrat	200
Austria – Nationalrat	183
Slovenia – National Assembly	90

Source: Own compilation based on diverse homepages of the national governments.

Obviously, one could also argue that due to the widely missing responsibility of the EP for the revenue side of today's EU budget the Parliament's incentives under the status quo are even more biased towards budgetary expansion. Although this is a valid argument, the common pool aspect does not justify large optimism that the EP's spending incentives will be substantially reduced once the EP gains more responsibility for the revenue side if this shift of responsibilities is not accompanied by additional restrictions.

The European Commission

The European Commission can use its agenda-setting power within the legislative and political process to shape policy outcomes and to promote its institutional interests (Pollack, 1997). If applying conventional reasoning from the theory of bureaucracy, the Commission should, first of all, be expected to have an interest in promoting European integration and EU competencies since this should imply the delegation of more executive power from the Council to the Commission and greater Commission influence in a larger number of policy domains. Moreover, in the everyday bargaining process of EU politics, the Commission has an incentive to support key member states and influential societal groups and private interests in order to secure the approval of its policy proposals by the Council and the EP. Hix (2005), for instance, reports that the Agriculture Directorate-General obstructed CAP reforms in the 1970s and 1980s to protect its position and the interests of its support groups. In a similar vein, Marks (1993) interprets the European Commission's introduction of the principles of additionality, partnership and concentration in the 1988 reform of the structural funds as a deliberate attempt to bypass member state governments in the implementation of policy and to promote decentralisation and federalisation within the member states.

The Commission as the central European bureaucracy is not directly responsible for European voters and taxpayers resulting in pronounced distortions of budgetary cost-benefit calculus. While additional expenditures are clearly in the interest of that institution, the costs in the form of additional taxes on EU citizens are far less relevant in the objective function of Commissioners or Commission civil servants (who are not even subject to national taxation).

The typical pattern of negotiations on financial frameworks in the past clearly supports the view that the Commission regularly lobbies for an aggressive expansion of the budget. In the latest negotiations on the FP 2007-2013, the European Commission proposed in July 2004 that the total commitment appropriations within the FP should amount to 1,025 billion EUR (equivalent to 1.24% of GNI) (see Table 5). The final amount continuously decreased in the course of the bargaining process (European Parliament (974 billion EUR), Luxembourg proposal (871 billion EUR), UK proposal (847 billion EUR)) before in December 2005, the members of the European Council decided unanimously that the EU budget should amount to 862 billion EUR (1.045% GNI).

Against this background, the common pool problem also exists in the case of the European Commission and is probably even the most pronounced for that budgetary player.

Regional Jurisdictions in Federal States: "Austrian Model" Versus "Central Level Pays All"

The incentives of the regional jurisdictions in federal states are not identical to those of the national level. The reason is that a region (e.g., a German Bundesland) may be confronted with a very different cost-benefit calculus with regard to EU spending compared to a country as a whole. The new German Laender are a good example: They are the main beneficiaries of EU cohesion spending within Germany but only contribute to German tax revenues below population proportionality.

Table 5. Proposals and final bargaining result of the new Financial Perspective 2007-2013

		EU Commission (July 14, 2004)		European Parliament (June 8, 2005)		Luxembourg proposal (June 17, 2005)		UK proposal (Dec 5, 2005)		European Council (Dec 19, 2005)		Inter-Institutional Agreement (June 14, 2006)	
		€ bill.	in %	€ bill.	in %	€ bill.	in %	€ bill.	in %	€ bill.	in %	€ bill.	in %
1a	Competitiveness for growth and employment	132.8	13.0	120.6	12.4	72.0	8.3	72.0	8.5	72.1	8.4	74.1	8.6
1b	Cohesion for growth and employment	338.7	33.0	338.5	34.7	309.6	35.5	296.9	35.1	307.6	35.7	308.0	35.6
2	Conservation and management of natural resources	404.7	39.5	396.2	40.6	377.8	43.4	367.5	43.4	371.2	43.0	371.3	43.0
	of which: Agriculture - market support measures and direct payments	301.1	29.4	293.1	30.1	295.1	33.9	293.1	34.6	293.1	34.0	293.1	33.9
3	Citizenship, freedom, security and justice	24.7	2.4	19.4	2.0	11.0	1.3	10.3	1.2	10.3	1.2	10.8	1.2
4	EU as global partner *	95.4	9.3	70.7	7.3	50.0	5.7	50.0	5.9	50.0	5.8	49.5	5.7
5	Administration	28.6	2.8	28.6	2.9	50.3	5.8	49.3	5.8	50.3	5.8	49.8	5.8
6	Compensation	0.2	0.0	0.8	0.1	0.8	0.1	0.8	0.1	0.8	0.1	0.8	0.1
Total commitment appropriations		1,025	100	974.8	100	871.5	100	846.8	100	862.4	100	864.3	100
% of GNI		1.240		1.182		1.057		1.030		1.045		1.048	

* Not included in the negotiations of the European Council is the expenditure for the European Development Fund totalling 22.7 billion EUR.

Sources: European Commission (2004d), European Parliament (2005), United Kingdom Presidency of the EU (2005), European Council (2005), European Parliament, European Council and European Commission (2006).

Apart from these differences which are a function of regional disparities within a country and should, in this respect, be cancelled out, there are more systematic differences between the national and the regional level which strongly depend on the way the EU contributions are financed. As our expert interviews show (see section 3.3.2), in almost all countries the national level bears the entire financing burden of the EU contributions. Only in Austria do the regions also contribute to the financing of the EU budget.

These differences affect the extent of the common pool problem. On the expenditure side, the regional level is an important recipient of transfers through cohesion policy and the rural development part of the Common Agricultural Policy. Hence, regions have a certain interest in the expenditure side of the budget. If national fiscal federalism does not constitute a link between national own resources payments to the EU budget and regional budgets, a systematically distorted cost-benefit-calculus on the regional level will be the consequence. Under the Austrian model of refinancing national payments to the EU budget, federal states have a more balanced view of EU spending compared to the German Laender.

Summing up, the extent of the common pool problem on the sub-national level cannot be generalised but heavily depends on national institutional arrangements. The common pool problem is less intensive in the case of the Austrian federal states than in the case of the German Laender.

3.5.4 Advantages and Disadvantages of the Status Quo

The existence of the common pool problem is helpful in evaluating the advantages and disadvantages of the current financing of the EU budget. The disadvantages are clearly connected to the current situation of the EU as an entity "sui generis", i.e. the combination of intergovernmental and supranational decision-making. Due to the intergovernmental set-up of the European Union, decision makers are strongly influenced by a regional or national perspective whereas the promotion of European public goods is less attractive. This, in turn, might explain the high relevance of policies which are focussed on regions and countries, respectively. The CAP and the Cohesion policy have a high relevance in the current EU budget since, according to the common pool logic, they are directly connected to the national and/or regional level. This stems from the decision makers' success in fighting for pork barrels for their respective constituency without sufficiently internalising the arising costs of spending. By contrast, the funding of European public goods, i.e. goods whose funding cannot be directly localised (e.g., Lisbon policies), is less pronounced.

Nevertheless, there are considerable advantages of the current system as well. First of all, there is a ceiling on the budget, which serves as a typical result of a successful contract approach (see Box 3). The level of the European budget is determined by the European Council whose members have a strong interest in capping the budget given that at least the net payers have to pay more for additional EU spending than they receive. As a consequence, taking into account the unanimous decision rule and the fact that there is no right to borrow, the current system succeeds in capping the EU budget and, thus, counteracts the expansionary pressure of the virulent asymmetry in the perceived costs and benefits of spending.

Furthermore, these aspects are strengthened by the fact that the EU budget is directly linked to the national budget. If the EU budget is increased, the member states are aware that they have to contribute to the rising budget according to their shares. This constitutes a high incentive for net contributors to cap the budget. The bargaining on the Financial Perspective clearly illustrated these preferences.

3.5.5 Findings for a Reform Perspective

Analysing the current EU financing system as a common pool problem delivers interesting conclusions for possible future reforms of the EU financing. First of all, the general common pool problem could be alleviated if those who call for certain expenditures have to co-finance the European spending. If, for example, a region in France demands additional resources for rural development, it would have to co-finance these EU expenditures. Thus, the regions would better internalise the arising costs resulting in a less regionally focussed attitude and in an increase in budgetary efficiency.

Furthermore, the common pool logic helps to conclude that many proposals that are currently discussed in the context of a reform of the EU budgetary system would not solve the problem. The introduction of a European tax would not improve the situation because the member states and/or the European regions would retain the incentive to fight for pork barrels for their countries because they do not internalise the full costs. Moreover, one positive feature of the current system is that the member states of the European Council (especially the net payers) have a strong interest in capping the European budget at a present system because the EU budget is directly linked to the national budget. If the EU budget is reduced, the national budget is increased by the national share of the reduction. Introducing a European tax would destroy this link. Thus, there is the danger that this would lead to overspending.

Increasing the responsibility and the right to say of the European Parliament would shift the common pool problem from the European Council (as the most important actor of the current system) towards the European Parliament. As discussed in section 3.5.3, the MEP would fight for pork barrels for their constituencies so that they do not internalise the total costs of financing. Additionally, the contract (own resources ceiling) might be endangered once the intergovernmental European Council loses direct budgetary self-interest in the EU budgetary discipline.

Finally, introducing majority voting in the Council or the European Parliament would not alleviate the problem either as the incentives towards regionally oriented EU spending would remain unchanged. Instead, majority voting would enable the majority to redistribute resources from the minority. The large recipients of EU funds, for example, can outvote the large net contributors. This might, in turn, aggravate the common pool problem.

3.6 The Drivers of Redistribution

3.6.1 Introduction

Before turning to the quantitative assessment of proposals for a reform of the system of own resources, it is important to take a look at the redistributive effects of the current system. Although this approach is, to a great extent, in line with the "juste retour" thinking which has generally been criticised when discussing reforms of the EU budget (and whose existence is often put forward as one of the main arguments for a reform), a quantitative analysis of the current system gives us guidelines in two different aspects:

1. Any reformed system of own resources must not deviate too much in its redistributive effects from the status quo to be politically feasible. As unanimity is the prerequisite of any change of the status quo, a proposal which would change the distribution of resources between the countries in an asymmetric way would not be supported by countries suffering from such a change.
2. The distributional effects of the system of own resources cannot be seen isolated from their counterparts on the expenditure side. The history of the system shows that adjustments on the revenue side are regularly driven by the perception of expenditure flow misbalances. Therefore, the current distribution of the expenditure is important in explaining current anomalies on the revenue side, such as occurring in the form of rebates granted to several countries.

3.6.2 The Simulation Model

The basis for the following quantifications is a detailed modelling of the revenue and the expenditure side for the budget of the EU-27 which was developed at the Centre for European Economic Research (ZEW) in the run-up to the negotiations on the Financial Framework 2007-2013 on behalf of the German Federal Foreign Office. It was designed to convert any allocation of commitment appropriations over the different budget headings into explicit allocations of payments and revenues between the member states and over time.

For the calculation of the annual net positions resulting from the actual figures finally agreed upon in the Financial Framework, several underlying assumptions of the model regarding the macroeconomic environment and the system of own resources were updated, based on the most recent information available (see Table 6). For the calculation of the traditional own resources and the VAT resource, for all countries the share of traditional own resources and VAT base in GNI is assumed to be constant over time; regarding the other revenues, a constant share in EU GNI is assumed, which corresponds to the level of 2005.

Table 6. Data sources revenue side

Item	Source
GDP / GNI	2007: European Commission (2006c), Economic forecasts autumn 2006. 2008-2013: European Commission (2004b), Multi-annual Financial Framework 2007-2013 Fiche no. 1b.
Traditional Own Resources	Average share of TOR in GNI, European Parliament (2006a, 2006b), Amending budgets of the European Union for the financial years 2005 and 2006; Romania and Bulgaria: Average of EU-10 minus Cyprus and Malta.
VAT resources	Average share of unlimited VAT base in GNI, European Parliament (2006a, 2006b, 2004), Amending budgets of the European Union for the financial years 2004-2006; Romania and Bulgaria: Average of EU-10 minus Cyprus and Malta.

The allocation of the own resources payments takes place according to the most recent changes in the system of own resources confirmed in the Financial Framework as determined in the Inter-Institutional Agreement of June 14, 2006. This explicitly comprises the fixing of the VAT call rate at 0.3% (and its respective reductions for four member states), the reduction of the GNI resource payments for two member states and the adjustment to the UK correction mechanism.

For the modelling of the expenditure side, it is important to differentiate between commitment and payment appropriations. In many policy areas, accepted commitments for one fiscal year translate into payments with a time lag of several years. The commitment appropriations over the different budget headings and years were fixed in the Financial Perspective 2007-2013; an indicative breakdown of expenditure was published afterwards by the EU Commission (European Commission, 2006d). In order to assess the chronological accruement of the payments resulting from the agreed commitments as well as from commitments remaining from the previous fiscal years ("reste à liquider", RAL), several assumptions were made based on statements by the European Commission (2004c).

Finally, it is essential for the calculation of net positions to break down the overall payments from the EU budget to national allowances. For this purpose matrixes were calculated, differentiated for all policy areas which show for every year how 100 EUR of payments appropriations are broken down to the 27 member states. Several publications of indicative allocations published very recently by the

EU Commission now allow us a very detailed approximation for some of these matrixes. For others, projections have been calculated based on past allocations and figures arranged with the accession countries in their negotiations. The underlying sources for the most important policy areas are given in Table 6.

Table 7. Data sources expenditure side

Budget Heading	Sources
Cohesion / Regional Convergence	Indicative allocation by member state of the commitment appropriations for the Convergence objective for the period 2007-2013 from 8/4/2006 (2006/594/EC) and amendment from 3/28/2007(2007/191/EC).
Regional Competitiveness and Employment	Indicative allocation by member state of the commitment appropriations for the Regional competitiveness and employment objective for the period 2007-2013 from 8/4/2006 (2006/593/EC).
Territorial Cooperation	Indicative allocation by member state of the commitment appropriations for the European territorial cooperation objective for the period 2007-2013 from 8/4/2006 (2006/609/EC).
Agriculture	Approximation based on the average allocation to the EU-15 2002-2005 (Allocation Report 2002-2005), Copenhagen package (source: European Council, 2002), Multi-annual Financial Framework 2007-2013 Fiche no. 24 (REV).
Rural Development	Annual breakdown by member state of the amount for Community support to rural development for the period from January 1, 2007 to December 31, 2013 from 9/12/2006 (2006/636/EC).
Fisheries	Commission decision on final fixing an annual indicative allocation by member state for the period from January 1, 2007 to December 31, 2013 of the Community commitment appropriations from the European Fisheries Fund from 3/28/2007 (2007/218/EC).

As the reference for the calculations below, the year 2010 was chosen which will be the first fiscal year after the revision planned for 2008/2009. Moreover, it will be the first year when the reformed regulation of the UK rebate will be applied almost in full. In 2010, the correction payments will be reduced through a reduction of the overall attributable expenditure by a share of 70% of the expenditure allocated to the new member states (except for CAP). The consideration of the full reduction of this expenditure which will start in the subsequent year would mean a further decrease of the UK rebate by 850 m EUR which is equivalent to 15% of the country's received correction payments in 2010. However, it has to be pointed out that this degree of reduction will not stay constant until 2013. According to our calculations, the overall capping of the reduction of 10.5 billion EUR will be exceeded in 2013 leading to higher correction payments to the UK in that year compared to the years before.

3.6.3 Expenditure Side Versus Revenue Side Redistribution

Although the revenue side is the focus of this report, it is also essential to briefly regard the contributions of the expenditure side to the overall distributive effect of the EU budget. An isolated view of the revenue side would also be incomplete because the historical overview has shown that expenditure side outcomes have always been key drivers of revenue side reforms (see section 3.3.1).

In Fig. 3 the distributive effects of the revenue side and the expenditure side are contrasted. The countries' net positions are broken down to contributions of the expenditure and revenue side and expressed as a share of the country's GNI. A positive value indicates a positive contribution to the net position (a higher share in allocated expenditures than in GNI or a lower share of own resources payments than in GNI, respectively), a negative value indicates a negative contribution. Therefore, the overall net position of a country results from the addition of both figures.

As can be easily seen from the picture, the overall net position is clearly largely determined by the expenditure side and not by the contribution of the own resources payments. This means that misbalances are predominantly driven by the budget's expenditure side. Moreover, there is generally a negative relationship between the net positions on the expenditure and on the revenue side. This holds true both for the countries with large positive net inflows and for the five countries with the lowest share of allocated expenditures to GNI (and the most negative overall net position as is shown in the chapter 9, Table 13): These five member states (namely the United Kingdom, Germany, Austria, Sweden and the Netherlands) are at the same time the countries with the highest positive net position regarding the payment of own resources.

This clearly indicates that the revenue side details serve as a buffer against distributive effects of the expenditure side which are obviously politically inacceptable in their original size. Thus, this analysis reiterates the result from the historical overview that expenditure side pressure impacts on the revenue side specifications.

Fig. 3. Redistributive effects of the EU budget

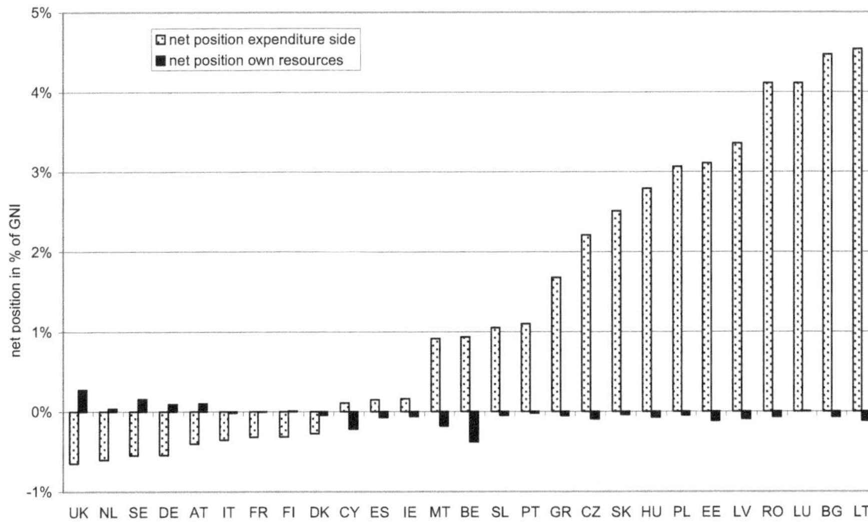

Source: ZEW calculations. Simulation results for the year 2010.

While the drivers of redistributive effects on the revenue side will be examined in greater detail in section 3.6.4, the two largest policy items on the expenditure side are shown in Fig. 4. This comprises the structural policies and the common agriculture policy. Not shown are the administration expenditures from which almost exclusively those countries benefit where most EU institutions are located, namely Belgium (57.1% of the total expenditures) and Luxembourg (19.8%).[8] Therefore, this constitutes the main driver of the relatively high share of payments attributed to these relatively small countries while having almost no redistributive effect on other countries.

By plotting the member states with decreasing GDP per head (in purchasing power standards, data estimated for the year 2008) from the left to the right, Fig. 4 reveals very different redistributive effects of the two policy areas. It can be seen that the payments from structural and cohesion funds clearly show a progressive development with negative net positions for the 12 richest countries and positive ones for the other countries, mainly the CEE countries. This is in line with the general assumption that these budget items should display a certain redistributive character and lead to transfer payments from the better off to the poorer member states in order to meet with the aim of cohesion. However, it has to be emphasised that, even if this is true for the overall payments from cohesion and structural

8 However, it is debatable whether the expenditure within this policy area should be attributed to member states, as mainly representatives from other member states do benefit from it. Therefore, it does not only increase consumption in the country to which the money is attributed.

funds, it does not necessarily mean that this proposition holds for every objective which is pursued by single funds. For instance, it will be shown in 5.1.2 that the distribution pattern of payments to "Competitiveness and Employment Regions" can, by no means, be described as progressive as these payments mainly benefit wealthier countries.

Fig. 4. Redistributive effects of the expenditure side

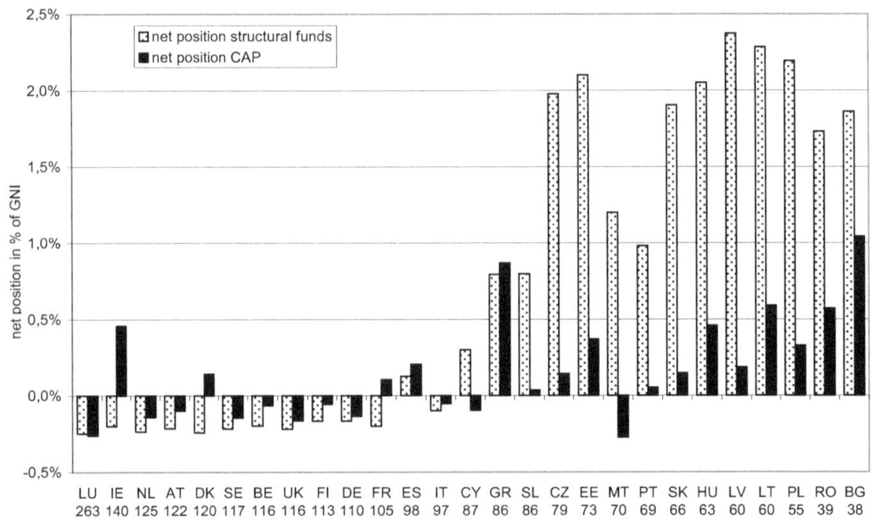

Source: ZEW calculations; subscript: GDP per head (PPS) estimated for 2008 by Eurostat, average of EU-25 = 100. Simulation results for the year 2010.

The payments within the Common Agricultural Policy, however, show a different dispersion. Here, the distributional effects seem to be dispersed rather arbitrarily. The very poor countries in particular do not benefit to a much higher degree than several Western European countries with a far higher GDP per head. This mainly affects countries such as Denmark, Ireland or France, which belong to the group of net recipients of the CAP in spite of their relatively high income level.

One further noteworthy aspect of the new Financial Framework is the inflation of additional clauses under the budget heading "Cohesion for Growth and Employment" (see also section 3.4). These various measures, which can be regarded as the discretionary pendant of the rebates on the revenue side discussed beyond, increased to an amount of over 12 billion EUR for the period 2007-2013. In absolute figures, Spain and Italy are the biggest recipients receiving more than half of the share. But as can be seen in chapter 9, Table 12, the distributional effects are rather limited, due to the relatively low absolute amount of the payments. The only country with a significant increase is Cyprus (+0.31 % of GNI), benefiting from assigning the country the status of a Phasing-in region; Spain, the main beneficiary in absolute terms, only improves its net position by 0.03% of GNI. For other countries the redistributive effect is fairly low, leading to a negative net position of only -0.01% of GNI for those countries not benefiting at all from these payments.

3.6.4 The Redistributive Effects of Different Own Resources

As was shown above, only few countries show a positive net position regarding the own resources, which means that they pay less than the amount they would have to contribute under an own resources system with payments that are completely proportional to GNI. In the following, the redistributive effects of the different own resources are analysed in order to explain these different net positions on the revenue side. The decomposition of the net positions is depicted in Fig. 5. The main findings are summarised below.

Fig. 5. Distributive effects of the system of own resources per item

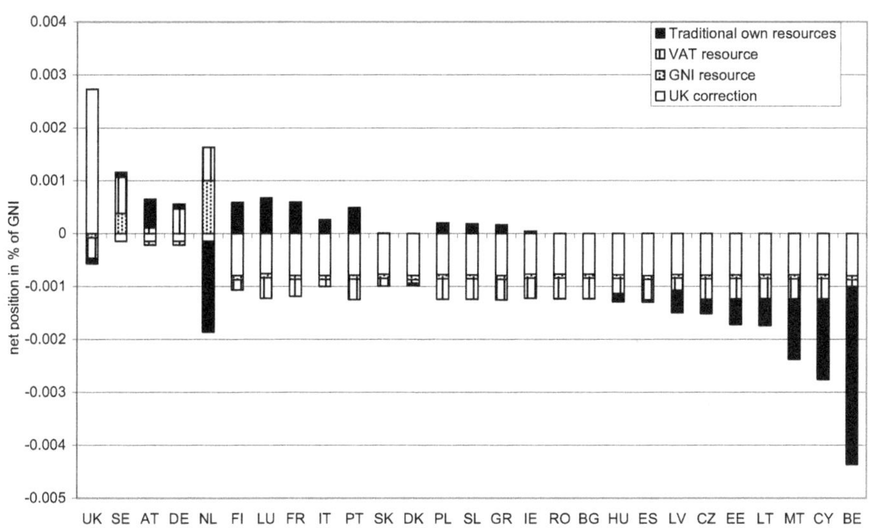

Source: ZEW calculations. Simulation results for the year 2010.

Traditional Own Resources

The redistributive effect of the traditional own resources can be characterised as the most asymmetric one. Few countries pay relatively much compared to their share in GNI while a large number of countries' net positions are positively affected, albeit to a small extent. The countries with an exceptionally high burden are most notably Belgium and the Netherlands, which are the main gateways for EU imports due to their important harbours; this effect is, therefore, also known as the Rotterdam-Antwerp effect. However, since the last accession rounds, the two island states of Cyprus and Malta can also be assigned to this group. It should, however, be stressed that the nexus between formal incidence (which country pays?) and material incidence (which country carries the final economic burden?) is particularly loose in the case of TOR so that these distributive effects have to be interpreted with particular care (see section 3.7.3).

Similar to the diagrams above, deviations from completely GNI proportional payments are shown for each resource; positive values indicate lower payments than under GNI proportionality, and negative values indicate higher payments than under GNI proportionality. The country order follows the size of the revenue side net position, i.e. the UK benefits the most, Belgium the least from the revenue side.

VAT Resource

The national differences in the impact of the VAT resource are dominated by the effects of the reduction of the rate of call for the four member states of Austria, Germany, Sweden and the Netherlands. Therefore, these countries are greatly disburdened and pay relatively low contributions compared to their share of GNI (all show a positive net position) while the other countries are affected slightly negatively.

Although there are partially huge differences regarding the ratio of the harmonised VAT base to GNI between several countries (which will be discussed in the context of a proposed EU tax based on VAT in section 5.2.4), these differences do not lead to high redistributive effects via the VAT own resources. The payment breakdown does not show big differences to a GNI share breakdown. This can be attributed to the capping of the VAT base, which restricts the payments of countries with a high consumption rate. Moreover, the relatively low share of the VAT resources in the overall revenues restricts the absolute amount of redistribution via this channel. Thus, even countries with a very low consumption rate (such as Italy or Denmark) do not benefit to a great extent from this resource as its amount is relatively low and other member states do not excessively contribute due to the capping of their VAT base.

GNI Resource

At first sight it appears surprising that the contributions of the GNI resource are not completely equal to the respective national shares in overall GNI. However, two exemptions have been introduced in the new Financial Framework which invalidate a perfect proportionality: The rebates for Sweden and the Netherlands are directly subtracted from their obligations within the GNI resource, thus leading to a significant reduction of their payment (and a positive net position) whilst slightly increasing the shares of the other countries' payments under this resource compared to their share in GNI. While the improvement of the Dutch net position is particularly striking, the overall redistributive effect seems to be rather restricted for the other countries.

UK Correction

The highest redistributive effect, in absolute numbers, stems from to the UK rebate. It reduces the net payment position of the UK by almost 0.3% of the country's GNI. The redistributive effects for the other countries which pay for the rebate are also significant: While it is highly limited in size for the four countries to which the "rebate on the rebate" was granted, it reduces the net positions of all other countries by 0.08% of their GNI.

Overall Revenues

On taking a closer look at the overall figures for the revenue, it is striking that mainly the biggest net payers have an advantageous position within the current system of own resources. It becomes obvious that particularly the several exemptions existing in the current system, beginning with the UK rebate and ending with the discretionary exemptions agreed in the new Financial Framework, aim to compensate some richer countries on the revenue side for their low backflows on the expenditure side. This mainly affects the UK, whose negative net position is reduced by 38%, but also Germany (-9%), Sweden (-22%) and Austria (-14%). Moreover, all other countries, including the poorer countries of Central and Eastern Europe, pay more than their corresponding share of GNI. Belgium, Malta and Cyprus have the most negative positions because of their higher share of TOR followed by the main receivers of EU payments in Eastern Europe as well as Spain and Greece.

Summing up, the redistributive effects of the current system of own resources differ from the progressive character of national tax systems. Here, the rate is the highest for those countries with the smallest base – at least based on GNI comparisons at nominal exchange rate.

However, one should be cautious classifying this own resources system as "regressive" since the picture is very different if one replaces the GNI shares calculated at nominal exchange rates by GNI shares calculated at purchasing power standards (PPS). Fig. 6 presents a reproduction of Fig. 3 where PPS shares in EU GNI now replace GNI shares calculated on the basis of nominal exchange rates. In this perspective, also the own resources system in isolation is progressive by posing a larger burden on the wealthier countries.

3.6.5 Conclusions for the Reform Debate

As has been shown in the preceding quantitative analysis, redistributive effects of the EU budget are largely driven by the expenditure side of the budget. Here, major differences appear regarding the two dominant expenditure categories: While the payments of the structural funds are clearly progressive (and, therefore, acceptable on the basis of traditional solidarity considerations), the redistributive effects of the CAP payments are more or less arbitrary.

In contrast, the redistributive effects on the revenue side are comparably low. The revenue side counteracts the expenditure side redistribution to a small extent and moves the net positions closer to a balanced GNI ratio by making a small group of net payers benefit from exceptional rules. This reflects a tendency of using the revenue side to partly offset the redistributive effects of the expenditure side and clearly indicates that the negative net positions of these countries are regarded as excessively high. The reasons for this can mainly be found in the agricultural policies: Here, an allocation of the payments only loosely related to relative wealth can be observed, which clearly discriminates against some member states, which in turn are partially compensated by corrections on the revenue side.

Fig. 6. Redistributive effects of the EU budget (GNI shares calculated on PPS basis)

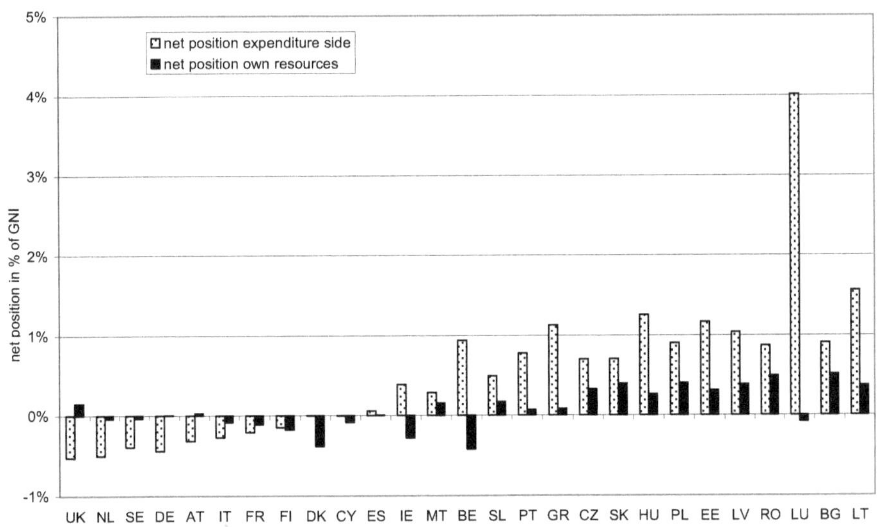

Source: ZEW calculations. Simulation results for the year 2010.

Evidence on the politically relevant determinants of redistribution comes from Kauppi and Widgrén (2004), who identify two different drivers for redistribution: First, there is the needs view, indicating that national income levels and the importance of agriculture determine the national backflows from the EU budget. However, the second view suggests that power politics play a role, meaning that politicians try to allocate as much money as possible to their countries. Rodden (2002) empirically proves that the second view contributes to a very high degree to the actual allocation of resources by showing that smaller countries which are over-represented in EU institutions (and, therefore, have a higher voting power) receive relatively more than bigger countries for agricultural and regional development spending, the two biggest parts of the budget. One example for such payments is the additional provision of payments for structural policies agreed upon in the Financial Framework.

From this digression, one can conclude that the expenditures, despite being bound to the rules as defined by the Financial Framework, nevertheless give room for redistribution in addition to the intended one, which is mainly driven by the aim of cohesion. Although it seems difficult and unfeasible to explicitly connect voting power of the member states to their shares in contributions (as proposed by the Advisory Council of the German Federal Ministry of Economics and Technology, see Wissenschaftlicher Beirat, 1998), the status quo clearly shows that under the current allocation of expenditures there is a demand for a correction on the revenue side. Expenditures obviously do not match an allocation where the redistributive effects follow the postulate of horizontal equity. Instead, single countries benefit due to higher voting power or a larger agricultural sector; this observation clearly hints at a visible connection between the revenue and the expenditure side, which ensures that undesirable redistribution on the expenditure side may be at least partially corrected on the revenue side.

3.7 Detail Problems of Own Resources Items

3.7.1 GNI Resource

Regarding the components of the current system of own resources, the GNI-based own resources usually receives strong support regarding its appropriateness as own resources. National payments of the GNI resource are very easy to calculate compared to any other resource as the statistical concept of GNI is widely established and calculated by the European statistical agencies anyhow. As its determination is very simple, it can easily be understood by the citizens, and as it is seen as a good indicator for the national capability to pay, it generally receives public appreciation.

Furthermore, by changing the rate of call it is very easily possible to generate any intended amount of revenues, therefore, guaranteeing stability and sufficiency of the EU budget in the short-run as well as in the long-run. It also shows a high degree of equity from a theoretical point of view as it is not subject to national peculiarities or preferences.

However, equity between the member states requires the calculation of GNI to follow the same rules in all countries, thus, ruling out biases due to different methodologies of the calculation. An evaluation by the European Court of Auditors (2000) shows the difficulties that arise in attempting to ensure equity, which demands the comparability, reliability and exhaustiveness of the data. Therefore, since its introduction, many efforts have been made to reach a sufficient harmonisation of the statistical determination of the GNI base leading to the European System of national and regional accounts ("ESA 1995"). However one has to concede that the calculation of the GNI has not yet reached perfection, as is the case for any purely statistical measure. This was most recently indicated in October

2006, when the National Statistics Office of Greece undertook a revision of their national account data which led to an increase of the country's GNI level by about 25%. Nevertheless, with regard to the size of the correction, this has to be seen as an isolated case as most of this revision was due to a better coverage of the informal sector, therefore, correcting errors made many years ago.

In spite of this weakness, we hold the view that statistical sources such as the GNI are a reliable indicator for measuring the national capacity as the monitoring of the national statistics improves and the national account is at least not subject to errors to the same degree as other indictors of national capability such as tax bases. For instance, the GNI is not exposed to distortions due to national differences in tax fraud and the size of the informal sectors, like many tax bases, as its calculation allows for different degrees of fraud in the societies (Raddatz & Schick, 2003).

The GNI resource also offers the flexibility to establish any intended redistributive effect on the revenue side by changing the degree of progressiveness. This was also the idea behind the Spanish proposal in 1998 which advocated for an increase of the redistribution on the revenue side by establishing a progressive system of own resources. In their view, this new resource should be raised on the basis of the GNI on which "modulation coefficients" should be applied which reflect the relative wealth or prosperity. This may be achieved using the GNI per capita of the respective country relative to the EU average or applying the same coefficient to groups of countries with similar GNI per capita (European Commission, 1998). Obviously, such a mechanism could also be applied to introduce a regressive own resources, a fact that emphasises its flexible character.

Summing up, we conclude that the use of a measure derived from the national accounts such as the GNI has met with great approval. Nevertheless, it may be disputable whether the GNI is the perfect indicator for the national contribution capacity; instead, the use of GDP or the provision for purchasing power standards may be considered. This will be discussed in section 5.3.2 in greater detail.

3.7.2 VAT Resource

The criticism of the VAT resource, which was the predominant resource until the introduction of the fourth resource, has always been severe. In the past, mainly its regressive character was criticised by the poorer member states. As one generally assumes that the share of private consumption expenditure and, therefore, the VAT base declines with increasing wealth, poorer countries would have to contribute more to the EU budget relative to their wealth (measured in GDP or GNI) than the richer ones. Moreover, countries with a higher share of tourism also show a higher consumption rate. This was generally regarded as dissatisfying in the light of fairness and horizontal equity as countries with a higher consumption ratio were discriminated against although this does not allow a judgement of the national contribution capacity. Hence, in the past the capping of the base was introduced and subsequently the cap was reduced several times in order to disburden the poorer countries, and the reduction of the uniform rate of call diminished the quantitative importance of the VAT resource even further (for details of this process see 3.3.1).

But while solving the problem of regressiveness, this development puts the existence of this resource into question. As more and more countries are affected by the capping of their VAT base (in 2005, 13 member states were affected, see European Commission, 2006a), this resource has become in its distributional effects similar to the GNI resource as these countries pay their contributions to the VAT resource according to their share of GNI. However, there are several disadvantages compared to a purely GNI based resource: First, it creates higher administration costs as the harmonised base must be exclusively calculated for this purpose. Secondly, it is unnecessarily complex and, therefore, difficult to understand for the citizens, thus, contributing to the intransparency of the EU budget.

Another negative aspect of using VAT revenues as a base for levying own resources is the fact that, because of national differences regarding tax fraud and administrative efficiency, the postulate of horizontal equity is also violated. As the rate of VAT evasion and fraud (ranging in the 1990s from 2.4% in the Netherlands to 34.5% in Italy, see Nam, Parsche & Schaden, 2001) as well as the efficiency of the national tax collection differ highly between the EU countries (Raddatz & Schick, 2003), countries with higher fraud or lower collection efficiency have a VAT base which is relatively lower to their wealth than comparable countries. Therefore, they have to pay lower VAT contributions which violates the principle of equity.

3.7.3 Traditional Own Resources

The general purpose of customs duties and agricultural levies is usually called into question by economists as it restricts world trade which leads to losses in efficiency, and it is also connected with high administration costs for custom authorities. It is, therefore, important to emphasise that generating revenues is not the aim of these arrangements but merely a side effect of common European trade and agricultural policies.

One argument in favour of assigning traditional own resources to the EU budget is the regional arbitrariness problem which is particularly obvious in the case of duties. These accrue mainly at the border regions of the Union so that countries with large ports like the Netherlands or Belgium levy high revenues from customs on imported goods although these countries are not the destination of the goods, and the burden of the duties is borne by the customers in other member states. The breakdown of these duties to the member states, however, would be difficult and connected with very high costs. Therefore, it appears to be appropriate to assign the autonomy over these resources to the EU and directly channel the revenues to the EU budget.

Although the TOR seem to be a prime example for the assignment of fiscal autonomy to the European level in the theoretical sense, it cannot play a major role in financing the EU in the future as its revenues should not be increased for fiscal reasons. Due to an increasing number of free trade agreements, the share of

TOR revenues has already heavily declined since the 1970s and is sure to decline even further in the future. As it currently only constitutes a share of about 13% of the EU budget, it is obvious that it fails the criterion of sufficiency. Although it is desirable to keep the TOR as part of the future system of own resources, it can only provide a small part of the resources which is probable to diminish even further in the future.

One point of criticism is the share of administrative costs retained by the collecting countries. Some authors argue that this amount is not connected to the true costs of this task (Euler, 2005). It is even suspected that the increase of the allowance from 10% to 25% in 2000 mainly served as a kind of hidden rebate for the Netherlands, one of the countries with the highest net payments. This view was also held by the EU Parliament (see European Parliament, 2001). In order to make the whole system of own resources more transparent and simple, this allowance should be cost covering while any measures intended for a redistribution of the burden should be transparently executed. Moreover, such a hidden rebate always runs the risk of producing unwanted side effects. In this case, it means an unjustifiable discharge of further countries with a high quantity of traditional own resources (mainly Belgium) and at the same time a higher burden for the other countries which have to contribute more to the EU budget through GNI resources in order to finance the gap produced by increasing the allowance.

However, one should not neglect that an increasing share of retained administration costs may also have a positive effect as indicated by Raddatz (2005). This higher share increases the incentives for the national authorities to improve the administration and the control of the raising of the levies, hence, the moral hazard problem is better addressed. However, this problem does not seem to be valid in the case of the EU in practice as the EU's control is currently very strict. Moreover, the moral hazard problem may also be addressed by introducing flexible additional payments for countries which are successful in collecting TOR and fighting evasion, as proposed by the European Parliament (1999).

While for the time being the principle assignment of TOR to the EU budget appears appropriate, attention has to be paid to the cost-benefit balance for that revenue source. With the desirable continuation of liberalisation revenues will fall. At the same time the administrative burden for collecting these revenues remains high. This may be a reason to reconsider the assignment of that revenue source in the future.

3.7.4 UK Correction

Finally, the major point of criticism concerning the current system of own resources is undoubtedly the existence of the UK correction. The UK rebate only privileges the United Kingdom (other net contributors only benefit from lower participation in its financing). While this might have been justifiable in the face of a seemingly unfair burden in the 1980s due to the country's low backflows from the Common Agricultural Policy and its high payments due to a high consumption rate, this correction mechanism has become more and more unjustifiable since then. The reduction of the relative share of the common agricultural spending as well as the increasing wealth of the UK compared to the rest of the EU have made it difficult to justify the existence of this one-sided mechanism. Currently, other countries show net positions similar to the UK. Therefore, a rebate granted exclusively to one country obviously violates the principle of horizontal equity as it privileges British tax payers. This has understandably aroused suspicion among the citizens of the other countries as it is regarded as unfair.

Furthermore, the UK correction system is the item mainly responsible for eroding the understandability and transparency of the whole system. The many changes conducted since its introduction have made it so complex that it can now only be demonstrated by large formulas. This has made it practically impossible for the citizens to understand it.

However, it may be argued that the still low share of agricultural payments to the UK would create undesired redistributive effects which would discriminate the country. It seems clear, however, that the rebate in its current state is not appropriate, its discriminative character and lack of transparency excludes it as an admissible correction mechanism for a reformed system of own resources.

3.8 Summing Up: Strengths and Weaknesses of the Current System

3.8.1 Necessity of a Holistic Assessment

The strengths and weaknesses of the current system of own resources can now be summarised with regard to the assessment criteria developed on the outset (chapter 2). For the overall assessment it is important to recall a general insight of the presented analysis: A meaningful analysis even if it is focussed on the own resources system must not ignore that:

- the own resources system and the expenditure side are mutually interdependent and
- the own resources must be assessed within the context of overall budgetary institutions and incentives of the important budgetary players.

Mutual Interdependence of Both Sides of the Budget

We regard it as inappropriate to look at certain types of own resources in isolation. A holistic approach taking account of all these dimensions is superior not only with respect to the analytical content and systematic stringency. It can also be expected to arrive at more realistic reform conclusions compared to the isolated approaches. If the link between the distributive effects of the expenditure side and the resulting pressure for compensation mechanisms on the revenue side is ignored, this will probably result in politically infeasible strategies.

With respect to the mutual interdependence of both sides of the budget, the historical overview (see section 3.3.1) and the quantitative calculations (section 3.6) indicate that the direction of causality runs from the expenditure side effects to adjustment on the revenue side rather than the opposite direction: The UK rebate, its subsequent adjustments including "rebate-rebates" for further countries but also adjustments to single own resources items of a seemingly technical nature (e.g., the administration compensation for the TOR) have been the consequence of expenditure side distribution effects which have not been regarded as fair and acceptable by certain veto players. Given that policies like the CAP produce distribution patterns only loosely related to relative wealth we find it hard to criticise this demand for compensation in principle even if the current compensatory mechanisms are dissatisfactory.

Incentives Within Overall Institutions

The manner in which a budget is financed is of relevance for the interest of all those players who have a formal or informal say in budgetary decisions. Good institutions should be characterised by setting balanced incentives to important decision makers with regard to both the benefits and the costs of spending. The common pool problem widely acknowledged in the literature on national budgetary systems is even more relevant at the EU level given the fact that the EU pool of public revenues largely exceeds any national pool. If due to this or other problems there are excessive spending incentives, appropriate institutions must safeguard budgetary discipline.

3.8.2 The Status Quo in the Light of Our Four Groups of Criteria

Box 4 summarises the strengths and weaknesses as they have already been explicitly or implicitly described in the preceding sections. First of all, as shown in section 3.5.4 negative incentives associated with the common pool problem bias expenditure policies against policies of a European public goods type. At the same time, the incentives to over-expand the budget are successfully contained through the cap on the budget in the form of the own resources ceiling. An important advantage of the status quo is also the contribution-based link between the EU budget and the national budgets, which explains the self-interest of Council members to press for fiscal discipline at the European level.

Therefore, it should be stressed that this link between national budgets and the EU budget through the current own resources system is a key advantage of the status quo in the light of the criteria of "fostering efficient public goods production" and of guaranteeing "fiscal discipline". The incentive analysis has made it clear that the Council plays a decisive role as an institution where revenue costs are paid more attention to compared to the budgetary calculus in the Commission or the EP. This (beneficial) incentive heavily depends on the current link between the national budgets and the EU budget. Savings on the European level flow back into the national budget and increase the fiscal leeway for national policy makers.

Box 4. Strengths and weaknesses of status quo

Fostering efficient public goods provision

Advantages:

- Compatible with principle of subsidiarity: No conflict with heterogeneous tax preferences or heterogeneous federal arrangements at the national level
- Cap on the level of the budget

Disadvantages:

- Crowding out of European public goods below the cap set by the own resources ceiling

Constraining narrow self-interest and creating budgetary discipline

Advantages:

- Link between costs of EU budget and fiscal revenues at the national level: Council with self-interest to limit EU spending (with regard to definition of cap and annual budgetary process)

Disadvantages:

- Common pool problem highly virulent for important players and reinforced through spending priorities on expenditure side

Integration compatibility

Advantages:

- Multi-annual framework is channelling and reducing costs of budgetary disputes
- GNI resource widely perceived as fair in administrative terms

Disadvantages:

- Inflation of rebates and special provisions
- Increasing complexity and low transparency

General principles of taxation

Advantages:

- GNI resource with many favourable characteristics: perceived as fair, stable, reliable, neutral, cost-effective

Disadvantages:

- VAT resources (revenue importance has strongly declined) with deteriorating cost-effectiveness

One can also argue that the cap of the own resources decision is an endogenous variable dependent on that incentive structure associated with the status quo of the own resources system. Hence, it is not realistic to expect a continuation of a relatively stable cap on the budget once the Council loses its immediate budgetary self-interest into a disciplined EU budgetary policy (which would be the case if the major part of budgetary finance would no longer have to be covered by national tax revenues).

A further not unimportant fiscal federalism advantage of the current system is that it does not interfere with national tax systems and preferences for redistribution. Member states are free to refinance own resources payments through autonomous tax policies reflecting their citizens' tax preferences. Neither does the status quo interfere with fiscal federalism structures within the member countries. In this sense, the principle of subsidiarity is respected by the current fiscal constitution.

While the status quo, thus, has its merits in the overall institutional assessment, the problem remains that once the cap on the budget is set, important actors will have spending preferences for policies characterised by national, sectoral or regional benefit profiles. Policies involving distributive patterns that are impossible to identify will risk being crowded out.

With regard to the criterion of "integration compatibility", the status quo has the advantage that conflict resolution is effective as can be seen from the fact that annual budgetary crises have been absent since the multi-annual framework is being applied. However, the manner in which conflicts are solved – the inflation of rebates and special provisions, the existence of a rebate privilege for a single country – constitutes a burden for the credibility, the perceived fairness and acceptance of the system. Thus, conflict resolution in the current system has come at the price of an increasing complexity, intransparency and a perceived breach of horizontal fairness considerations. Moreover, transparency is restrained due to the plurality of revenues sources and the complexity of the calculation of the VAT resource and the UK rebate.

Finally, on looking at general principles of taxation, it is fair to say that the system performs increasingly better because of the continuously rising importance of GNI resources. The GNI resource has good characteristics with respect to most principles. It is not only perceived to imply an equitable key for the fiscal burden, it is also relatively cost-efficient in administrative terms, stable, reliable and, as such, does not imply any price distortions (although distortions may occur in the national refinancing of these payments). The overall system has also succeeded in endowing the EU with stable and reliable revenues, thus, guaranteeing the match of revenues and expenditures. Furthermore, it has the advantage that member countries are free to decide on how to refinance. Countries are also free to incur deficits for this purpose. From this perspective, one could argue that, to a certain extent, the GNI resource also implies a decentralised deficit facility of the EU: Proceeds from national deficits can be channelled as own resources payments to the EU budget. Compared to a centralised deficit facility (a direct EU level competency to borrow), this regime is clearly advantageous as it is in line with the spirit of the no-bailout clause of TEC Art. 103 which implies a decision against the pooling of European public debt. Compared to the GNI resource, more problems are linked to VAT resources and also to TOR, for example, with regard to administrative cost-effectiveness.

4 Background Analyses

4.1 Introduction

Before we proceed to the analysis of reform options for the revenue side, two background analyses are presented. First, the degree of tax system and tax preference heterogeneity within the EU is scrutinised. Secondly, an overview is given on revenue systems of international and supranational organisations.

The study on tax system heterogeneity sheds light on the question to which extent a continuing divergence of national tax preferences in Europe exists. One argument which, in principle, speaks in favour of the current system of EU own resources is that this de facto contribution system gives member countries free choice of how to refinance their payments to the EU budget – at least with respect to GNI and VAT own resources which constitute the bulk of current revenue. By contrast, any movement towards a uniform EU tax would tend to eliminate such autonomy. This argument is even more important the more diverse taxation systems and taxation preferences are among EU countries. The freedom to choose how to refinance contributions to the European budget is a greater advantage if member countries still differ with regard to their tax system preferences.

A glance at international organisations is helpful for comparisons and may function as a source of inspiration for the development of EU reform options. Given that the EU has achieved a much deeper level of integration compared to any other international organisation, naïve comparisons would be inadequate. However, this does not preclude the usefulness of these case studies.

4.2 Tax System Heterogeneity

4.2.1 Introduction

This excursus' function is to collect evidence with regard to the current degree of divergence in member countries' tax systems and preferences. Before embarking on the exposition of statistical details, the following consideration is important: A national tax system as it is observable today is hardly exclusively driven by national tax preferences. As well-known from the field of corporate taxation (Overesch, 2005; Winner, 2005), competitive pressure arising from corporate mobility may cause some convergence of corporate tax rates even if national preferences are not converging. Hence, tax system convergence does not necessarily reveal tax preference convergence. If, on the contrary, tax system divergence is a stable empirical fact in spite of globalisation pressure, this can be taken as a strong indicator of continuing divergence of tax preferences.

In the following, different approaches are presented to derive insights about the current divergence and the past evolution of differing tax preferences among EU countries. First of all, direct value judgements with a close logical connection to tax preferences stemming from the World Value Survey are presented. Secondly, time series of important tax system parameters are scrutinised. Thirdly, a cluster analysis is presented indicating which sub-groups of EU countries have a high degree of tax system similarity.

A further methodological remark is important: Often similarity of tax systems is assessed on the basis of tax revenue data (e.g., the share of indirect taxation to GDP versus the share of direct taxation). Since revenues are a complicated consequence of the interplay of tax system characteristics and its diverse incentive effects, we do not regard tax revenue GDP shares as the appropriate starting point for this excursus. Instead, we focus on key tax system parameters – most important statutory and effective tax rates – in order to describe a national tax system's properties.

4.2.2 Divergence in Tax-Relevant Value Judgements

The most direct way for measuring tax system preferences is based on a direct measurement of basic value judgements of a country's citizens. Since the tax system offers key instruments for societies to realise their redistributive preferences, a first important insight with regard to tax system preferences is to which extent fundamental value judgements differ among EU countries with regard, for example, to the efficiency-equity trade-off.

The European and World Value Surveys (European Values Study Foundation & World Values Survey Association, 2006) offer a rich database which allows studying the cross-section properties of these judgements. Currently, four waves of surveys (wave 1: 1981-1984, wave 2: 1989-1991, wave 3: 1995-1998 and wave 4: 1999-2001) are available.

For the most recent wave, Table 8 presents the means for EU countries where available for the following questions:

- *Equal pay*: "Imagine two secretaries of the same age doing practically the same job. One finds out that the other earns considerably more than she does. The better paid secretary, however, is quicker, more efficient and more reliable at her job. In your opinion, is it fair or not fair that one secretary is paid more than the other?"

  Answers: 0 "not fair", 1 "fair".

This question reveals the acceptability of performance-related wage differentials in a society. Although it does not directly reveal tax system preferences, it could be also regarded as an indicator to which extent a society may accept income differentials.

- *Freedom or equality*: "Which of these two statements comes closest to your own opinion?
  I find that both freedom and equality are important. But if I were to choose one or the other, I would consider personal freedom more important, that is, everyone can live in freedom and develop without hinderance.
  Certainly both freedom and equality are important. But if I were to choose one or the other, I would consider equality more important, that is, that nobody is underprivileged and that social class differences are not so strong."
  Answers: 1 "Freedom above equality", 2 "Equality above freedom".
  Tax systems also serve the function to correct market incomes whereas the price, at least in the perception of many taxpayers, is a limitation of personal freedom. This question indicates how a country evaluates this possible trade-off.
- *Equality versus incentives*: "Incomes should be made more equal" vs. "We need larger income differences as incentives".
  Answer scale from 1 "Incomes should be made more equal" to 10 "We need larger income differences as incentives".
  Similarly to the preceding question, this question serves to indicate a country's citizens' preferences with regard to a trade-off, this time the trade-off between equality and efficiency.
- *Cash instead of taxes*: "Please tell me for each of the following statements whether you think it can always be justified, never be justified, or something in between, paying cash for services to avoid taxes."
  Answer scale from 1 "Never justifiable" to 10 "Always justifiable".
  This question covers a specific aspect, the idea of transferring tax-financed public services into fee or market price-financed (private) services. The answers may reveal to which extent voters would accept a larger degree of user fees in traditionally tax-financed fields such as education, health or other.

Due to incomplete country coverage in earlier waves of the World Values Survey (WVS) no analysis of tax preference heterogeneity over time is possible. However, Table 8 shows that there are today marked differences in the answering behaviour of EU countries. Interestingly, formerly communist countries like the Czech or the Slovak Republic are today characterised by the largest acceptance of performance-related wage differentials. At the same time, these countries' respondents also tend to weigh freedom relatively strong in relation to equality. Extreme positions with regard to the equality-efficiency trade-off are taken by Austria, Finland and France (strongest preference for equality) on the one hand and Luxembourg, the Netherlands, Ireland and Italy (strongest preference for incentives) on the other hand. The largest openness for fee-based public services can be detected in Belgium, Denmark and the Netherlands, the largest opposition in the Czech Republic, Italy and Portugal.

Table 8. Value judgements related to tax system preferences: Country means

	Equal pay	Freedom or equality	Equality versus in-centives	Cash instead of taxes
Austria	0.89	1.39	4.56	3.15
Belgium	0.71	1.51	5.50	4.25
Czech Republic	0.97	1.38	5.49	2.38
Denmark	0.82	1.28		4.31
Finland	0.76	1.45	4.60	3.64
France	0.77	1.47	4.85	4.15
Germany	0.87	1.35		2.69
Greece	0.88			4.02
Hungary	0.85	1.50		2.64
Ireland	0.65	1.48	6.11	2.89
Italy	0.78	1.55	6.02	2.50
Luxembourg	0.81	1.45	6.83	3.99
The Netherlands	0.75	1.41	6.18	4.26
Poland	0.88	1.44	6.09	2.73
Portugal	0.75	1.49		2.28
Slovak Republic	0.91	1.28		3.68
Spain	0.66	1.45	5.06	3.35
Sweden	0.76	1.35		3.80
United Kingdom	0.73	1.35	5.60	3.49
Mean (unweighted)	0.80	1.42	5.57	3.38
Minimum	0.65	1.28	4.56	2.28
Maximum	0.97	1.55	6.83	4.31
Range	0.32	0.28	2.26	2.03
Standard deviation	0.08	0.08	0.67	0.68

Source: Own calculations based on European Values Study Foundation & World Values Survey Association (2006, wave 4: 1999-2001).

For indicative purposes, in Fig. 7 these findings are condensed in an indicator describing the efficiency orientation as it can be derived from the WVS results. For that purpose, in a first step, all four variables of Table 8 are z-transformed (standardised by subtracting the mean and dividing by the standard deviation). In a second step the variables signs are adjusted so that a positive sign represents a relative strong weight to efficiency. In a third step the mean of all four (equally weighted) variables is calculated.

Fig. 7. Indicator of efficiency orientation of tax preferences

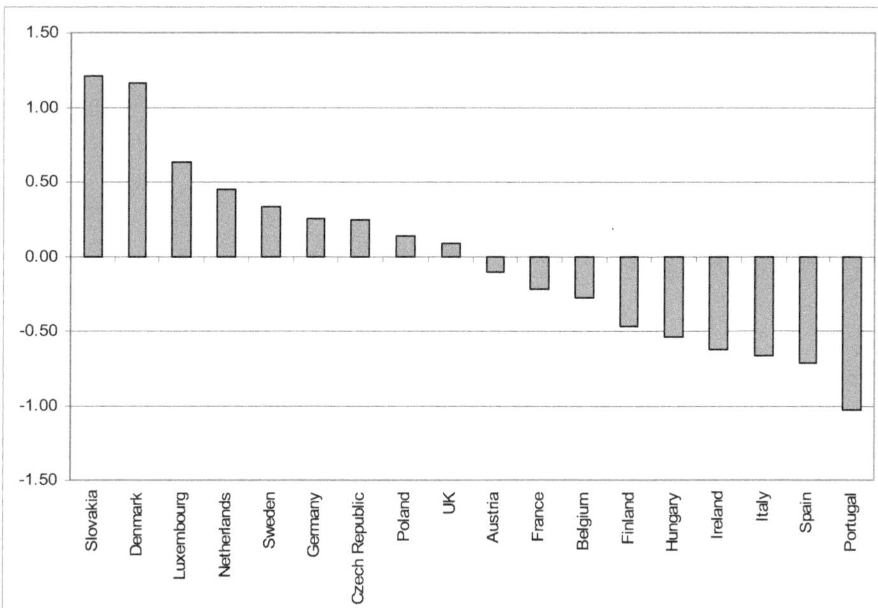

Source: Own calculations; for indicator construction, see text.

While some results – for example, the relatively low weight of efficiency compared to equality in Southern Europe or France – are hardly surprising, other results may come as a surprise such as the strong efficiency orientation of some Scandinavian countries like Denmark and Sweden. An explanation could be that answering behaviour may be strongly influenced by the desired change of the system. In that sense, Danish or Swedish preferences for a more efficiency-oriented approach must also be seen with the background of a tax and transfer system in place which has stressed equality strongly for decades and where nowadays a correction may be regarded as desirable.

4.2.3 Convergence of Tax Structure Parameters

The next analytical step immediately focusses on central parameters of the tax system. Here we have collected time series on:

Indirect taxes:

- VAT, standard rate,
  Source: European Commission (2007).
- Petroleum tax (Euro per litre),
  Source: IEA (International Energy Agency) (2005).

Direct personal taxes:

- Top income tax rate,
  Source: IBFD (2006).
- Top income tax rate bracket relative to average compensation of employees,
  Source: IBFD (2006).
- OECD tax wedge,
  Source: OECD (2007).

Direct corporate taxation:

- Corporate tax rate,
  Source: IBFD (2006).
- Effective average tax rate (EATR),
  Source: Elschner and Overesch (2007).
- Effective marginal tax rate (EMTR),
  Source: Elschner and Overesch (2007).

Inheritance tax:

- Inheritance tax revenues/GDP,
  Source: IBFD (2006).

With the exception of inheritance taxation all measures constitute key properties of the tax tariffs and, thus, are not directly influenced by tax payers' reactions. However, as explained in the introductory remarks, national autonomy to determine these parameters substantially differs among tax types. For VAT, EU harmonisation measures have defined a corridor for normal rates. For corporate taxation, tax competition increasingly sets restrictions. Hence, only taxes for which neither harmonisation nor competition significantly cuts into national leeway, tax parameter divergence can be taken as an indicator of differing national tax preferences.

Table 9 and Table 10 summarise the mean and standard deviation of tax parameters for EU countries. Data availability differs widely among countries and over time. In order to avoid a distortion of the depicted development over time by a changing composition of included countries, all statistical measures are calculated for a country sample which is constant over time but which differs across tax parameters. Hence, the indicated changes in tax parameter divergence over time are no statistical artefact resulting from the inclusion or exclusion of countries along the time axis.

Table 9. Tax parameters for EU countries over time – Indirect taxation and personal taxation

	VAT (normal rate, in %)		Petrol tax (in Euro per litre)		Top income tax rate (in %)		Tax bracket top income tax (in % of average employee compensation)		OECD tax wedge (in %)	
	mean	stdv	mean	stdv	mean	stdv	mean	stdv	mean	stdv
1981									41.0	7.3
1982										
1983									43.1	6.8
1984										
1985									43.8	6.4
1986										
1987									43.9	6.7
1988	18.4	4.1								
1989	18.4	4.1							43.6	7.1
1990	18.4	4.1					2.5	2.0		
1991	18.5	3.4			53.0	7.9	2.5	2.1	42.6	6.5
1992	19.0	3.7			51.3	7.6	2.4	2.2		
1993	19.1	3.4			50.8	7.3	2.2	1.7	43.3	6.5
1994	19.2	3.4	0.4	0.1	51.8	7.8	2.3	2.0	43.6	6.7
1995	19.3	3.3	0.4	0.1	52.6	7.5	2.1	1.6	44.1	7.2
1996	19.5	3.3	0.4	0.1	52.3	8.0	2.0	1.5	44.1	7.4
1997	19.5	3.3	0.4	0.1	52.5	8.0	2.0	1.4	44.3	7.8
1998	19.6	3.2	0.4	0.1	50.8	6.9	1.7	0.7	43.6	7.5
1999	19.6	3.2	0.4	0.1	50.7	7.0	1.7	0.7	43.3	7.7
2000	19.6	3.2	0.4	0.1	50.0	7.0	1.7	0.6	42.8	7.9
2001	19.7	3.2	0.4	0.1	48.6	6.7	1.6	0.6	41.8	8.2
2002	19.7	3.2	0.7	0.1	48.0	6.9	1.6	0.5	41.0	8.4
2003	19.8	3.1	0.5	0.1	47.5	6.7	1.4	0.5	40.9	8.3
2004	19.8	3.1	0.5	0.1	47.0	6.3	1.4	0.4	41.3	8.0
2005	19.8	3.1	0.5	0.1	46.6	6.3	1.5	0.7		
2006	19.7	2.8			45.8	6.7	1.5	0.6		
2007	19.9	2.6								

Mean and standard deviation (stdv) are calculated for a sample of EU countries constant over time but differing across included tax parameters.

Source: Own calculations.

Table 10. Tax parameters for EU countries over time – Corporate and inheritance taxation

	Corporate tax rate (in %)		EATR (in %)		EMTR (in %)		Inheritence tax (revenues relative to GDP)	
	mean	stdv	mean	stdv	mean	stdv	mean	stdv
1981							0.003	0.001
1982	44.7	12.6	40.7	11.5	34.4	12.1	0.003	0.000
1983	44.0	12.5	40.5	11.5	34.3	12.2	0.004	0.002
1984	44.4	11.9	40.5	10.9	34.3	11.4	0.003	0.000
1985	44.4	11.7	40.8	10.7	33.9	10.7	0.003	0.001
1986	42.7	11.4	38.9	10.4	32.2	10.3	0.003	0.001
1987	42.1	11.6	38.2	10.6	31.7	10.4	0.004	0.002
1988	41.9	11.5	37.6	10.4	31.0	10.4	0.004	0.002
1989	41.2	11.7	37.3	10.4	31.3	9.9	0.004	0.002
1990	39.6	10.3	35.7	9.2	29.2	9.3	0.004	0.002
1991	37.1	10.0	33.7	9.0	27.4	9.4	0.004	0.002
1992	37.0	10.9	32.7	9.2	26.5	9.5	0.004	0.002
1993	35.8	11.2	31.9	9.5	26.2	9.9	0.005	0.003
1994	34.9	11.0	30.6	9.1	24.2	9.5	0.005	0.003
1995	35.1	11.1	30.9	9.5	24.6	10.0	0.005	0.003
1996	35.8	11.2	31.5	9.5	25.5	10.0	0.005	0.003
1997	35.8	11.2	31.1	9.0	24.4	8.6	0.005	0.004
1998	34.0	8.9	29.5	7.5	20.7	8.1	0.005	0.004
1999	33.6	8.8	29.2	7.4	20.4	7.9	0.005	0.004
2000	33.4	8.6	29.1	7.3	20.0	8.5	0.005	0.003
2001	32.7	8.2	28.7	7.0	20.0	9.3	0.005	0.003
2002	32.6	8.1	28.3	6.2	19.7	8.9	0.005	0.003
2003	32.1	7.0	28.3	5.8	21.6	6.2	0.005	0.003
2004	31.8	6.8	28.1	5.6	21.5	6.1	0.005	0.003
2005	30.3	7.0	26.9	5.5	20.5	5.8		
2006	30.2	7.0						
2007	29.5	7.3						

Note: Mean and standard deviation (stdv) are calculated for a sample of EU countries constant over time but differing across included tax parameters.

Source: Own calculations.

As expected, all parameters related to corporate taxation reveal both a falling tax burden and increasing convergence. Both statutory corporate tax rates and included effective tax rates show that compared to the early 1980s the standard deviation has halved. Convergence is also observable for VAT. Contrary to corporate taxation, this convergence is combined with increasing rates. The picture of direct personal taxation is less uniform. A slight decline of top income tax rates is accompanied by a marked fall of the tax bracket at which the top income rate sets in. At the same time, the tax wedge driven both by taxes and social security contributions appears to have peaked at the end of the 1990s and has declined since then. These tax wedges are even characterised by an increasing divergence whereas the top income rates appear to converge slightly and the (relative) tax bracket for the top income rate strongly. No convergence is observable for petrol taxation and inheritance taxation. For the latter, our indicator even points towards increasing heterogeneity.

All together this descriptive evidence draws the picture of some convergence in the fields where competition and EU harmonisation are driving forces. For those parts of the tax system where national autonomy is prevailing, no similar convergence patterns can be detected. This could be taken as a cautious hint for continuing tax preference heterogeneity. One should add that missing historical data for the new Eastern European member countries led to their exclusion from our calculations. In this sense, the depicted measures of tax parameter heterogeneity may even underestimate the true divergence. In order to find out more about the current diversity, we proceed to the next analytical step, a cluster analysis for the enlarged EU.

4.2.4 Cluster Analysis: Tax System Classes

The preceding analysis is now supplemented by an analytical approach based on a cluster analysis. This technique (for details see, e.g., Bortz, 2004) allows us to identify to which extent certain groups ("clusters") of countries are characterised by a high degree of internal similarity and between group dissimilarity. For that purpose we proceed as follows:

In a first step, a dimension-limiting technique (principal component analysis) is applied in order to reduce the number of included dimensions to three as follows:

- VAT tax rate and petrol tax are condensed into a principal component "indirect taxation";
- top marginal income tax rate, the tax bracket for that top tax rate and the OECD tax wedge are condensed into a principal component "direct personal taxation";
- the statutory corporate tax rate, the EMTR and the EATR, are condensed into a principal component "direct corporate taxation".

Inheritance taxes are excluded due to missing data. This reduction of dimensions is necessary in order to avoid an implicit different weighting of these three fields of taxation which would otherwise result from the different number of available variables.

In a second step, a hierarchical cluster analysis is performed. As a distance measure the Euclidean distance is applied, the country merger follows the Ward Algorithm (for details, see Bortz, 2004). The analysis is based on the year 2003 since this year offers the most complete country coverage. In addition to 18 EU countries, Norway and Switzerland are included. Missing data led to the exclusion of the UK, the Baltic States, Slovenia, Malta and Cyprus. Romania and Bulgaria could neither be included due to the data situation.

Five clusters with a relatively high degree of internal homogeneity emerge from the algorithm (see Fig. 8):

- Cluster 1: ("Eastern European cluster") Czech Republic, Poland, Slovak Republic, Hungary and Ireland;
- Cluster 2: ("Small countries") Luxembourg, Norway, Greece and Portugal;
- Cluster 3: Switzerland;
- Cluster 4: ("Nordic cluster") Austria, Finland, Denmark, Sweden and Belgium;
- Cluster 5: ("Large continental EU countries") Italy, the Netherlands, France, Spain and Germany.

Fig. 8. Cluster analysis for similarity of tax systems

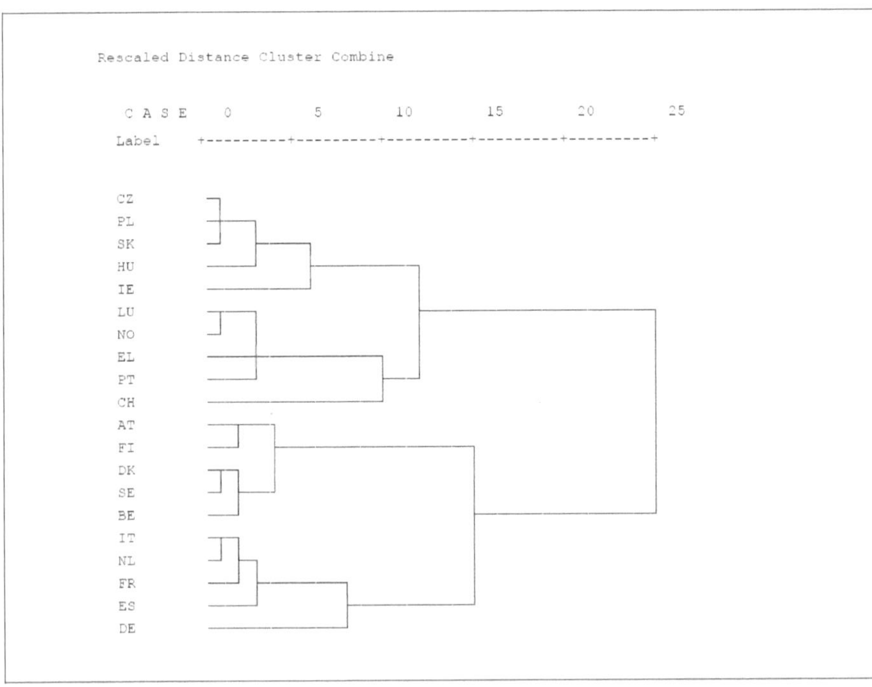

Source: Own calculations, Ward algorithm and Euclidean distance measure based on 2003 tax parameters.

This clustering reveals that the new members on the eve of EU entry were characterised by tax systems parameters which could best be compared to the Irish setting (cluster 1). The isolated position of Switzerland (cluster 3) is hardly surprising given the fact that this country is not restricted by VAT harmonisation and uses this freedom to stick to a much lower VAT normal rate (7.6%). The Scandinavian EU countries (cluster 4) are united in one single cluster together with Austria and Belgium indicating that there is, indeed, a "Nordic" tax model while the large continental EU countries (cluster 5) also reveal a high degree of similarity. A further cluster (cluster 2) finally combines smaller European countries.

Table 11. Cluster profiles of tax parameters

	Indirect taxaton		**Direct personal taxation**			**Corporate taxation**		
	VAT	Petrol tax	Top inc. tax	Tax bracket top rate	OECD tax wedge	Corporate tax rate	EMTR	EATR
Nordic cluster: Austria, Finland, Denmark, Sweden and Belgium								
Mean	22.6	0.5	55.0	1.2	46.9	31.0	19.3	27.1
Stdv.	2.30	0.1	3.6	0.4	4.7	2.8	4.2	2.9
Eastern European cluster: Czech Republic, Poland, Slovak Republic, Hungary and Ireland								
Mean	22.0	0.4	38.4	1.4	39.4	23.0	15.5	20.4
Stdv.	1.9	0.1	3.9	0.8	8.7	7.2	2.3	4.1
Large continental EU countries cluster: Italy, Netherlands, France, Spain and Germany								
Mean	18.1	0.6	48.8	1.7	43.7	36.8	29.6	34.5
Stdv.	2.0	0.2	3.1	0.4	7.1	2.6	5.3	2.3
Small countries cluster: Luxembourg, Norway, Greece and Portugal								
Mean	19.0	0.4	41.6	1.8	37.3	32.8	19.9	27.0
Stdv.	3.7	0.1	4.0	1.0	5.7	4.7	3.7	2.6
Switzerland								
Mean	7.6	0.5	41.0	9.2	29.0	24.1	16.3	21.8
Stdv.								
Total								
Mean	19.9	0.5	45.9	1.9	41.4	30.5	20.9	27.0
Stdv.	4.1	0.1	7.4	1.8	7.6	6.8	6.5	5.9
F-test signif.	0.00	0.03	0.00	0.00	0.11	0.00	0.00	0.00

Source: Own calculations.

Table 11 summarises how these clusters differ with regard to average values of tax parameters and indicate significant differences based on an analysis of variance for the difference of means among clusters. With the exception of the tax wedge the differences in tax parameters between clusters are significant, with petrol tax always with the highest level of significance (see F-test). The Nordic and the Eastern European clusters are characterised by high VAT and moderate (Nordic) to low (Eastern Europe) corporate taxation. Both clusters are very different with regard to personal taxation where the Nordic countries show a much more aggressive approach compared to the Eastern Europeans. The large continental

European cluster depicts the highest burden on corporate profits; at the same time it has moderate VAT (but the highest petrol tax of all clusters).

The cluster analysis allows to gain additional insights with regard to tax system heterogeneity in Europe. Definitely, the EU membership of the Central and Eastern European countries has increased tax system heterogeneity since these countries have established a relatively unique type of tax system as these countries immediately form a cluster of their own (together with Ireland). It is hardly possible to decide solely on the basis of the cluster analysis whether this increasing tax system heterogeneity only reflects a different competitive approach or differing tax system preferences as well. The results from the WVS data exploration, however, indicate that new EU member countries' populations look at efficiency-equity trade-offs differently compared to many old EU member countries.

4.2.5 Conclusion

Doubtlessly, the presented statistical evidence leaves many questions unanswered. Surprisingly, the issue of international tax preferences heterogeneity is a largely under-researched issue, and much more needs to be done to arrive at definitive answers. Thus, it must be left to future research to disentangle more precisely to which extent a limited convergence of tax parameters actually only reflects the effect of tax competition or harmonisation measures on the one hand or converging tax preferences on the other hand. However, three key results indicate a substantial and stable (or even increasing) heterogeneity of tax preferences among EU countries:

- First, tax parameter convergence is less observable on fields where countries do not face pressure from tax competition or harmonisation rules.
- Secondly, direct indicators on tax preferences derived from surveys reveal substantial difference how voters across EU member countries judge certain trade-offs which are essential to determine a tax system.
- Thirdly, the unique tax model of new EU member countries indicates that the spectre of tax system preferences has become more diverse with enlargement.

In the analysis of EU own resources reform options, the theoretical point has been made that it may be an advantage of any own resource if it offers the EU members flexibility how to refinance the contribution. This excursus indicates that this aspect is, indeed, relevant given the current European situation.

4.3 International Comparison: Financing of International Organisations

This section aims at presenting the different types of financing of international and supranational organisations (IO) in order to gain insights for possible reform options for the financing of the EU. The analysis shows that concerning the financing of IO two aspects are of special concern: the type of funding and the decision rules regulating the decision-making within the IO. While the former is related to the distinction between contribution schemes and systems of own resources, the latter is related to the question who, within an IO, decides on the level and type of contribution and tax revenues, respectively. These questions are addressed in the following.

4.3.1 Types of Financing for IO

Contribution Schemes

Most international organisations are funded by contributions of its members. Contributions are payments collected from each member state, which permanently profits from the membership in the IO. The extent of use of the service of the IO does not play a role. Contributions are payments from the national budgets of the member states to the IO in order to guarantee the financing of the main tasks of the organisation. Consequently, the terms of the distribution of the contributions among the member states have to be determined. However, contribution schemes are characterised by the fact that each member is free to choose how to refinance the contributions.

Generally, there are three different ways of how to distribute the contributions among member states (Euler, 2005; Meermagen, 2002; for illustration, see Fig. 9): The easiest way is to equally share the contributions, i.e. each member pays the same amount. The Western European Union (WEU) was financed like this until 1990. Currently, the Organisation of Petroleum Exporting Countries (OPEC) and the Central Commission for Navigation on the Rhine are financed by equal contributions. Big advantages of this principle are simplicity and clarity. However, the fact that small and large member states have to pay equal amounts is considered to be unfair and inadequate. As a consequence, only very few international organisations use this type of financing.

Another type of financing is characterised by the fact that all members within a certain contribution scale pay the same amount of money. In this respect, two different configurations can be distinguished. The classification into a group can either be based on the decision of the member states themselves as in the case of the International Telecommunication Union (ITU). Since this principle frequently entails that member states do not truthfully reveal their preferences, the classification is usually made by the IO. Examples for this kind of financing are the World Intellectual Property Organisation (WIPO) and the Universal Postal Union (UPU).

Using contribution schemes allows only for a rough division of contributions among the member states. In order to ensure individual-tailored levels of contributions, most international organisations use contribution quotas. The allocation of these quotas is determined by one of the two following fundamental principles of fairness: the ability-to-pay principle or the principle of equivalence (for a discussion, see Euler, 2005).

The principle of equivalence states that the amount to be paid by the member state should either be equal to the utility the member state gains from being a member or it should be equal to the costs resulting from membership (Peffekoven, 1981). Due to difficulties in finding an appropriate indicator, the principle of equivalence has been used only rarely. The operationalisation is relatively easy if the indicator is directly related to the assignment of tasks to the IO. The World Trade Organisation (WTO), for example, allocates the contributions according to the percentage shares in world trade. The Intergovernmental Organisation of International Carriage by Rail (OTIF) uses the percentage share of the length of the railway system of each member state as indicator. Moreover, between 1958 and 1970 the European Economic Community (EEC) and the European Atomic Energy Community (Euratom) were funded according to both the economic power of the member state and the interests of the member states in the work of the IO (Meermagen, 2002). International organisations using the principle of equivalence are often characterised by a clearly restricted assignment of tasks and a relatively low budget. It is less suitable for IO aiming at redistribution between the member states because it is not connected to any fiscal equalisation scheme (Peffekoven, 1981).

Frequently, the application of the principle of equivalence is difficult because it is not possible to distinguish between costs and benefits of the membership in a specific IO (Meermagen, 2002). The use of the population as an indicator – as used by the German Confederation ("Deutscher Bund") and temporarily by the Council of Europe – is criticised because of its regressive effect (Euler, 2005). Nevertheless, it should not be ignored that the principle of equivalence plays an important role in the current discussion of fair allocation of contributions to the EU budget that is characterised by arguments asking for a "juste retour".

Most international organisations are financed according to the principle of ability-to-pay. In that respect the level of contributions is connected to the economic capacity of a member state. Again the big question is which indicator to use in order to determine the ability-to-pay. Frequently, measures like the gross national product (per capita) or the national income (per capita) are used. In many cases, these measures are applied in a slightly modified version. The United Nations (UN), for example, use floors and caps to limit the contributions. Beyond, the UN temporarily took into account the foreign debt in order to control for member states' balances of payments. In general, the advantages of using these indicators are (i) that they are technically easy to handle and (ii) that they retain the member states' financial autonomy by leaving the free choice to them of how to finance the contributions (Euler, 2005). Thus, there is no rivalry concerning the tax bases.

As a consequence, the principle of ability-to-pay is suitable for those international organisations that are characterised by a broad variety of tasks, so that costs and benefits of a membership are difficult to quantify. Furthermore, this principle is appropriate for those IO aiming at redistribution between its member states.

Fig. 9. Financing of International Organisations

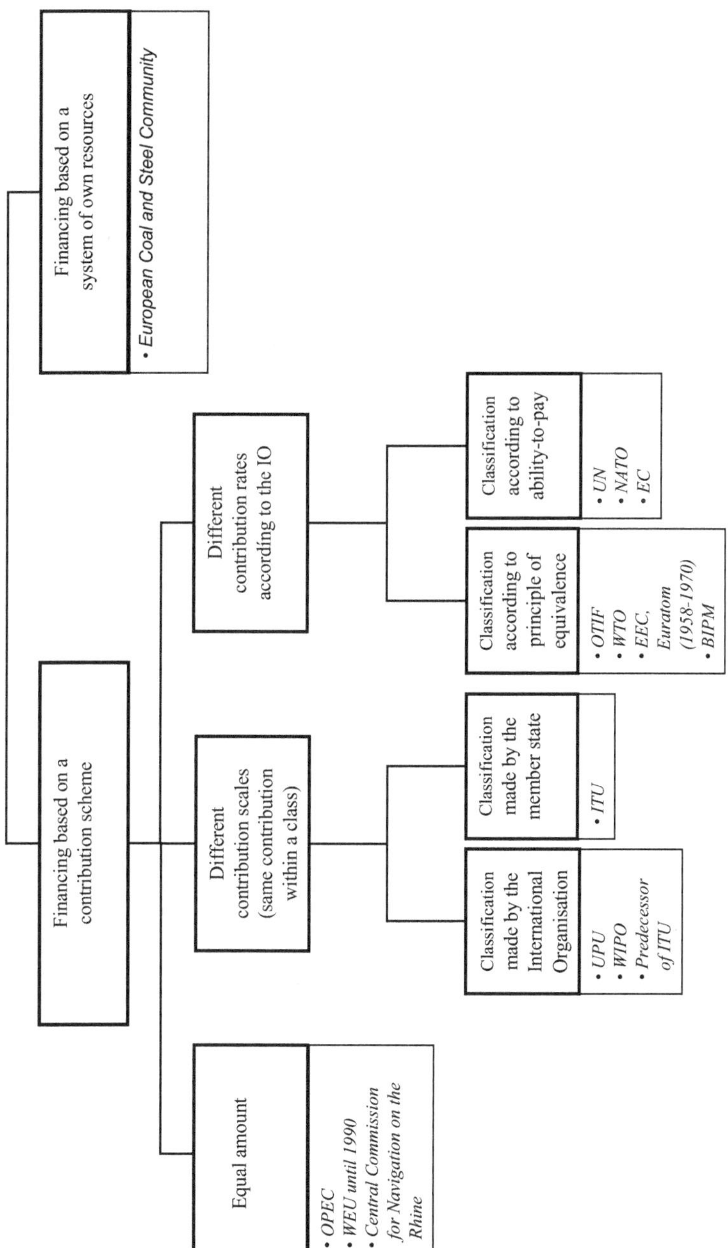

Source: Own illustration.

Generally, the use of contributions to finance IO is linked with a high degree of autonomy for the member states and a low degree of autonomy for the IO. One problem results from the question of how federal states allocate the payments within their country. Another problem is that there is a foreign exchange risk if contributions are paid in foreign currency. Additionally, some IO (especially the UN) have to cope with bad payment morale of single member states.

System of Own Resources

In contrast to contribution schemes, the level of payments arises independently of the budgetary decision-mechanism of the member states (Euler, 2005). One main difference to contribution schemes is that a system of own resources is not revenue oriented. By contrast, the level of revenues is not determined ex ante. Systems of own resources provide for the financial autonomy of the IO in several ways. First of all, the own resources are not dependent on yearly budgetary decisions of the national parliaments. Furthermore, own resources do not have to be listed in national budgetary plans. If they are listed – as it is the case for the own resources of the EU – it is for informative purposes only. Consequently, systems of own resources transfer legislative powers and the power to determine the revenues to the IO leading to greater financial autonomy of the IO. The administrational rights, however, are not necessarily transferred to the IO (Meermagen, 2002).

In reality, only a few examples for systems of own resources can be found because national states do rarely want to give far-reaching power to the IO. The prototype of a system of own resources was the levy of the European Coal and Steel Community (ECS). The ECS was founded as the first of the three European Communities. In contrast to EEC and Euratom, it was endowed with far-reaching financial autonomy since the very beginning. Thus, ECS had the power to determine the level of the levy on coal and steel production. Consequently, it had never been dependent on national contributions of the member states. As the Treaty of the ECSC expired in 2002, the levy was only collected until 1997.

It is doubtful whether the European Communities can be characterised as a system of own resources. Even though the European revenues do not require a yearly approval by the national parliaments, the EU currently lacks financial autonomy (see section 3.2). The EU revenues are no tax revenues in the real sense but they are dependent on the previously determined level of expenditures. This is obvious in the case of GNI resources. But even in the case of VAT revenues, the European Court of Justice judged that the rate of call of VAT resources has to be reduced if VAT revenues and other own resources exceed the financial requirements of the EU (Meermagen, 2002). Consequently, characterising the current financing of the EU as a system of own resources is due to the lack of financial autonomy of the EU and due to similarities to contribution schemes quite "misleading" (Huber, 2001).

4.3.2 Decision Rules

Apart from the choice of the type of financing of the IO, the decision rules of who decides on the sources of financing within an IO are to be investigated in more detail. First of all, it is important to analyse who has the right to prepare the budget and how this right is legally defined. Normally, the right to budget is assigned to that body that is responsible for the special interests of the member states. As all member states participate in financing the IO, they take part in the preparation of the budget. Frequently, the body decides with majority voting so that the minority has to agree on the decision. For example, the UN budget decisions are implemented by a two-thirds majority in the General Assembly. One exception for this was the League of Nations that implemented the budget by unanimity which often resulted in decision deadlocks.

Moreover, another important regulation is on what the particular decision-making body is allowed to decide. In some cases the level of contributions is (statutorily) regulated in the foundation or the accession treaties of the organisation. This applies to those organisations that are financed from equal amounts of each member state as well as those that are financed from the same amount within a contribution scale. Furthermore, Euratom and EEC (until 1970) regulated the level of contributions in their treaty. By contrast, most IO using quotas for financing did not regulate the level of contributions statutorily. Generally, the right to determine the quotas and the budget is to the decision-making assembly. Furthermore, the regulations of updating the quotas are important because number and wealth of members may change over time. Concerning this, OECD annually updates the calculations of the quotas.

Finally, one important question is what sanctions an IO is allowed to impose to the member states if the contributions are not paid on time. The Council of Europe, for example, regulated that every member state has to pay at least one third of its contribution in the course of the first two months of the year and that the balance is payable before the end of a period of six months (Art. 39 of the Statute). Member states that have not paid their entire contribution before the end of the period of six months will be required to pay a simple monthly interest of 0.5-1% on the amounts remaining unpaid. If a contribution remains unpaid in whole or in part at the end of the financial year, the budgetary receipts account shall be credited with the amount of the contribution called, the unpaid amount being debited to a debtors account.

4.3.3 Taking a Closer Look: The Financing of the OECD and the UN

This section shortly presents the financing of two international organisations (OECD and UN) in more detail. The OECD consists of 30 member states and is governed by a Council consisting of representatives of all its member states. The organisation is primarily funded by assessed and voluntary contributions from its member countries within the framework of a biennial programme of work and budget. It determines the amount of contributions to be paid by members after taking into account other resources of the organisation. The size of the OECD budget (336 m EUR in 2006) as well as its programme of work are determined on a biennial basis by the member states represented in the OECD Governing Council.

All OECD member countries fund the Budget for Part I programmes accounting for about 80% of the consolidated budget. This part is based on a scale of contributions proportional to the relative size of their economies with a floor of 0.1% and a cap of 24.975%. The largest contributors are the United States (24.975%), Japan (17.5%) and Germany (9.3%). The scales are calculated according to the relatively adjusted national incomes based on the gross national products of each member state. The formulas are a series of mathematical calculations prepared by the OECD's Statistics Directorate. The scales are updated each year based on a three-year rolling average of national income and other data. The formulas are only modified by consensus of the member states with the latest modifications in 2004 and 1999. Part II programmes (20% of the budget) are limited to a number of member states with special interests. It is funded according to a scale of contributions or other agreements among the participating countries.

The financing of the United Nations can be divided into three components: (i) assessed contributions according to an assessment scale, (ii) mandatory contributions (for peace keeping operations) and (iii) voluntary contributions. The assessment scale is changed every 3 years by the General Assembly after recommendation of the Committee on Contributions. The Committee on Contributions applies the principle of ability-to-pay. Since December 1997, the member states' contributions are calculated in two steps: Firstly, the relative amount of the single member state is calculated according to its share of world GDP. Secondly, this ranking is changed by taking into account a low-income discount (less contributions for countries with high population but low GDP). Furthermore, there are ceilings (25%) and floors (0.01%). According to the assessment scale, 14 countries accounted for 85% of the expenditures in 1998.

4.3.4 Conclusion

By analysing the financing of international organisations it is possible to derive insights for the reform debate on the EU revenue side even if the different quality of integration between IO on the one hand and the EU on the other hand precludes any direct imitation. A first conclusion is that without a doubt an ability-to-pay approach is appropriate for the revenue system of the EU. Given the variety of policies the EU has taken responsibility for, it is unrealistic to quantify contributions based on the principle of equivalence and, hence, related to the Union's usefulness for each individual country. A revenue system related to relative GNI is, therefore, also a reasonable element of an EU revenue system in this comparative perspective.

Beyond this insight the OECD type structuring of the budget might offer inspiration for the European reform perspective. Here, we differentiate between the financing of programmes which have the character of benefiting a limited number of members and a more general budget. Although we do not believe that this approach should be copied for the EU, it may hint at a promising direction of reform: differentiating the revenue formula by policy areas. This idea will be elaborated on in chapter 6.

5 Reform Approaches

5.1 Link Between Expenditure and Revenue Reform Debates

During the course of the upcoming budgetary review scheduled for 2008/2009, not only the revenue side of the budget will be inspected but also the expenditure side. Both in the conclusions of the EU Council (European Council, 2005) and in the new Inter-Institutional Agreement (European Parliament, European Council & European Commission, 2006) an explicit reference is made to a revision of the UK correction and, on the expenditure side, of the Common Agricultural Policy. This broad view of the reform perspective is in line with our finding (see section 3.6) that many revenue side characteristics reflect compensation measures for perceived misbalances on the expenditure side. Therefore, it is not unrealistic to assume that any fundamental reform of the revenue side (with the reform of the UK correction as the prime objective as shown in section 3.7.4) is conditional on changes of the expenditure side. As the Lamassoure report (2007: 10) holds it,

> the political link between a reform of revenue and a review of expenditure is inevitable and perfectly reasonable, especially as long as the logic of financing Community policies through revenue stemming from national budgets is still the Union's guiding principle.

The calculations given in the following sections are based on the assumption that no radical solutions will materialise with regard to the expenditure side. In this short excursus we intend to sketch which modifications may emerge to our results if – against our expectations – a fundamental restructuring of expenditures could be achieved. Here, it should be stressed that many of our arguments with regard to single own resources items hold independently from expenditure side developments. What will be subject to change in the case of fundamental expenditure side reform, however, are the distributive effects. In the following, some of the possible reforms on the expenditure side are briefly presented, and their implications for the design of the revenue side are shown.

5.1.1 Co-Financing of CAP

The co-financing of CAP is probably the most frequently discussed option for a reform on the expenditure side (as proposed, e.g., by Sapir, 2004). This means that financing of CAP would partly be assigned to national budgets, thus, reducing the overall spending of the EU in this area.

In Fig. 10 the distributive effects of two reform options for the Common Agriculture Policy are shown: the co-financing (with an assumed national co-financing rate of 50%) as well as the complete phasing-out of this policy. In both cases it is assumed that the funds which become available due to reduced CAP spending are not spent by the EU for other purposes but lead to a reduction of the size of the EU budget. As a benchmark for the status quo the results from section 3.6 have been added. We would like to underline that we do not regard the complete CAP phasing-out as a realistic reform option and that the consequences of co-financing for spending behaviour at the EU-level and the national level are hard to predict. Nevertheless, for analytical purposes this thought experiment is helpful.

Fig. 10. Net positions for different CAP reform options

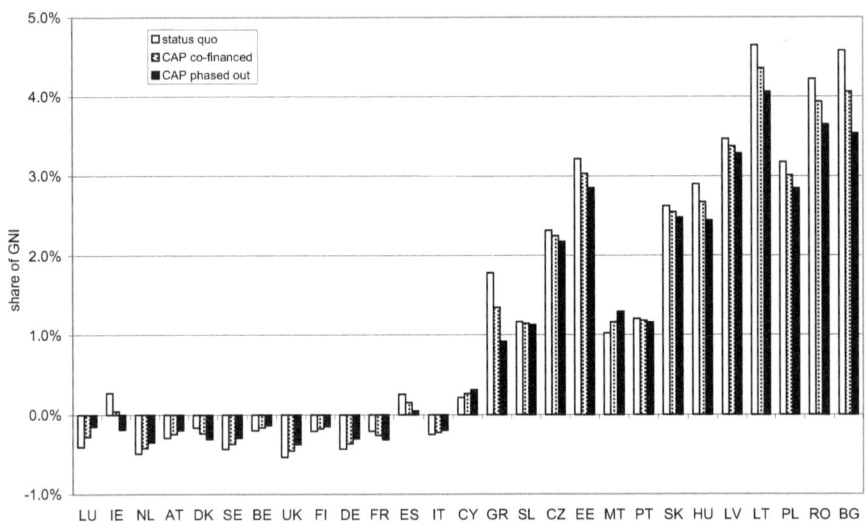

Note: Payments for Administration have not been attributed.

Source: ZEW calculations.

It can be seen that the impact on the overall distributive effect of the expenditure side differs very much between the member states. Obviously, these differences are driven by the national net positions regarding the CAP spending as discussed in section 3.6.3. Generally, it can be observed that the expenditure side would lose part of its progressive character by decreasing CAP spending as poorer countries tend to worsen their positive net positions. But it can also be seen that several anomalies of the status quo would be overcome: The sound net positions of several relatively better off member states are corrected downwards (Spain, Greece) or even turn negative (Ireland). At the same time, some countries with very negative net positions on the expenditure side, mainly the beneficiaries of the status quo's abatements, disclose a significant improvement of their position which brings them more in line with the other countries of the same wealth.

Under the current system of own resources, a reform which leads to a decrease of CAP spending automatically leads to a discharge of the member states which is approximately proportional to their shares in GNI. The only major deviation of proportionality is the effect of the UK rebate: As the total attributable spending to other countries is reduced, the total amount corrected by the correction mechanism is also reduced. From around 3.5 bn EUR the UK saves at the introduction of co-financing due to their pro-rate reduction in the GNI resource, around 1 bn EUR is passed up due to a reduced amount of correction payments.

All in all, it can be concluded that any reform of the CAP spending induces major distributive effects compared to the status quo which would substantially change the restrictions for revenue side reforms. As the overall redistribution is reduced and the net positions of several countries which are net payers of the CAP are improved and put in line with other countries of similar wealth, the case for special provisions only benefiting single countries would be resolved in a just manner. However, the perpetuation of the current system of own resources in combination with a CAP reform would not lead to a reasonable adjustment of these abatements. Only the UK correction mechanism is affected and cut significantly, but it still puts the country in a better overall net position than other countries with similar wealth (UK: -0.35%; Germany: -0.41%; France: -0.40%). The special provisions benefiting the four other beneficiaries are not even affected at all by a CAP reform as neither the rebates of the VAT resource nor the flat rate rebates on own resources payments are affected. This reflects the problems which are connected to such flat rate reductions as they continue to exist even when misbalances as due to the CAP spending are resolved.

5.1.2 Reformed Structural Policy

One possible direction of a future reform in structural spending may be the accentuation of the cohesion target in the structural policy. This would imply the abolition of payments to relatively well-off regions. These expenditures come under the heading "Regional Competitiveness and Employment" in the Financial Framework 2007-2013 and consist of payments to "Competitiveness and Employment Regions" and "Natural Phasing-Out Regions" ("Phasing-In Regions"). Such a reform may be reasonable as it can be argued that the support of these regions can rather be viewed as side payments to countries which do not benefit from other structural fund objectives than as a contribution to the aim of cohesion. In Fig. 11 the distributive effects of a hypothetical complete phasing-out of "Regional Competitiveness and Employment" by 2010 is outlined.[9] It depicts the effects of a shift of funds from "Competitiveness and Employment Regions" and "Phasing-In Re-

9 Due to the fact that most of the commitment appropriations lead to payments at a date several years later, this scenario is unrealistic. However, it is intended to clarify the distributive effects of the payments to "Competitiveness and Employment Regions".

gions" to expenditures which benefit all member states according to their GNI. Again, we would like to add that we do not regard this radical reform as realistic in the short-run but this assumption is helpful in analysing the distributive consequences of reform tendencies.

Fig. 11. Net positions for structural policy reform option

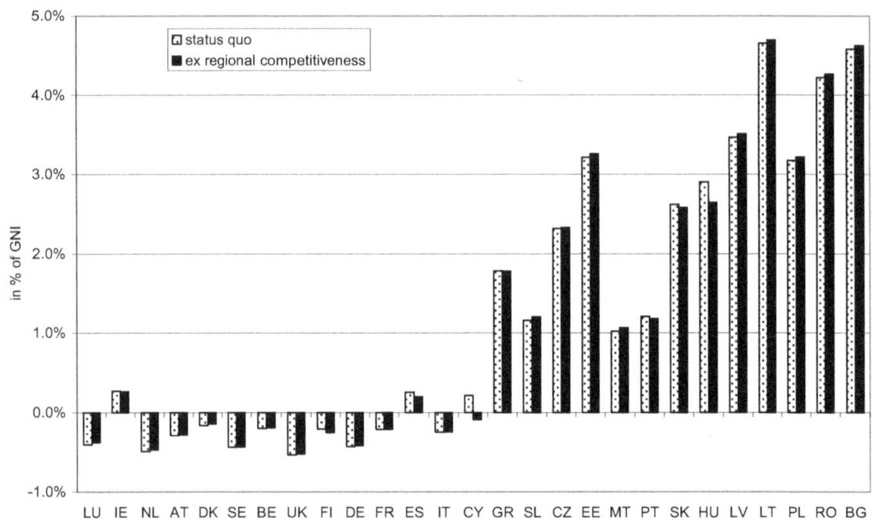

Source: ZEW calculations.

As it can be seen, the abolishment of structural payments benefiting "Competitiveness and Employment Regions" alone does not have a significant effect on the overall redistribution on the expenditure side.[10] This is plausible as the main beneficiaries of this policy area are the better off member states and, hence, the countries which contribute most to the funding of this policy with their payments of own resources.

Major distributive effects are possible, however, in the case of an ulterior use of the vacant funds than for the hypothetical GNI proportional reimbursement of these funds. In case these funds are merely used to increase the endowment of other structural funds (Cohesion or Regional Convergence expenditure), the overall redistributive effect of the expenditure side will be strengthened, thus, leading to an increased demand for a regressive system of own resources to achieve a similar overall redistribution as today.

10 The only major impact on a country's net position in the case of Cyprus is due to the country's classification as a phasing-out region.

5.1.3 Reducing the Progression on the Expenditure Side

A rather long-term reform option which would, however, induce the most meaningful change to the environment of the reform of the current system of own resources would be a significant change of the expenditure structure which leads to a major change of the redistribution. This change might take place due to a reduction of the progressiveness on the expenditure side, for instance, to pursue the often made claim for a shift from redistributive dominated expenditures to European public goods (see, e.g., Sapir, 2004). Although this is currently not on top of the reform agenda and only imaginable on the long-run, models for such a development are advocated by some academics.

As the structural policy funds currently play the dominant role regarding the redistribution of funds from richer to poorer countries, reforms with a major impact on the overall redistribution would have to pick up there. Huber (2001), for instance, argues from an economic point of view against both the current use of conditional structural grants and against the use of unconditional grants as these would even increase the incentives of the poorer countries to demand for redistribution. In contrast, he argues that the intended degree of redistribution would be best obtained by assigning the cohesion function to the revenue side. The author argues that this might be achieved by the introduction of the financing via GNI contributions and the application of a progressive rate increasing with higher GNI per head.

Although such a far-reaching reform on the expenditure side seems to be unrealistic with respect to the upcoming budgetary review, it is yet useful to become aware of its consequences for the system of own resources in a long-term perspective. This reform option would demand a system of own resources which is flexible regarding its degree of progressiveness as it would imply an increasingly progressive system. For instance, as discussed by Huber (2001), the GNI resource could fulfil this task as it may be easily adjusted by changing the rate. In contrast to this, other resources which will be discussed in the following are not adequate as they would create a fixed degree of progressiveness in the long-run.

5.2 EU Tax

5.2.1 Introduction and Frequent Suggestions

As it was discussed in chapter 3, the status quo of the system of own resources is marked by several shortcomings, therefore, the need for a reform of the system is widely undisputed. However, the direction of a reform, i.e. whether the best way to offset the existing shortcomings should be via systemic or parametric adjustments, is up for discussion. One reform option which would imply far-reaching changes compared to the status quo would consist of the introduction of a tax directly payable to the EU which would constitute a "genuine" own resource. But this proposal also provokes the most controversial discussions among academics as well as politicians and the broad public. Supporters of this "EU tax" expect from such a reform a solution for several deficiencies of the status quo, opponents fear and criticize, among others, the increasing fiscal burden for the citizens. The introduction of a tax-based own resource demands two choices, which, however, are mutually interdependent, (1) the design of the tax system and (2) the choice of a tax base.

Regarding the first choice, Raddatz and Schick (2003) present three different designs how a tax-based system of own resources might be designed. These designs mainly differ in the degree of harmonisation of the tax systems which is needed. The highest degree of harmonisation is needed in a "linked system" with the EU participating from the revenues of a certain tax levied in a uniform way in all member countries. Such a system requires both the tax bases and the tax rates to be identical in order to guarantee horizontal equity between the citizens of the different member states. Less harmonisation is required by the second alternative, the "surcharge system". For this variant only the harmonisation of the tax base is required; the EU would have the autonomy to levy a uniform EU-wide rate in addition to the national rates which might differ. These two designs are relevant for taxes whose revenues exceed the amount attributed to the EU. Finally, in a "separation system" the EU would have the full and exclusive autonomy to tax a specific base. This design would be highly relevant in case of an introduction of a new EU tax which does not exist in the member states yet.

Regarding the choice of the tax base, several authors applying different sets of assessment criteria similar to ours as introduced in chapter 2 sometimes arrive at quite different conclusions regarding their preferable tax. However, all supporters have one feature in common: Nobody argues that their preferable alternative is the "perfect" solution for an EU tax as every alternative is seen as problematic in certain points, even if it is considered as the most useful alternative by its proponent.

In the most prominent proposal, the European Commission (2004a) suggests the introduction of a tax-based own resource by 2014 and offers three "main candidates": energy consumption, a modulated value added tax (VAT) and a corporate income tax. Recent comments by tax Commissioner Kovács suggest that the Commission favours the idea of VAT at the moment (Kovács, 2006). An expert advisory board installed by the former president of the European Commission, Romano Prodi, and led by the former French finance minister, Dominique Strauss-Kahn, regarded company taxation as the "natural candidate" (Strauss-Kahn, 2004). Another influential report of the Commission, the Sapir Report (2004), mainly demands the allocation of sources with a clear EU dimension and argues that seigniorage, capital income taxes and stock exchange taxes fulfil this criterion. A recent analysis by the Austrian research institute WIFO supports the idea of a tax on financial transactions and a kerosene tax (Schratzenstaller & Berghuber, 2006). The former Austrian Chancellor Wolfgang Schüssel proposed exactly these two alternatives in his role as Head of Presidency of the European Council (Schüssel, 2006). A detailed proposal from politics comes from three German Members of Parliament of the Green Party, who propose to finance the budget for the medium-term with harmonised gasoline taxes and in the long-term with revenues from emission trading or corporate taxes (Lührmann, Schick & Steenblock, 2006). In academics, it is not uncommon to find an explicit consideration based on scores reflecting the advantages and disadvantages of certain taxes. By applying this, Begg and Grimwade (1998) propose the introduction of a modulated VAT own resources complemented with communication taxes. Gros and Micossi (2005) also argue in favour of VAT but propose the perpetuation of GNI resources as shock absorbers. And finally, some academics explicitly demand the introduction of a mix of resources in order to offset the disadvantages created by a single resource (Goulard & Nava, 2002). Other influential analyses, such as the Lamassoure report (2007), stay vague with regard to their preferred tax.

Cattoir (2004) and the European Commission (1998) list the most commonly proposed candidates for an EU tax. These comprise direct taxes, namely (1) corporate income tax and (2) personal income tax, as well as indirect taxes, such as (3) VAT, (4) excise duties (on tobacco or alcohol), (5) energy taxation (on kerosene, motor fuel or CO_2 emissions), (6) taxes on financial transactions and (7) communication taxes (on telephone lines or air and road transport).

The following discussion will concentrate on the general suitability of tax-based own resources. A detailed presentation of these proposed alternatives as an EU tax is dispensable since extensive evaluations of single taxes can be found, for instance, in Cattoir (2004), Le Cacheux (2007) or Euler (2005). The distributive consequences of different types of EU taxes are simulated in detail as it may be assumed that these are crucial from the perspective of national governments when evaluating the adequateness of a tax-based system of own resources.

5.2.2 The Pros

In the following section, several arguments which are usually put forward in favour of the introduction of an EU tax are presented. Moreover, they are critically discussed as it is often neglected by the supporters of an EU tax that several arguments in favour of a tax-based own resources are only valid for a restricted number of proposed taxes and that several features of tax-based own resources which are regarded as "improvements" compared to the status quo are not as undisputed as they are described by their supporters.

Visibility

One of the most popular arguments put forward by advocates of an EU tax is the increase of transparency of the budget which would occur by introducing an EU tax. Indeed, it is generally acknowledged that the current system of own resources with its multitude of revenue sources and abatements performs poorly regarding transparency and is, therefore, not visible to the citizens. Thus, the EU citizens are not able to assess their contribution to the EU and the added value of EU politics. It is claimed that this deficiency contributes to the democratic deficit of the EU. The weak role of the European Parliament enforces this deficit (see section 3.2).

Goulard and Nava (2002: 10) state that the European Parliament "is the only parliament in the world that debates expenditure but has no competence to determine the revenue that must be collected in order to finance that expenditure". This view claims that if the Parliament was not only responsible for the expenditure but also for the revenues towards the citizens, this would increase the involvement of the voters in European policies.

With regard to that argument at least two qualifications are important. First, as argued extensively in chapter 3, transparency may be a necessary but by no way sufficient condition for budgetary discipline. Secondly, it has to be asked which taxes are in fact visible to the citizens as obviously only these can have the positive effects discussed above. In this respect, it is often neglected by supporters of an EU tax that this is by far not fulfilled by every tax which is up for discussion. From the tax options mentioned above, we only regard taxes which are tangible for the vast majority of the citizens appropriate to increase visibility but not those taxes which only affect a small portion of the tax payers. Thus, the choice would be reduced to the following taxes: VAT, personal income taxes and, with limitations, excise taxes on gasoline. Huber (2001) goes even further and argues that only a direct tax like a personal income tax would be tangible for the citizens while indirect taxes would only have an impact through higher consumption prices and, thus, would not be tangible.

Other taxes that are exclusively imposed on companies or small groups of people, such as smokers or consumers of alcohol, can obviously not fulfil the criterion of tangibility so that they are not visible to most citizens. They would not be "recognisable and identifiable as such by the public", as one of the supporters of an EU tax, former EU Budget Commissioner Michaela Schreyer (2001: 225) demands it from an EU tax. Moreover, the postulate of horizontal and vertical equity is violated by introducing taxes that are imposed on a smaller part of the EU population. First, especially excise taxes on alcohol and tobacco mainly hit poorer citizens who consume relatively more of these goods leading to a regressive effect.[11] Furthermore, horizontal equity is hurt as the financing is only borne by a small part of the society, for example, smokers. Both would have a negative effect on the citizens' attitude towards European integration as it gives the impression that only a small, not prosperous group of the society is responsible for the financing of the EU.

Nevertheless, we agree on the fact that an advantage is created if the citizens are able to assess the costs connected with the membership of the EU. However, it could be seen as doubtful if the visibility of the costs of the EU indeed increased the popularity of the EU institutions as claimed by many proponents of an EU tax. As a recent poll by Eurobarometer (2006) shows, only 11% of the respondents stated that the replacement of national income tax by a European income tax would strengthen their feeling about being a European citizen.

A key assumption of many proponents of an EU tax is that nowadays people overestimate the burden due to the fact they are not able to quantify the costs of

[11] However, as it is discussed in section 8.1, a regressive tax within a national tax system is not problematic per se and even desirable when it fulfills an incentive function.

EU (Goulard & Nava, 2002). However, this view is problematic because if more visibility does in fact lead to a better assessment of the costs of the EU, it would be imaginable that, once confronted with a sudden perception of the individual burden from EU spending, the public support of the EU by its citizens may even decline (Belafi, 2006). Apparently this view is also shared by the Commissioner László Kovács who promoted the use of VAT as an EU tax in a newspaper interview and stated that direct taxes would have a direct effect on citizens and companies and might, therefore, cause an anti-EU sentiment (Kovács, 2006). Consequently, it is important to keep in mind that especially a highly tangible tax, while increasing transparency, might also have a negative impact on the citizens' attitudes towards integration. As Goulard and Nava (2002: 18) point out, this would mainly affect newly introduced taxes as "any new tax would be unpopular", which makes them unsuitable for integration enhancing goals.

Autonomy

An increase in autonomy is one of the main arguments in favour of introducing an EU tax (e.g., European Commission, 2004a). However, even from official statements of supporters of an EU tax it is not clear how far this autonomy should go and whether in their view this would be identical to fiscal sovereignty in the sense that EU institutions are allowed to increase the rate of a tax once assigned to the EU. Although it is often put forward that autonomy would only imply autonomy over the revenues of a certain resource, many politicians beyond Brussels still oppose even such an increase in autonomy of the EU institutions.

As it has been discussed in chapter 2, we hold the view that autonomy is not an end in itself as this claim could simply reflect the ambition of European institutions to increase their influence. However, one general advantage is frequently granted to transferring the revenue autonomy over a certain tax to the EU: The reliability of EU revenues could be secured if the Union was no longer dependent on national contributions. Although this problem has not yet appeared in the case of the EU, financing via national contributions always entails a certain potential for blackmailing the EU by their member states by holding back their payments (Begg, 2004). As it is discussed in section 4.3, this problem is highly virulent in international organisations, such as the UN, on which the member states put pressure by depriving their contributions in order to achieve certain political goals.

However, it is doubtful whether this argument is valid to give support for an EU tax. First, it has to be emphasised that a withholding of EU payments is still a violation of binding international contracts today; therefore, due to its legal deterrence the danger of holding back revenues is low compared to international organisations (see section 3.2). Moreover, even if the possibility of a holding back was assumed theoretically, an EU tax would not reduce the danger. For none of the taxes discussed above would the EU be able to adopt the administration of the tax by itself. The Union would still depend on the work of the national tax administration and, in this case, the possibility to withhold payments would be as high as in the case of national grants. Therefore, an EU tax would hardly make a difference compared to the status quo in this regard.

Public Choice Aspects

Several authors argue that the pressure on budgetary expansion caused by the common pool problem and bureaucratic self-interest (see section 8.1.3) may be best met by increasing the Parliament's autonomy through the introduction of an EU tax. In formal terms, Biehl (1996) derives the "principle of correspondence" from the theory of fiscal federalism in order to achieve a more efficient EU budget. This principle claims "fiscal equivalence", i.e. the identity of a "match between those who receive the benefits of a collective good and those who pay for it" as it was already introduced in the seminal literature on fiscal federalism by Olson (1969: 483). Following this view, the European Parliament as the authority responsible for expenditures should also be responsible for the decision-making on how to finance the EU budget. As this would increase their accountability to their voters, it would put pressure on a more efficient budget.

But this optimistic view towards an increase in budgetary discipline through an EU tax is too simplistic. It is problematic to assume that only through the assignment of tax power to the European institutions a more efficient budget would automatically evolve. The incentive analysis in section 3.5 has clarified that this issue is much more complex.

In addition, inefficient budgetary outcomes may also appear because of reduced tax competition. Following the view of Brennan and Buchanan (1980), tax competition serves as a constraint to the tendency of public institutions to maximise the budget. The assignment of an EU tax to the EU as the highest tier of government would imply a complete harmonisation of it and, hence, disable competition regarding this tax. Therefore, the tax revenue may be increased in the following by the European politicians without having to fear negative effects due to evasion within the EU.

Moreover, it is doubtful whether the control of the European institutions by the people, i.e. checks and balances, is sufficient, as "European voters have practically no means of sanctioning EU policy makers for "bad" budget decisions" (Caesar, 2001: 232). As it has often been stated, the interest of the citizens in EU affairs is by far not as pronounced as on the national level as, for example, reflected by the voter participation rates of the elections to the European Parliament. This may limit the effective control of EU politicians. As a consequence, there is a real danger that giving more revenue autonomy to the European Parliament would lead to an inefficient increase of spending.

Finally, as it has been extensively discussed in chapter 3, the substitution of national contributions would lower national governments' incentives in constraining the EU budget.

Political Struggles

Among others, the European Commission (2004a: 11) argues that the "juste retour" thinking can be overcome by the introduction of an EU tax which would create "a sufficient degree of autonomy from national treasuries to reduce the tendency towards a narrow focus on national interest".

However, it is questionable whether the assignment of a revenue source to the EU would automatically remove the "juste retour" discussion. Although the national payments would no longer be directly displayed, it would be an easy task to calculate the national shares from their tax payments to the EU. As no tax option allows for a tax collection by a common European tax authority since this would be too costly, an EU tax would still be collected by national authorities, thus, enabling the calculation of national contributions (Mutén, 2001).

Another aspect is that it is also imaginable that taxation by EU authorities may serve as a scapegoat for national politicians. They might blame the EU for the fiscal burden of their citizens, which would even increase the conflict potential between member states and European authorities.

Moreover, as it was shown in section 3.6.3, the redistributing effects from the budget do not arise from the revenue but mainly from the expenditure side. It should be stressed that most struggles regarding the revenue side, for instance, in the discussion on the new Financial Framework, did not arise because the four own resources were not regarded as fair but because the revenue side served as a counterpart to the expenditure side with its partly unsystematic redistributive effects. Thus, the most efficient reform to avoid further struggles should take place on the expenditure side (Caesar, 2001).

Regional Arbitrariness

With regional arbitrariness there is no close connection between the regional revenue of a fiscal source and the true economic regional distribution of its burden. If a revenue source is characterised by regional arbitrariness, this will give strong support to its assignment to the EU. Sometimes this argument is also given to justify the assignment of taxes to the EU. However, obviously this problem only affects very few taxes where it is not possible to assign the revenues at least roughly to the countries. Corporate and capital transaction taxes are taxes where regional arbitrariness is put forward as an argument for the use as an EU tax (Schratzenstaller & Berghuber, 2006). The intuition behind this is that gains of multi-national companies are often not taxed in that country where they have been created. However, the argument is not as convincing as in the case of TOR, where revenues directly result from European policies and where national revenue is a very poor indicator for a country's true economic burden. As a consequence, in our view it is not a sufficient reason for the assignment to the EU.

Fiscal Externalities

Another argument often put forward in favour of assigning a certain tax to the level of the EU stems from the existence of fiscal externalities. This mainly affects taxes with a very mobile tax base, namely the taxation of interest or corporate income.

But as discussed in section 8.1.2, it is controversial whether competition for mobile tax bases or its abolishment – which would be the consequence of the introduction of an EU tax – is desirable. Even if there were a consensus in the EU that competition for certain taxes is not wanted, this would not necessarily mean that the centralisation of the tax should be strived for. Instead, the member countries might agree on certain minimum tax rates, thus, reducing the degree of unwanted tax competition while still granting them a certain degree of autonomy to allow for diverging national preferences (Euler, 2005). Apart from that, it should not be neglected that the EU member states do not only compete with other EU members for mobile tax bases but also with non-EU countries. Therefore, potentially harmful competition would not be completely abolished but at best be reduced.

As differences regarding taxation between member states generate cross-border shopping, fiscal externalities are also often assumed regarding VAT, excise duties or petrol taxes. This is also seen critical due to its negative effect on the environment because of additional traffic. But as analogical evidence shows (Cnossen, 2001), this only happens in regions close to national borders and only generates comparatively low fiscal externalities, thus, not justifying the complete harmonisation through the assignment of these taxes to the EU level.

5.2.3 The Cons

The proposal of the introduction of an EU tax has often been criticised both in the academic and in the political debate. In the following, several often-cited deficiencies of an EU tax as well as some rather new objections against it are discussed.

Increasing Financial Burden

Supporters of an EU tax claim that any reform of the system of own resources should not be accompanied by an increase in the financial burden of the citizens (Schreyer, 2001) or ensure "cost neutrality" (Haug, 2001). The Lamassoure report (2007) even demands that this should be ensured by the supervision of the national and European Courts of Audit. However, there are at least two arguments which make the claim of cost neutrality doubtful. First, as shown above, it is ambiguous whether the increase in financial autonomy of the EU authorities would have a positive or a negative effect on the budgetary discipline. Secondly, an EU tax necessarily limits tax competition for the involved type of tax. Advocates of tax competition argue that any such step would simplify the financing of budgetary expansion.

The reduction of tax competition would depend on the quality of harmonisation steps involved. The harmonisation of a certain tax base for the purpose of establishing a common EU tax would reduce the tax competition between the member states in this area or even abolish it completely in the case of a linked system, which would even mean the alignment of tax rates in such sensitive areas such as corporate taxation. A problem may emerge from the introduction of a surcharge system which may give rise to harmful vertical tax competition. Vertical tax competition is given if two or more tiers will have unrestricted access to a common tax base through their autonomy to choose the tax rate. Wigger and Wartha (2003) and Müller (2006) analyse this argument analytically. If no coordination between the different tiers of a federation exists, policy makers with a certain degree of self-serving behaviour do not incorporate the negative externalities of their choice of tax rate on the common tax base and, therefore, on the tax revenue of the other tier which has the right to tax the same base. This might lead to a reciprocal increase of the rates and, consequently, to an excessive taxation which violates both the citizens' preferences as well as the claim for efficiency.

Moreover, any model of the introduction of an EU tax put forward by their supporters assumes that the abolition of national contributions would completely be handed over to the citizens by reducing national taxes, thus, holding their overall fiscal burden constant (Euler, 2005). But under the assumptions of public choice theory, self-interested politicians might use this occasion to raise their revenues by not handing over all of their saved contributions. This may allow them to increase their tax revenues and blame the EU for the tax increases; as Caesar (2001: 233) holds it, this would be "a very comfortable excuse". It is important to highlight that this danger is the greatest in the case of the introduction of a new tax which is totally assigned to the EU. If an existing tax (or parts of it) were assigned to the EU, this would automatically reduce the national tax revenues by the same amount. In the case of a new tax, the money saved by the national governments would call for the cut of other taxes to keep the tax payer's burden unchanged. This, however, might be resisted by the politicians as the resulting tax increase on the national level would not be visible to the citizens.

Preferences

Any option of a tax-based own resource demands a certain degree of harmonisation. This might only affect the tax base (surcharge system) or both tax base and rate (linked and separation system). In any case, this will lead to inefficiencies if the preferences for taxation differ between the member states. As it is discussed in section 4.2, tax preferences indeed appear to be substantially heterogeneous in Europe so that this argument is empirically valid. This problem is especially severe within a linked system as it claims the harmonisation of both the tax base and the tax rate.

Interference with National Federal Structures

In several countries of the EU, federal structures exist which give lower tier governments the right to levy certain taxes. These domestic relationships would be disturbed by the introduction of certain EU taxes. For example, Germany would be affected insofar as the revenues of some taxes proposed to be assigned to the EU do not accrue to the federal government but to the Laender or are shared among both. This mainly affects the VAT, the personal and the corporate income tax, which are shared among both levels.

The assignment of one of these taxes to the EU would, thus, reduce the tax revenues of the lower tiers in the respective federal state and limit its autonomy in cases where the lower tier today has the autonomy to set the tax rate. Then, a rearrangement of the responsibilities between the different tiers of the federal state would be unavoidable, which would meet with the strong disapproval by lower tier politicians and would, moreover, cause further adjustment costs in the affected countries.

Compliance Costs

Any introduction of a new tax to finance the EU would automatically be connected with increasing administration costs. But the assignment of an existing national tax to the EU would entail additional costs as well. These would be caused by increasing administration costs due to the monitoring by the EU which is necessary to prevent fraud. The EU would have a vital interest in putting through a very strict control of the national tax administrations as it could not accept national differences in collection efficiency. These may be caused by existing differences in fraud or by principle-agents problems as the national institutions would not participate at all (or at least to a lower extent than today) in the levied revenues and, therefore, do not have a strong interest in strict controls anymore. Any difference in collection efficiency would cause unequal national contributions and might lead to struggles between the member states about an unfair sharing of the financial burden. These controls might cause very high costs in relation to the additional benefits which would arise from the monitoring as it may be assumed to be the case of today's levy of traditional own resources.[12]

Apart from that, additional costs would also arise before the introduction of an EU tax to a great extent due to the indispensable full harmonisation of existing tax bases. As it is discussed in the literature (e.g., Cattoir, 2004), there are major differences regarding the current degree of harmonisation of the candidates for an EU tax. There are only few tax options which have already highly standardised tax bases, for example, excise duties on alcohol, tobacco or petrol.

Sufficiency

From the group of taxes proposed as EU taxes, there are only very few fulfilling the criteria of sufficiency. As argued in chapter 2, this criterion must be cautiously applied since scarcity of revenues has the advantage of constituting a hard and disciplining budget constraint. However, taxes for which revenue would by far not cover budgetary needs have the obvious disadvantage that numerous different sources would have to be combined. This would not serve the claim of visibility as an increasing number of resources automatically increase the complexity of the system, thus, reducing the transparency.

Cattoir (2004) estimates the maximal shares of GNI that different resources can supply: tobacco 0.7%, alcohol 0.3%, airport tax 0.1%, telephone lines 0.1%, aviation charge 0.1%. Hence, the consideration of one of these taxes necessitates the use of further revenue sources and would, thus, be confronted with the need to establish a system based on a multitude of revenue sources.

---

12 The extent of today's control intensity can be seen in European Commission (2006b).

In addition, several tax proposals do not guarantee sufficient resources in the long-run even if the share of the EU expenditure in GNI stays constant over time. As VAT revenues grow slower than GNI, the use of this tax as own resources would require frequent adjustments of the call rate to ensure the endowment with sufficient resources (Begg & Grimwade, 1998).

Flexibility

One problem of all proposed tax options compared to a system based on national contributions is that they are fixed regarding the degree of progressiveness. Once introduced, the degree of redistribution is determined according to the national shares in the agreed tax base; future changes would result from changing national shares in the tax bases but cannot be influenced by changing the EU-wide identical tax rate. However, an adjustment of the progressiveness on the revenue side might become desirable in the long-term due to changes on the expenditure side or changed preferences for redistribution as it was discussed in section 5.1.3.

Stability

As a matter of fact no tax option exists which is able to ensure the same degree of stability of revenues for the EU budget as the GNI resource does today. Any tax is, to a certain extent, unpredictable in its revenues, thus, showing higher volatility resulting in either too low or too high revenues. Both the business cycle as well as structural changes in the economy have an impact on tax revenues. Business cycle effects are the strongest for corporate income taxes while VAT or excise duties show the highest stability over the business cycle – but may be affected by other trends like world trade growth or changes in consumption.

As shown above, apart from the controversial question whether the advantages of an EU tax would outweigh the disadvantages, the introduction of a purely tax-based system of own resources (plus the TOR) would technically not be feasible within the existing framework of the budget which prescribes a balanced budget for every year. The reason for this is that there is no tax imaginable whose revenues are flexible enough in order to exactly match the amount of money which is fixed by the Financial Framework. In the following, some options discussed in the literature to solve this dilemma are presented, which are all afflicted with further problems.

GNI as Residual

The option implicitly or explicitly underlying most proposals for a tax-based system of EU own resources is the perpetuation of the GNI resource as residual. This means that the GNI resource would keep the same role as it has in the status quo where it is intended to balance the difference between a cyclical resource (today: VAT resource) and the amount of spending fixed by the Financial Perspective. Although the maintenance of the GNI resource as residual seems to be the most adequate way to establish a tax-based system of own resources, several disadvantages arise.

One main disadvantage would be the major reduction of visibility. The number of resources would stay the same as in the status quo (while the EU tax replacing the VAT resource), which would not contribute to an increase in simplicity (Fehr, 2001). Moreover, the GNI resource would necessarily continue to be of major importance in order to create a buffer large enough to cope with the volatility of the EU tax. Obviously, only a part of the revenue would be visible to the citizens through their tax payments giving them a wrong impression of the true costs of the Union. Consequently, the additional gain of the EU tax concerning the visibility compared to the status quo would be limited.

Right to Borrow

Another option often put forward to solve the problem of unstable revenues is to entitle the EU with the right to borrow if the revenues are lower than the expenditure due to cyclical effects. This would enable the EU to choose a tax which balances the budget in an average year, thus, avoiding the use of a further residual resource. In addition to that, economists may justify the right to borrow with several other features (for an overview, see Caesar, 1996). In that respect, mainly the Keynesian view of a stabilisation function in order to smooth the business cycle is mentioned. However, this view is highly controversial as it is undisputable that the current amount of the budget is far too low to have a stabilising impact.

If one assumes self-interested public agents as done in the public choice literature, the granting of the right to borrow to the EU needs to be critically assessed. This would automatically lead to a relaxation of the budget constraints and raises the pressure towards an increase of the budget. As Caesar (1996) stresses, this problem would be even more severe than on the national level as on the EU level an effective mechanism for sanctioning of the parliamentarians is missing, which might counteract an increase in the budget. Furthermore, the EU would – at least initially – face even less capital market restrictions than EU member countries with lower ratings. Thus, it seems justified that a deficit competence is rarely mentioned as a reform option for the EU own resources system.

Increase of Flexibility on Spending Side

A further way to cope with the variability of the revenues of an EU tax is to make the spending side more flexible. This would mean the reversal of the current situation where the fixed expenditure side determines the amount of revenues. Instead, the collected tax revenues would determine the level of spending.

Similarly to the right to borrow, such a reform would have to be critically viewed regarding the budgetary discipline. The limitation of spending as achieved through the Financial Framework would be abolished, and therefore, the major institutional constraint on the size of the budget would cease to exist which could open the floodgate for further spending expansion. In the view of the "common pool" problem, this would be the worst case scenario. There are no constraints which limit the incentives of national representatives to strive for increased spending paid out of the common resources provided by the EU tax.

Practically speaking, this reform is not compatible with the current policy objectives of the EU as a majority of spending is dedicated to long-ranging projects (especially in the structural funds) which demand the stability of spending.

"Rainy-Day Fund"

A further academic proposal is put forward by Le Cacheux (2007) who proposes to choose a higher tax rate than necessary to be able to balance the budget even in the case of a recession. The excessive revenue in "normal" and "good" years will be accumulated in a "rainy-day fund", which would be decumulated in the years when the tax revenues are unable to cover the expenditures.

Obviously, this proposal is also problematic as it leads to a softening of the budget constraint due to the fact that it generates more revenues than fixed in the Financial Framework and, therefore, widens the scope for increasing expenditures. Experience with national budgetary policy has impressively demonstrated that budget policy has hardly ever succeeded in building up reserve funds even under highly favourable revenue developments. Instead, an extraordinary revenue situation regularly results in new spending. A realistic expectation is that such a strategy would result in an increase in EU spending and a higher burden for the citizens.

5.2.4 A Digression: Distributive Consequences of EU Taxes

As it has been emphasised in section 3.5, for a full analysis it is also indispensable to take the interests of the players involved in the budgetary process into account in order to evaluate the prospects of an EU tax. As discussed above, public choice theory implies that an EU tax would surely find the support of the European Commission and the Parliament as both institutions would gain in importance and prestige. However, regarding the European Council and the national parliaments, the situation is more ambiguous. Here, the distributive consequences are of importance. A problem for the acceptability of any reform proposal emerges if the distributive consequences substantially deviate from the current distribution of the contributions, which is roughly proportional to GNI as shown in section 3.6.4. In this case, one of the following two consequences would arise:

- One or several countries which are disadvantaged compared to the status quo would use their veto in the Council to avert the introduction of the respective EU tax. The tax option would, therefore, be unfeasible as EU tax.
- The Council might still agree on the introduction of the respective tax but, then, only after granting compensations to the negatively affected countries. Thus, the demand for abatements for the affected countries would be even higher than today. This development would risk an offset of the (possible) gain in transparency through an EU tax and violate the principle of equity.

In the following, the distributive consequences of several EU tax proposals are revealed. For this purpose, the distribution of the respective tax base over the member states is estimated and compared with a distribution according to the national shares in GNI.[13] An additional burden (relief) resulting from a specific EU tax is represented by a positive (negative) value. Percentages relate to the reference point of GNI proportionality. A value of +*X*% for country *Y* for tax *Z* means that – compared to a GNI-proportional own resource – country *Y* is confronted with an increase of the financial burden by +*X*% in the case of tax *Z*.

Indirect Taxes

Value Added Tax

Fig. 12 shows the distributive consequences of a shift from GNI proportional contributions to payments of a harmonised value added tax. The distribution of the harmonised VAT base has been calculated according to the average national harmonised bases from 2004 to 2006 which are calculated by the Commission for the purpose of the determination of the VAT resource payments (European Parliament, 2004; 2006a; 2006b).

Fig. 12. Distributive consequences of an EU value added tax

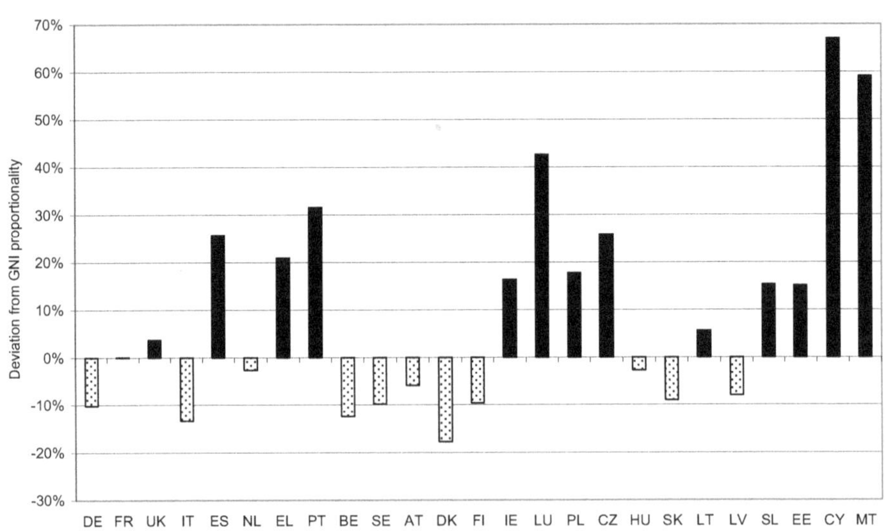

Source: European Parliament (2004; 2006a; 2006b); own calculations.

As it can be seen, the introduction of an EU VAT would cause major distributive consequences. These range from massively increasing contributions for some countries (e.g., Cyprus, which would have to pay almost 70% more than under

[13] For some taxes not all member states are included due to missing data.

GNI proportionality) to much lower contributions for other countries (almost 20% less for Denmark). Two main drivers for this unequal distribution are noticeable:

- The often-mentioned regressive character of VAT which burdens the poorer member states of Southern and Eastern Europe relatively more due to a higher consumption ratio;
- The "Marbella" effect, which mainly places a relatively higher burden on the Mediterranean countries with their higher share of tourism.

These results are not surprising. They are well-known from the debates on the VAT resources and have caused the complications and the essential phasing out of VAT resources as described in section 3.7.2.

Excise Taxes

In Fig. 13, the distributive effects of two excise taxes, of tobacco and alcohol, are shown. The distribution of the alcohol consumption was calculated based on the estimates of national consumption of pure alcohol per adult in 2003 following Cnossen (2006). The tobacco consumption was estimated on the basis of the annual cigarette consumption per person according to Mackay, Eriksen and Shafey (2006).

Fig. 13. Distributive consequences of an EU excise tax

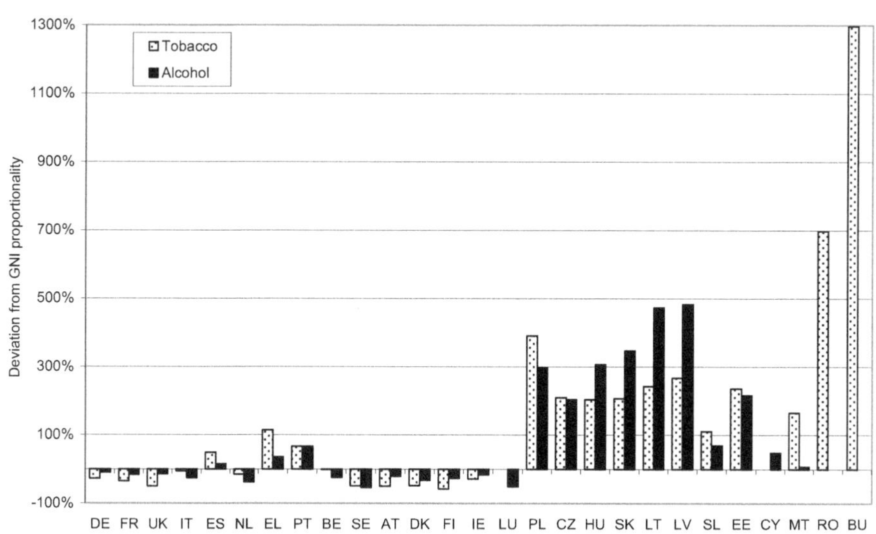

Source: Cnossen (2006); Mackay (2006); own calculations.

In Fig. 13, immense distributive effects of excise taxes can be seen. Both taxes would have extremely regressive effects as even on the per capita level the poorer member states from Eastern Europe have the highest consumption of the two taxable goods. Moreover, national preferences for drinking and smoking influence the relationship between the consumption of these goods and the GNI. A quantity tax might lead to an increase of their EU contributions up to a factor of 12 in these countries and to a halving of the contributions in some Western European member states.

Fuel Tax

In Fig. 14, the distributive effects of an EU fuel tax are shown. The national consumption of fuel is calculated as the sum of the total final consumption of motor gasoline and diesel for transportation (both in 2004) according to the International Energy Agency (IEA) statistics.[14]

Fig. 14. Distributive consequences of an EU fuel tax

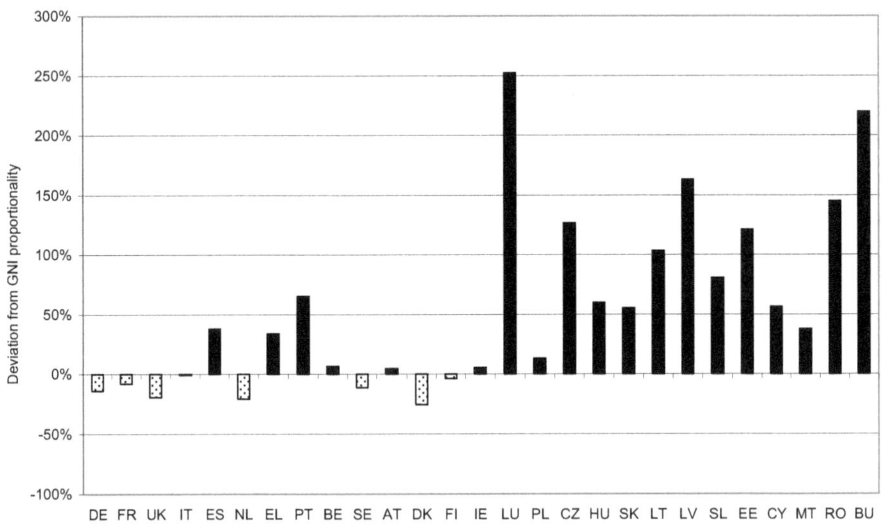

Source: IEA (2006); own calculations.

Also in the case of an EU fuel tax, a regressive effect can be observed with the Eastern European countries as the major losers of its introduction (in some cases burdened with about more than a doubling of their contributions). This reflects that the ratio of fuel consumption relative to GNI decreases with increasing national wealth.

Tax on CO_2 Emissions

The effects of an EU tax on CO_2 emissions are estimated on the basis of the national CO_2 emissions in 2004 (from IEA, 2006) and displayed in Fig. 15. As with the taxes discussed above, the distributive effect of a tax on CO_2 emissions would

14 These statistics are available at the IEA homepage, http://www.iea.org/Textbase/country/index.asp.

be a regressive one. It is primarily the Eastern European countries that have a high per capita emission of CO_2 due to their economic structure. By contrast, Western European countries, like France or Sweden, with a high share of nuclear power would be significantly disburdened.

Fig. 15. Distributive consequences of an EU tax on CO_2 emissions

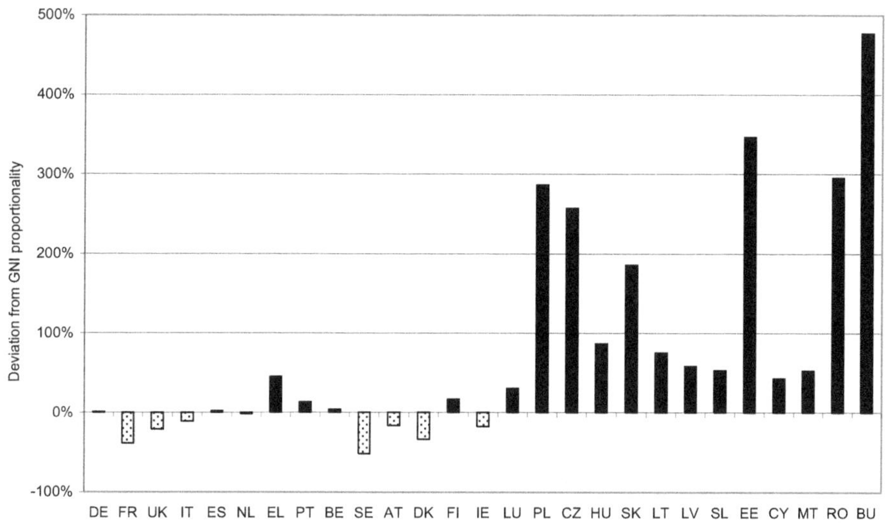

Source: IEA (2006); own calculations.

Kerosene Tax

The calculation of the distributive consequences of a quantity tax on kerosene is based on IEA statistics for total final consumption of air kerosene in 2004 (Fig. 16). This tax also results in major shifts of the national burdens leading to a quadruplication of the contributions of Cyprus and Malta whose location and tourism industry promote higher-than-average air traffic. Moreover, apart from economies with a high share of tourism, countries with major airline hubs (London, Amsterdam) are negatively affected. In contrast, several countries without major air traffic are almost entirely disburdened from any contributions to the EU.

However, it has to be considered that the incidence of this tax would only partially fall on the citizens of the countries which pay the taxes to the EU but mostly on citizens from other countries using the airports, for instance, tourists from other EU member countries. Nevertheless, there would still be opposition in the affected countries to a kerosene tax as it exclusively hurts their local industries and, thus, reduces their competitiveness.

Fig. 16. Distributive consequences of an EU kerosene tax

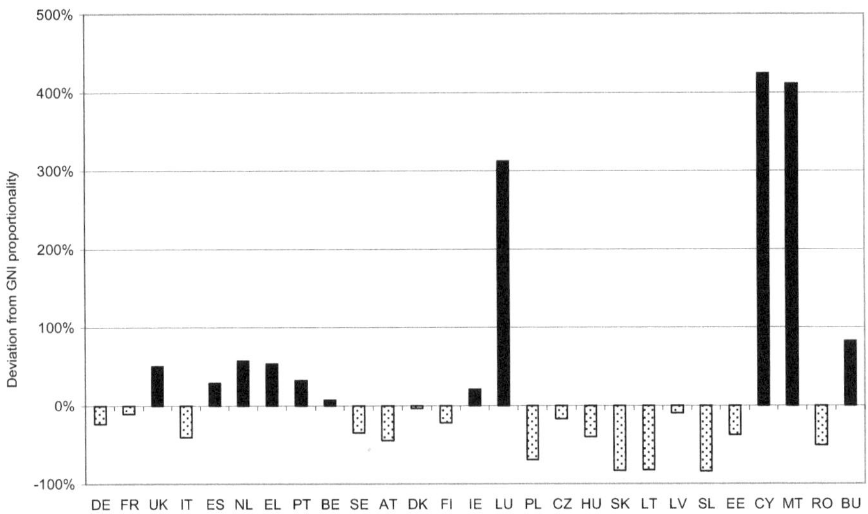

Source: IEA (2006); own calculations.

Fig. 17. Distributive consequences of an EU tax on foreign exchange transactions

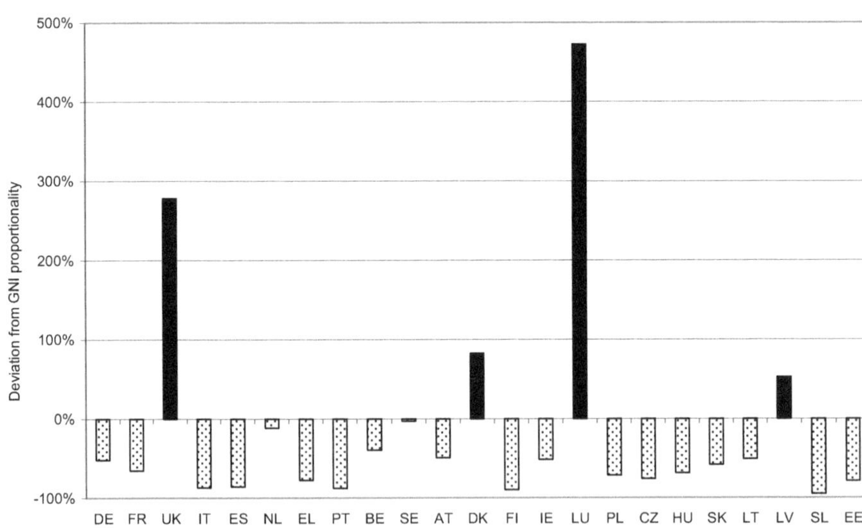

Source: BIS (2005); own calculations.

Tax on Foreign Exchange Transactions

Fig. 17 shows the distributive consequences of a tax on foreign exchange transactions as proposed by Schratzenstaller and Berghuber (2006) and the Austrian chancellor Schüssel (2006). The distribution of the tax base has been calculated from the daily averages of reported foreign exchange market turnover according to the Bank for International Settlements (BIS, 2005).

It is striking that a tax on foreign exchange transactions would not have a regressive character as most of the other indirect taxes discussed above. Instead, it would excessively burden few countries with important financial markets (in absolute figures mainly the UK with a European market share of almost 2/3) and disburden the overwhelming majority of member states.

Similar to the kerosene tax, the incidence of a tax on financial transactions does not fall in full to the citizens of the countries with important market places either. But these market places would lose much of their competitiveness and, hence, lose market shares to their competitors from overseas.

Direct Taxes

Personal Income Tax

The distributive consequences of a harmonised European personal income tax are much more difficult to estimate than the consequences of the indirect taxes discussed above. It does not only depend on the distribution of the tax base among the member states as in the case of indirect taxes but also on the design of the harmonised EU personal income tax, especially its progression. If a high degree of progressiveness is chosen, countries with a high inequality in its distribution of personal income will be burdened relatively more and vice versa.

A first indication that an EU personal income tax would also lead to a different distribution of national contributions to the EU budget than GNI proportionality can, however, be derived from the national shares of compensation of employees and self-employed persons. This was calculated via the national accounts data for the compensation of employees and was adjusted by the estimated compensation of the self-employed persons according to the method of Musso and Westermann (2005). The results for some member states are displayed in Fig. 18.

Despite the fact that the overall compensation of employees is obviously highly correlated with the national GNI, significant differences in its ratio can be observed for the European countries. Although this does not allow us to draw a final conclusion about the actual sharing of the burden of a personal income tax on the EU level, it helps to clarify that the diverging shares of labour income in the GNI of the member states would lead to a distribution pattern significantly different to GNI proportionality.

Fig. 18. Distributive consequences of an EU personal income tax

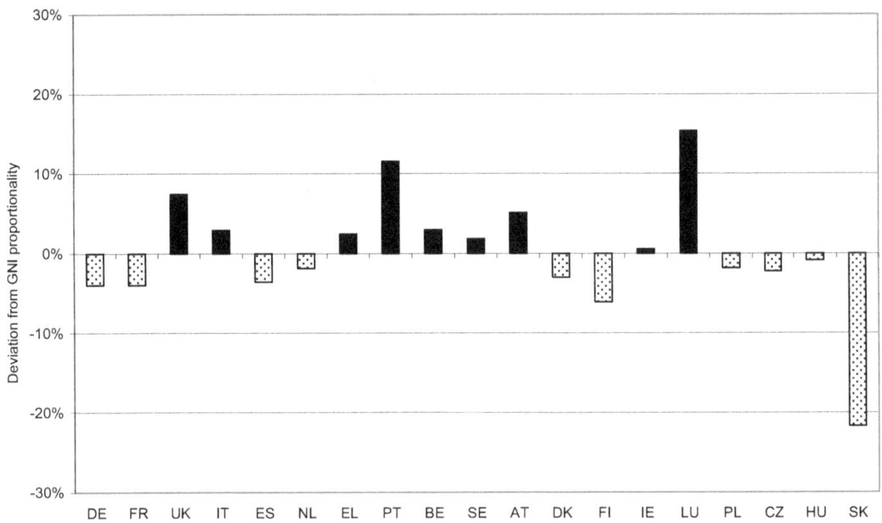

Source: Eurostat; own calculations.

Corporate Income Tax

Generally, there might be good arguments in favour of harmonising corporate income tax bases in Europe. This section only evaluates the suitability of a corporate income tax as an EU tax. Similar to the personal income tax, the distributive consequences of the introduction of an EU-wide harmonised corporate income tax are very difficult to estimate. Indicators for the hypothetical national tax burdens which are usually quoted, such as the share of income tax in GNI, are not very reliable as they are dominated by the impact of national differences in tax rates and bases. However, equivalent to the share of labour income in GNI, the share of corporate income can be assessed from national accounts data (see Fig. 19). The share of "gross operating surplus and mixed income" was reduced by the estimated share of compensation of those self-employed.

It can be seen that, due to diverging shares of corporate income in GNI, the shares in tax base derived from national accounts would substantially differ from GNI proportionality. But in the case of corporate taxation, another problem for the assessment of the distributive effects caused by an EU tax arises from the fact that the actual tax payments are determined by the definition of the tax base which is not equal to the corporate profits as measured by national accounts statistics. This implies that the actual distribution of tax payments also depends on the design of a harmonised corporate income tax which would be a prerequisite for the use as an EU tax. For instance, the design of depreciation allowances might have a major impact due to national differences in industrial structure or form of organisation.

Therefore, a conclusive assessment of the distributive effects of an EU tax based on a harmonized corporate tax is not feasible.

Fig. 19. Distributive consequences of an EU corporate income tax

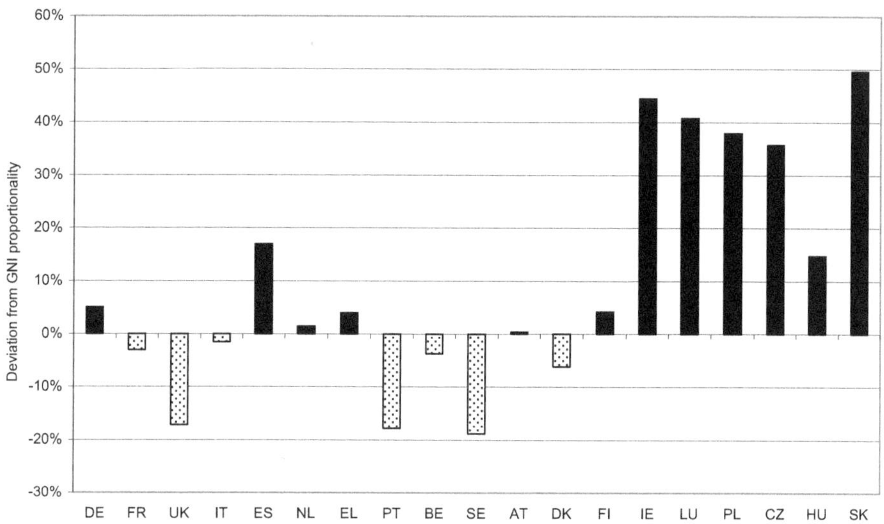

Source: Eurostat; own calculations.

5.2.5 Conclusion

As discussed in this section, there are many doubts about the desirability and feasibility of replacing the current system of own resources by the introduction of an EU tax. In our view, most of the aims usually put forward by supporters of an EU tax are respectable but it is doubtful whether an EU tax would be able to achieve significant improvements compared to the status quo. There are only few taxes imaginable which might cause an increase in visibility and simplicity of the system of own resources, which are generally emphasised as the main advantages of a tax-based system of own resources. Moreover, we do not agree that an EU tax would end political struggles due to the "juste retour" problem. Furthermore, the danger that an EU tax could be harmful is significant. This danger mainly lies in the fact that an EU tax may lead to less budgetary discipline on the European and on the national level resulting in an increasing fiscal burden on the citizens, which might finally erode their support in the EU. Moreover, an EU tax would interfere with diverse national preferences regarding taxation and in many designs also with national federal structures. Additional costs would also be caused by the necessary harmonisation of the national tax bases. Finally, there is no conclusive solution how to meet the problem of instable payments from an EU tax as this would either further increase the danger of declining budgetary discipline by giving the EU the right to borrow or increasing the flexibility of spending or it would remove any gain in visibility by adding further resources as residual.

The positive analysis finally even yields a more unfavourable result for the prospects of an EU tax. First, several of the proposed alternatives are likely to fail as it cannot be accepted that the Council can agree on a common tax base. This mainly affects taxes which are characterised by strongly diverging national preferences, especially personal and capital income taxes but also several excise duties. Secondly, and even more clearly, the quantitative analyses have shown that none of these proposed taxes have a distributive effect which comes at least close to that of the current system of own resources. It would cause arbitrary redistribution via the revenue side with significant divergence from GNI proportionality (winners and losers will depend on the type of tax which is chosen) and would even worsen today's situation where single countries only feel discriminated due to imbalances on the expenditure side of the EU budget.

Hence, the introduction of any of the proposed taxes would make a number of countries worse off, thus, either provoking their veto against the respective tax or it would call for an inflation of new abatements for disadvantaged countries. Even supporters of an EU tax agree that the redistributive effects of any EU tax would hardly be acceptable for all countries (see Le Cacheux, 2007). Le Cacheux (2007), therefore, proposes the introduction of a correction mechanism based on gross contributions in order to disburden countries with an excessive burden. Imaginable are the capping of the tax base (as in the case of the VAT resources today), reduced rates of call for single countries, general correction mechanisms or exception rules on the revenue side. Regardless which mechanism would prevail, it would surely offset the main advantages usually entitled to an EU tax, namely visibility and simplicity.

5.3 Parametric Adjustments Within the Status Quo

5.3.1 Elimination of VAT Resources

The most frequently proposed starting point for adjustments within the status quo is the elimination of the VAT resource and the extension of the GNI resource. As discussed in section 3.7.2, many deficiencies of the VAT resource can be observed compared to a system exclusively based on GNI resources (plus the traditional own resources). It seems that the GNI is a better and more transparent indicator for the national contribution capacity than the harmonised VAT base. Moreover, reducing the number of revenue sources is also desirable in order to reduce the complexity which is immanent in the current system of own resources.

The distributive effects of the elimination of the VAT resource were calculated in the simulation model introduced in section 3.6.2 for the year 2010 as a deviation from the status quo (see Fig. 20). A positive value of X% indicates that the country's overall gross contributions to the EU increase by X% whereas a negative value indicates a relief. As in the status quo the distributive effects of the VAT resource are dominated by the abatements which are granted to four countries as shown in section 3.6.4, two scenarios were calculated as basis for the status quo: (1) the inclusion of the currently reduced rate of call on the harmonised VAT base for Germany, Austria, Sweden and the Netherlands, and (2) the non-consideration of these abatements. In the hypothetical scenario (2), the four countries pay the full rate of call (0.3%) on their harmonised VAT base.

It can be seen that major changes in the pattern of distribution only emerge when the existing abatements are considered. In that case, all four beneficiaries of reduced rates of call face much higher contributions than under the status quo (Sweden would have to pay 8% more than today); the other member states are disburdened due to the phasing out of the rebates.

If the effects due to the phasing out of the abatements are ignored, as it is done in scenario (2), no major distributive effects of the elimination of the VAT resource can be observed. The most disadvantaged country would be Denmark even though its overall gross payments would only increase by about 2%.

Fig. 20. Distributive effect of elimination of VAT resource

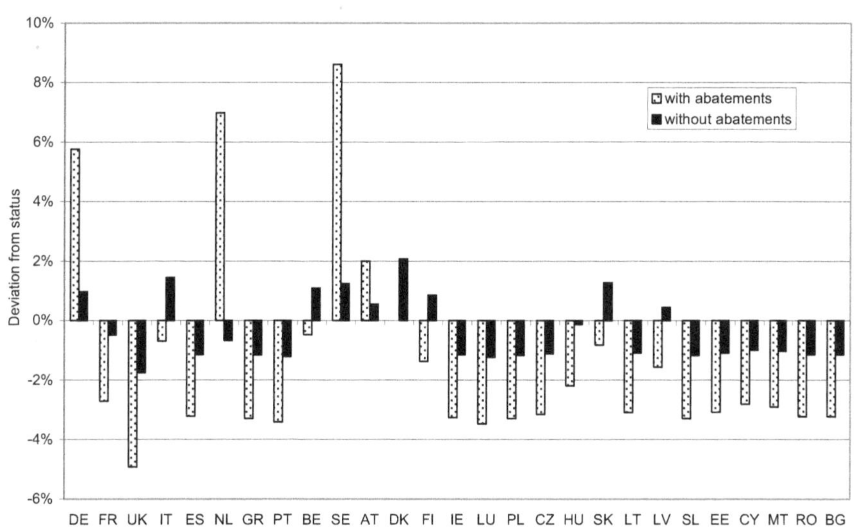

Note: % change refers to 2010 level of total own resources payments.

Source: ZEW calculations.

It seems that in contrast to the systematic reforms presented above, the proposed elimination of the VAT resource and the shift to an almost completely GNI-based financing of the EU budget seems to be feasible in terms of political enforceability. While the distributive effects of both resources greatly differed in the past, the consistent retrenchment of the harmonised VAT base and rate of call did not only reduce the quantitative importance of the source but also reduced its distributive effects. Despite the fact that there are still some countries which benefit from the financing via VAT resources due to low consumption rates (mainly Denmark and Italy), the quantitative benefit of the affected countries has become rather low; so this would probably not get in the way of the elimination of the VAT resource.

The main problem of an elimination of the VAT resource would be the dealing with the countries currently benefiting from a reduced rate of call. If the need for granting this abatement to these countries stayed unchanged due to enduring unwanted redistribution on the expenditure side, a compensation for these countries would have to be found in order to keep the overall distributive effect of the budget unchanged after the elimination of the VAT resource. This might be lump sum transfers, as today in the case of the Netherlands and Sweden, or a general correction mechanism as discussed in section 5.4.4. Thus, there are hardly any convincing counterarguments against a complete phasing out of the VAT own resources in the coming years.

5.3.2 Adjustment to GNI Resources

The conceivable abolishment of the VAT resource discussed above and, thus, the concentration on the fourth resource also put its currently used statistical concept up for discussion, which is the GNI at market prices. As it is shown in section 4.3, the use of GNI as an indicator for national wealth is not very common in international organisations where numerous different statistical aggregates are used. In the following, it will be discussed whether this macroeconomic aggregate is the most useful indicator for the economic capability or whether reform options are imaginable.

Choice of Base

As Euler (2005) discusses, reforms of the currently used statistical concept of GNI at market prices are imaginable in three dimensions, i.e. the use of (1) factor costs instead of market prices, (2) net values instead of gross values, (3) workplace instead of national concept. In contrast to market prices, the application of factor costs ignores the distortions of market prices due to governmental intervention. Technically, the transition from market prices to factor prices would imply the deduction of the balance between excise taxes paid and received subsidies. As received taxes increase the capability of the member state and as the concept of factor prices is not very common, the application of market prices is widely undisputed.

More crucial is the application of the currently used gross concept, which includes the gross investments and not the net investments as done in the net concept. Technically, the change to the net concept would imply the deduction of depreciations; this may be reasonable from an economic point of view as deductions do not increase the national capability. But it may be argued that macroeconomic depreciations suffer from methodological flaws which would lead to arbitrary results when using this for international comparisons (Euler, 2005). Moreover, the net concepts are not as common to the citizens as the gross concept, thus, its introduction would reduce the transparency of the system of own resources.

Finally, the most crucial dimension is the choice between workplace and national concept, hence, the choice between the GNI and GDP. The GNI follows the national concept and covers the income of all citizens living in the respective country. In contrast, the GDP covers the overall production in the respective country. Technically, the shift to GDP would mean the deduction of the balance of income from employment and wealth from abroad as well as the balance of subsidies received from the EU and levies of production and import paid to the EU.

Fig. 21. Distributive effect of shift from GNI to GDP proportionality

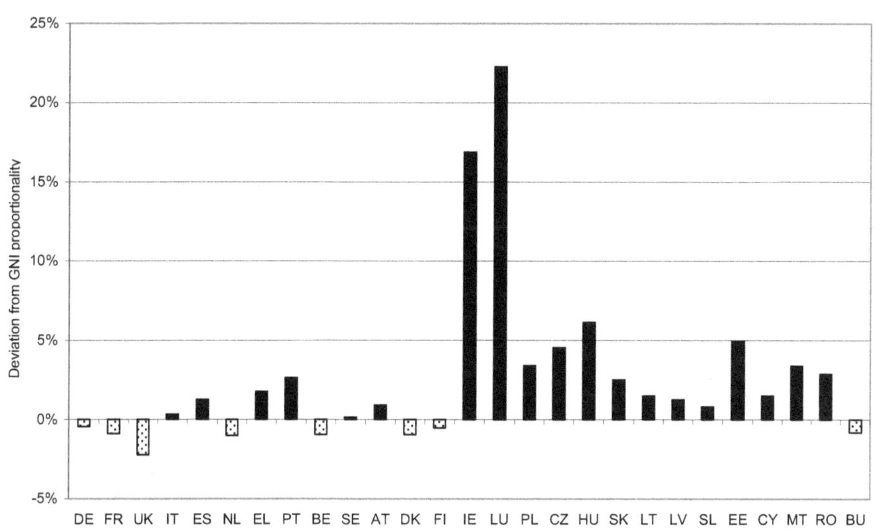

Note: % change refers to deviation from GNI proportionality in 2005.

Source: Eurostat; own calculations.

For the purpose of comparing the national economic capabilities, it is most often regarded as reasonable to use the GNI; as the European Court of Auditors (1998: 5) holds it, GNI "was chosen as an indicator of contributory capacity because it is supposed to measure the prosperity of a country and not, as is the case with GDP, its productive capacity". Raddatz (2005) concludes that the GNI is a better indicator to compare welfare internationally as it also includes flows of income from abroad and, hence, better reflects the total value of income and goods which can be disposed by the natives. However, it can still be argued that the GDP enjoys higher acceptance by the citizens as this aggregate is better known due to its more frequent use; from this point of view, a shift to GDP might increase the transparency of the system of own resources. In order to highlight the distributive differences between the use of GDP and GNI, Fig. 21 displays the distributive effects of the shift from complete GNI proportionality to GDP proportionality using data from 2005.

It can be observed that the distributive consequences for most member countries are rather low. However, the effects on Luxembourg (due to its high share of employees living abroad) and on Ireland (due to net capital imports) would be considerable as their contributions would increase by about 20%.

All in all, no strong support for a change from the current use of GNI at market prices towards the use of factor prices or the net concept can be found in the literature. Regarding the GDP, the situation is more ambiguous but, at least, this reform would cause considerable distributive effects for some countries. However, as it has been shown, there are no mandatory reasons to change the choice of the statistical base for the calculation of the fourth resource.

Nominal Exchange Rates or PPS

Another option to reform the GNI resource is the replacement of the current application of nominal exchange rates with purchasing power standards (PPS), which has been proposed several times in the past, for instance, by the ministries of finance of the German Laender in 1997 (Milbrandt, 2001). The use of PPS would account for national differences in the costs of living and is a well-established indicator in the EU as it is applied, for instance, for the allocation of structural funds. Its use on the revenue side can also be justified theoretically because the application of nominal exchange rates usually does not reflect the national capacities correctly as nominal exchange rates only regard traded goods. Moreover, nominal exchange rates are affected in the short-term by a number of further factors, like international capital flows (Raddatz, 2005). Applying exchange rates at PPS, the purchasing power of different currencies is equalised by using a common basket of goods, thus, giving a better impression of the national capability.

While the use of PPS may be preferred from a theoretical point of view, its methodological weaknesses are also considerable (for a critical discussion, see, among others, Raddatz, 2005). Especially the use of a common market basket is problematic as this does not adequately reflect different national consumption patterns and preferences. But this definition, as well as the choice of the price index, would determine the amount of contributions a country has to pay and would, therefore, be a crucial point of the calculation. Moreover, it may be criticised that the introduction of PPS as artificially calculated exchange rates would not contribute to the transparency of the system of own resources.

In Fig. 22, the distributive effects of the application of PPS instead of nominal exchange rates are shown for the GNI at market prices in 2005. It is clear that a transition to PPS would cause major shifts in the pattern of distribution of the national payments. Generally speaking, under PPS the poorer member states would have to face much higher financial burdens; most of the CEE member states would be confronted with an increase of the contributions between 50% and 100%; the contributions of Bulgaria would almost triple. By contrast, the contributions of the richer member countries in Western Europe would decline by up to 25%. This is explained by the higher price level for non-tradable goods in richer countries compared to poorer countries, known in literature as the Balassa-Samuelson effects (Balassa, 1964).

Turning to the positive analysis, it can be concluded that the massive redistribution of the financial burdens from the wealthy to the poorer countries makes the application of PPS unlikely. Keeping the expenditure pattern of the EU constant, they would have to face a dramatic worsening of their net positions compared to the status quo. The introduction of PPS would, therefore, only be feasible under a changed expenditure structure which would have to lead to even more extensive redistribution to the poorer member states than today in order to compensate them for the higher payments on the revenue side.

Fig. 22. Distributive effect of application of PPS

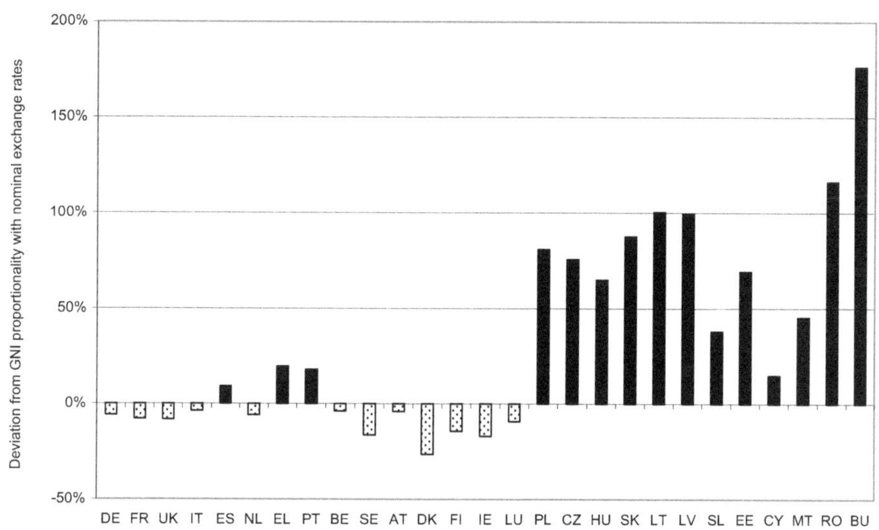

Note: % change refers to deviation from GNI proportionality with nominal exchange rates in 2005.

Source: Eurostat; own calculations.

5.3.3 Adjustments to Traditional Own Resources

Retained Amount for Administration

As it was discussed in section 3.7.3, it has often been criticised that the amount which is currently retained by the member states for the collection of the traditional own resources is not in accord with the true costs which accrue for this task. As this would have to be judged as a hidden abatement for some member states, it should not be integrated in the amount retained for administration but rather reported openly.

The distributive effects of a reduction of the retained amount for administration resulting from decreasing the rate from 25% to 10% were calculated using our simulation model for 2010 (see Fig. 23). As it could be expected, the contributions of the member states with high payments of traditional own resources (due to the discussed Rotterdam-Antwerp effect) would increase. However, this effect stays limited in size with the highest increase for Belgium by the amount of 5%.

Fig. 23. Distributive effect of the reduction of the retained amount for administration to 10%

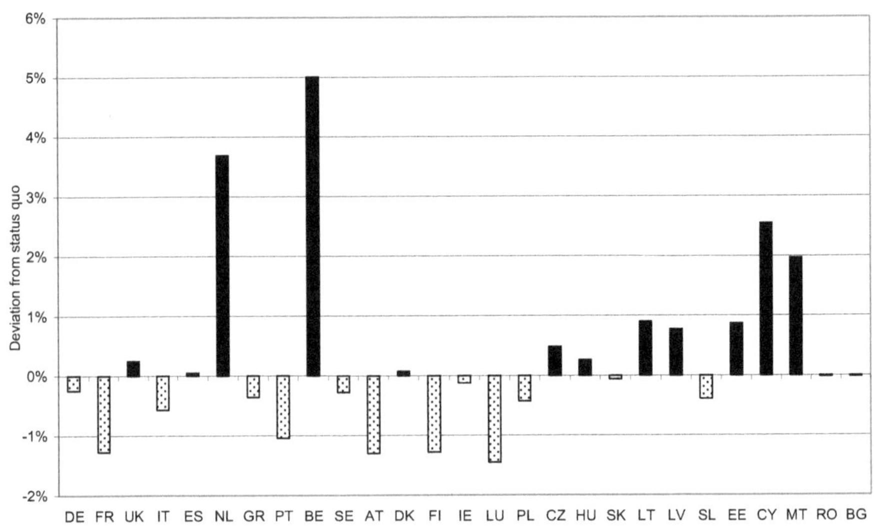

Note: % change refers to 2010 level of total own resources payments.

Source: own calculations.

Inclusion of ECB Seigniorage

One adjustment of the status quo which is sometimes proposed (e.g., by the Sapir report) is the inclusion of the ECB seigniorage[15] into the traditional own resources. This view usually receives strong theoretical support from the theory of fiscal federalism. Similar to the customs duties, the seigniorage also constitutes a byproduct

15 Technically, this means the monetary income of the European System of Central Banks (ESCB) which has to be differentiated from the overall profits of the ESCB; the overall profits include further revenues sources (see Cattoir, 2004).

which emerges from a common European policy. Its decisive feature is that these revenues cannot reasonably be geographically attributed to the member states which suggests the assignment to the highest tier of government, namely the EU.

This problem of regional arbitrariness is not sufficiently solved in the status quo. The current mechanism used for the allocation of the monetary income from the common monetary policy does not account for the source of this seigniorage (which would be the national shares in notes in circulation) but rather uses a formula which only regards the weighted national shares of GDP and population. As several authors remarked in the course of the start of the common monetary policy, even in the initial situation when the national monetary bases were still attributable, the use of this formula already distorted the true national shares and, hence, caused a redistribution of seigniorage wealth (Sinn & Feist, 1997).[16]

However, usually this potential source of revenues does not receive much support from advocates of an EU tax; in their eyes it fails several criteria for an appropriate EU tax. This mainly concerns the lack of a direct connection to the tax payers and, hence, no gain in visibility. Moreover, the revenues emerging from this source are far too low to cover the EU budget and show high fluctuations. These disadvantages could be connived due to the fact that the seigniorage would not constitute the autonomous "genuine" own resource which replaces the current system (as it would be the case with an EU tax) but would rather mean an adjustment of it and play a role similar to that of the custom duties today. Additionally, this limited amount of funds the seigniorage is able to generate also dispels doubts that the independence of the ECB might be challenged due to the EU's pressure of generating higher seigniorage in order to increase the EU budget. As any increase in revenues from the traditional own resources causes a reduction of GNI resources under the current framework, the overall expenditure level stays unchanged.

One main practical problem which would have to be solved is the integration of countries not yet participating in the common monetary policy. Goulard and Nava (2002) propose that these countries pay a share of their GDP which is calculated through a formula constituted of a linear combination of the share of the ECB seigniorage in the GDP of the Euro area and the share of the country's central bank's profits in the country's GDP. By applying this formula, a higher weighting of the second part would lead to an increase of most countries' contributions as the central banks outside the EMU usually generate higher profits due to higher inflation.

A much easier solution to this is imaginable by making the countries outside the Euro area pay according to their GNI shares. This is easy to realise by deducting the overall ECB seigniorage from the GNI contributions of the Euro area countries while making the other EU member states pay the GNI contributions in full. The distributive consequences of this method are shown in Fig. 24 for the actual Euro area countries based on national accounts data for the year 2005. It can be seen that poorer member states would lose from this approach: These countries

16 A transitional arrangement which partly offsets these redistributions is phased out until 2008.

save a certain part of their payments according to their share in GNI but lose the disbursements from the ESCB, which are higher than the payments of the GNI resource as their share in participation does not only incorporate their share in GDP but also their (higher) share in population. However, although these effects are high in percentages, it is not as important in figures as the absolute share of ESCB seigniorage would be restricted and not sufficient to cover the budget in full.[17] Assuming a share of 25% in the overall EU revenues, in the last resort Slovenia would have to pay around 10% higher contributions than today.

Fig. 24. Distributive consequences of seigniorage transfer to the EU

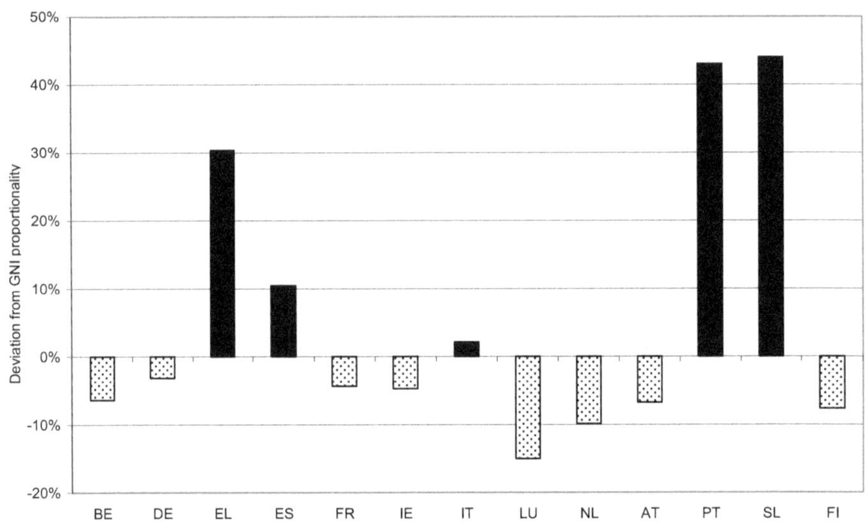

Source: Eurostat; own calculations.

While the fiscal federalism argument of regional arbitrariness clearly points to the inclusion of the ECB seigniorage into the traditional own resources, some practical and legal aspects oppose this view. First, the "Statute of the European System of Central Banks and of the European Central Bank" would have to be changed, which explicitly demands in Art. 33.1(b) the distribution of the ESCB's monetary income to its shareholders, which are the national central banks. This change would have a major impact on the construction of the current ESCB, which emphasises the independence of the national central banks and its decentralised character (SEP, 2005) and would, therefore, face much opposition. Another problem would occur at the level of the national central banks due to their different constitutions. The usual view on the distribution of the ESCB's net profits, which assumes that the payments once distributed to the national central banks are automatically transferred to the national treasuries, simplifies too much. First,

17 The share of the German Bundesbank's monetary income in the country's overall EU contributions was 22% in 2005 and 27% in 2006 (Deutsche Bundesbank, 2007).

there are differences in the accumulation of reserves, which reduce the budgetary revenues that actually accrue to the national budgets to a different degree. Moreover, several national central banks of the Euro System (e.g., Belgium, Austria and Italy) are partly or completely privately financed; therefore, they are owned by private shareholders with a claim for dividends (Rösl, 2002). Assigning the profit to the EU would make it necessary to find a compensation for these private shareholders.

5.3.4 Declaratory EU Tax

A declaratory EU tax is a proposal which is mainly put forward by academics who argue against the financing via a "true" EU tax (e.g., Caesar, 2001, and Schick & Märkt, 2002). Their idea is that the system of own resources continues to be based on non-tax-based contributions but that the amount of contributions paid from the national budgets to the EU is revealed directly to the citizens. This would be done by signalising a certain percentage of VAT on the bills or a percentage of the personal income rate as EU contribution.

Proponents of this procedure argue that it could make EU contributions visible without opting for an EU tax. It would enable the citizens to easily identify their personal contribution to the EU in a way very similar to a European tax. But simultaneously, it avoids several drawbacks which impair a "true" EU tax as discussed in section 5.2.3. Furthermore, any costs due to harmonisation as well as interferences of diverging tax preferences are avoided because the member states can choose themselves which of their existing taxes would be used as base for the declaratory EU tax. This does not forbid the use of different tax bases or different progressions in the case of a personal income tax.

However, several objections can be raised against this concept. First, the principle of horizontal equity might be violated in the eyes of the citizens as it seems as if comparable individuals are treated unequally in different countries. Due to differences in national contributions but also because of differences in the design of the tax systems, the impression would arise that the citizens in different countries differ in their contributions to the EU. For instance, differing progressions of personal income tax may give the people the impression that the burden of those better off compared to poorer citizens widely differs in the countries. This may give the people an impression of unequal treatment regarding the EU payments.

Moreover, it should not be neglected that a declaratory EU tax would be some kind of false labelling and, hence, misleading as it gives the citizens a wrong impression of the true tax autonomy of the EU. Finally, it would be a violation of the convention of not attributing general taxes like VAT or personal income taxes to special purposes. If doing this in the case of EU contributions, one has to wonder why this is not done in other cases in order to reveal the amount spent for the different national expenditure categories.

Nevertheless, this proposal shows that the lack of visibility, one of the most criticised deficiencies of the status quo, may also be solved by means other than an EU tax. Although a declaratory EU tax may go too far, this points out the potential of the governments to increase the visibility through a better communication policy even without an EU tax.

5.4 Reforming the Correction Mechanism

5.4.1 Introduction

As discussed above, the existing abatements for several countries are one major point of criticism of the current EU system of own resources. These abatements comprise the UK correction mechanism including the "rebate on the rebate" for the countries of Austria, Germany, Sweden and the Netherlands as well as the reduced rates of call for these four countries on the VAT resource and the lump sum rebates for Sweden and the Netherlands. Our discussion starts with a complete phasing out of any correction, then looks into possible adjustments of the UK rebate and finally into possible variants of a generalised correction mechanism.

5.4.2 Complete Phasing Out of any Correction

Even if the need for some corrections must be acknowledged, the current rebate with its focus on the UK is difficult to justify. As argued in section 3.7.4, due to the reduction of the relative share of agricultural spending as well as the increasing wealth of the UK compared to the rest of the EU, it has become difficult to justify the conservation of the status quo of the UK rebate. Moreover, the principle of horizontal equity demands the abolishment of the UK rebate. In addition, this is also true with respect to the abatements for the four other beneficiaries of corrections. In the following, the distributive consequences of a reform similar to the proposal of Lamassoure (2007), building up on the Finnish proposal from 2004, are presented. This reform includes:

1. Abolition of VAT resource;
2. Suppressing the UK rebate as well as all other abatements on the revenue side to zero in the medium-term.

In Fig. 25, the percentage changes of the countries' overall gross payments due to this reform are displayed for the theoretical phasing out of all abatements by 2010. As it can be seen, the effects of a complete phasing out of all rebates are immense. It is not surprising that the main loser would be the UK being confronted with contributions which increase by more than one third. However, Sweden and the Netherlands would also lose substantially as their payments would increase by more than 10%. The remaining beneficiaries of today's abatements are not affected so much with a slight increase of the burden for Germany and even a marginal reduction for Austria.

Fig. 25. Distributive consequences of Lamassoure proposal

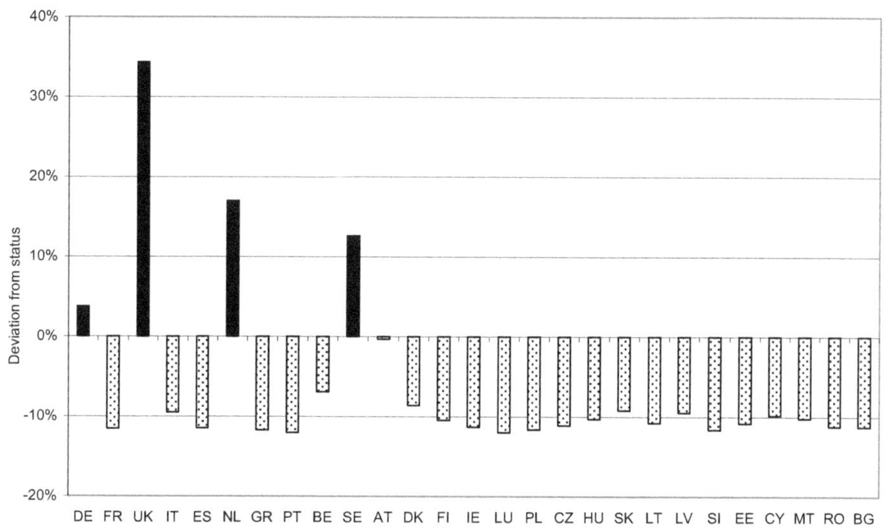

Note: Simulation results for % change of total own resources payments in 2010.

Source: Own calculations.

As the changes concerning the distribution of the financing of the Union are so immense, it is unlikely that this would be accepted by the negatively affected countries without simultaneously implementing reforms on the expenditure side. According to Lamassoure (2007: 12), the report's authors are "aware of the fact that an agreement on a new financing system along the lines of the Finnish proposal is only politically acceptable within the framework of a global negotiation process which also includes expenditure". This mainly includes a reform of the CAP spending as it was shown in section 5.1.1. Under the condition of an abolishment of the UK rebate without any substitution and given that the agricultural spending remains unchanged, the UK would become the largest net contributor.[18] Clearly, due to the unanimity rule in the European Council, such a worsening of the country's fiscal position would be unrealistic even if the claim was justified. Additionally, it should not be ignored that there is substantial public pressure which keeps any government in the UK from giving up the rebate without abolishing the CAP spending. In the center of this emotionally charged discussion is the often cited resistance of the British to "pay for the French farmers".

However, the other countries which are negatively affected by the abolishment of all abatements can also rightly refer to their under-representation on the expenditure side, even compared to countries with similar wealth. Hence, it can be concluded that if their overall net positions are not increased significantly, for exam-

[18] The corresponding net positions can be found in the Additional Tables in chapter 9.

ple, by the reduction of the spending for agricultural policy or special payments from structural funds, there will still be a need for a correction mechanism.

5.4.3 Parametric Corrections to the UK Rebate

Since its introduction, the UK rebate has experienced several technical adjustments to keep its correction payments stable in the face of enlargements of the EU or changes in the structure of its budget. While the fundamental principle of correction was maintained (see section 3.3.1), its design has become more and more complex and incomprehensible to the citizens. The last adjustments concern the participation of the UK in the financing of the enlargement costs for the acceding countries (see section 3.3.2).

This reflects that within the framework of the current UK rebate adjustments are imaginable which lead to a reduction of the amount reimbursed to the UK. If it will be possible in the future to reach further steps in this direction, several parameters could be adjusted in order to further reduce the reimbursed amount, as shown by Coussens (2004):

- A threshold could be introduced which would correspond to an acceptable net position (as a share of GNI); only a net position acceding it would be corrected.
- The correction factor (today 66%) could be reduced.
- The financing arrangement of the rebate (rebate on the rebate) could be revised by reducing or extending the number of beneficiary countries including the introduction of a contribution by the UK.
- Changing the definition of the net position, for example, by the exclusion of administrative or cohesion expenditure, would reduce the reimbursement.
- Finally, a very simple option would be the introduction of a ceiling for the overall reimbursement.

In spite of the variety of possibilities to reduce the rebate in order to make it more acceptable to other countries, it is obvious that they cannot solve the general problem of an unjustified privilege for one country. The principle of equity between the member states would still be hurt, and other net payers would still strive for equivalent corrections of their net positions. Instead, these proposals merely seem useful for a potential phasing-out process applied to transfer the current arrangement into a new system, for example, a new generalised correction mechanism. For this purpose, we regard a reduction of the correction factor as the most straightforward and transparent approach to phase out the UK rebate.

5.4.4 A Generalised Correction Mechanism

As shown in section 3.6.5, the anomalies on the expenditure side do indeed justify the establishment of corrections on the revenue side for countries which show an excessive negative net position due to low returns from CAP spending. Therefore, the optimal reform from a theoretical point of view, which is the abolishment of all abatements, is not realistic. However, we do not regard the status quo as an optimal solution for the compensation of countries with an excessive negative net position as discussed in section 3.8.2. Instead, we think that this may be better solved by a generalised correction mechanism in order to guarantee equity and transparency.

Beyond the severe discussion on the UK correction, one should not forget that it is not the only correction exemption granted for net payers. Other countries with similar net positions as the UK also have successfully strived for a reduction of their burdens leading to unilateral reductions. But the pertinacity of the UK rebate has shown that such unilateral correction mechanisms, or even exemptions like the ones granted to Sweden and the Netherlands within the new Financial Perspective, are not a satisfactory solution.

Thus, it is important to open a discussion which deals with the question about how a robust and simple generalised correction mechanism can be designed which can fulfil several normative and positive claims:

- It should automatically correct national net positions which exceed a generally accepted negative net position in a transparent way. This automatism enables that abatements for countries are automatically phased out when their net positions improve.
- It must not violate the principle of horizontal equity by benefiting only one or few predefined countries as in the past. The generalised correction mechanism should enable the equal treatment of countries with similar net positions and replace the current arbitrariness.
- It should be politically implementable, i.e. it should allow the current beneficiaries to agree on the abolition of the current UK correction as well as on the abolition of their rebates by generating a pattern of distribution which does not deviate much from today's pattern.

In the past, several proposals have been made regarding the introduction of a generalised correction mechanism. These are briefly presented in the following.

Focus on Gross Contributions

Even before the Fontainebleau decision in 1984, a generalised correction mechanism existed which was created in response to the UK's complaints about the country's excessive net position in 1975 (European Commission, 2002). This mechanism was provided to be triggered if three conditions were fulfilled: a member state's GNP of fewer than 85% of the Community's average, growth rate of the GNP per capita of less than 120% of the average and the actual gross payments to exceed 110% of the share of the country's GNP.

This mechanism has never been triggered because no country fulfilled all of these three criteria simultaneously. As Begg and Grimwade (1998) emphasise, it was not even fulfilled by the UK because the problem of the country was not a high gross contribution but a high net contribution, as it did not receive enough spending in return.

This is still the case today. As we have shown in section 3.6.3, the predominant driver of redistribution is the expenditure side. Therefore, a correction which is only focussed on the revenue side and, hence, gross contributions would not be sufficient to solve the problem of excessive net contributions. This can only be solved by connecting the spending with the revenues that a country receives; therefore, using the net contributions as the difference between gross contributions and backflows from the EU budget is superior to gross contribution systems.

Correction on the Expenditure Side

In contrast to the established approaches stated below, the mechanism proposed by the finance ministers of the German Laender in 1997 does not provide the correction on the revenue but on the expenditure side (Busch, 1998). It demands the introduction of a welfare-related base on the revenue side which can be best operationalised in their view by the GDP in purchasing power standards (PPS) (reduced by the amount of traditional own resources to account for the Rotterdam-Antwerp effect).

The correction of excessive net positions takes place on the expenditure side. It is demanded that the backflow to the member states shall be reversed proportionally to the national wealth, which is also expressed as GDP/PPS. This guarantees a fixed degree of redistribution as the richer member states pay higher contributions and receive lower spending from the EU budget. But as the structure on the expenditure side shall still be designed according to political criteria, the actual expenditures will not match the shares of national wealth. These differences to the wealth equivalent backflows for individual countries will be corrected in the budgets of the following years.

This mechanism creates the simplest solution imaginable for the revenue side comprising a very transparent source of revenues and the abolishment of any exception which makes the current system of own resources incomprehensible. However, the complexity of correcting the unacceptable net positions is shifted to the expenditure side. This must be criticised as it means that the expenditure side will even obtain a more distributive function than today in order to reach the intended degree of redistribution. It can be expected that this increases the "juste retour" thinking even more as there will be no room anymore for supranational projects which do not improve the net position for a single country. Instead, the money will go to funds benefiting single countries in order to achieve the intended fixed degree of redistribution and not to European public goods which might be more efficient.

Correcting Excessive Net Positions

Most correction mechanisms in the discussion are directly geared to the indicator of the national net position. While its concrete definition is more or less arbitrary as shown below, it seems to be widely agreed upon the fact that a national net burden is regarded as unacceptable if the difference between its gross contributions and attributable backflows from the EU budget exceeds a certain share of the national GNI. In the following, some approaches which center this consideration in the design of the correction mechanism are presented and critically discussed.

The most prominent model in the current discussion on the introduction of a generalised correction mechanism is the model proposed by the European Commission (2004a). It can be seen as an attempt to design a mechanism which can replace the current UK correction while reducing it in the amount which is reimbursed and while extending it to other countries with an excessive net position.

This basic mechanism is derived from a mechanism originally proposed by the German Ministry of Finance (BMF) in 1996 (Stark, 1996). The idea behind this generalised correction mechanism was to achieve a partial reduction of the net contribution of the net payers beyond a threshold of reasonability. Due to the similarity in design it can also be regarded as an extension of the UK rebate system to other net contributors who show an "unfair" net position. The concept of this mechanism is formally presented in the following (according to Euler, 2005):

$$\text{Reimbursement of country } i = \begin{cases} 0, if(NP_i - zY_i) \leq 0 \\ a \times (NP_i - zY_i), else \end{cases}$$

with NP_i = net position of country i; Y_i = GNI of country i.

This design of the generalised correction mechanism has several degrees of freedom which make this mechanism quite variable regarding the intended distribution of corrections: The adjustment factors in this mechanism are the values for a and z. The variable a can be regarded as a refund rate, its initially proposed value was 66%, whereas z determines the threshold for an acceptable net contribution, here the values of 0.3 and 0.4% were originally proposed.

The financing of the corrections should be carried out relatively to the national prosperity expressed in GNI. Regarding the participation of the beneficiaries of such a mechanism, in principle three different options exist:

- Originally it was proposed that the reimbursements for an individual country have to be financed by all other member states (including other recipients of correction payments) excluding the country itself.
- Member states which receive a correction also equally participate in the financing of the total correction, which means a lower sum of corrections compared to the BMF model.
- Member states which receive a correction might be completely excluded from the financing, which would lead to a higher sum of overall corrections.

The European Commission (2004a) resorted to the general principle presented above and only marginally diverged it from the original BMF proposal in the choice of the parameters. It proposed the values of 0.35% for z and 66% for a but added a further maximum available refund volume of 7.5 billion EUR. Moreover, it proposed that all countries should participate in the financing of the overall reimbursement according to their share in GNI; the total reimbursement would, therefore, be lower. It also put variable thresholds up for discussion: An increase of z with increasing GNI in PPS per head would discharge the poorer net contributors, especially Germany.

In Fig. 26, the effects of the generalised correction mechanism as proposed by the European Commission (2004a) on the member states' gross contributions are shown compared to the status quo, i.e. the perpetuation of all existing abatements. Two cases were regarded: (a) the full participation of the beneficiaries in the financing of the reimbursements, (b) no participation of the beneficiaries. The results of the application of the BMF mechanism, which assumes that the beneficiaries finance all but their own reimbursements, would lie in between these two alternatives. The situation without any abatement (as presented in section 5.4.2) was added in order to show the deviations caused by the GCM.[19]

Fig. 26. Distributive consequences of GCM

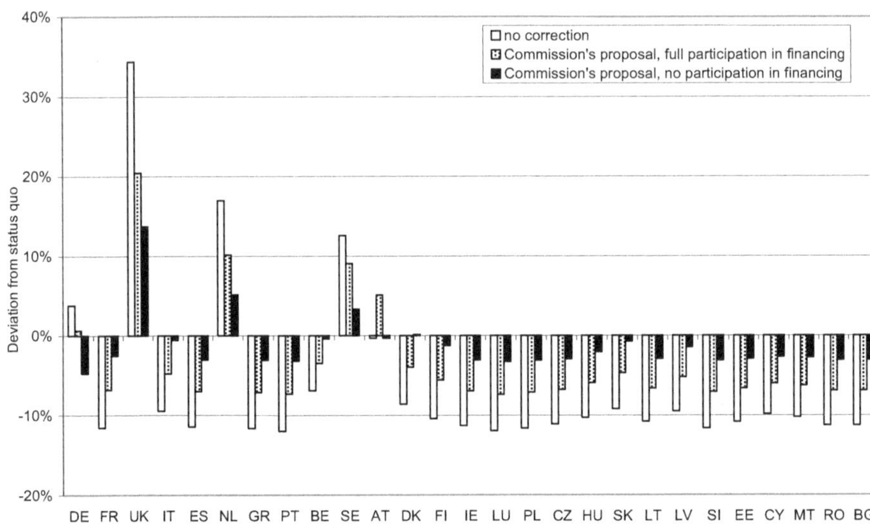

Note: Simulation results for % change of total own resources payments in 2010.

Source: ZEW calculations.

Generally starting from an assumed system of own resources without any abatements, the GCM moves the member states' gross contributions (and, hence, net contributions)[20] closer to the status quo. As it can be seen, the GCM is successful in at least partially compensating 4 out of the 5 countries which benefit from abatements on the revenue side today. The effect on the position of the UK is the most pronounced as its increase in contributions compared to the status quo is reduced from almost 35% to around 20%; the effects for the Netherlands and Sweden are also considerable. However, two special cases arise: If excluded from the financing, Germany even benefits from the replacement of the current abatements

[19] All calculations on correction mechanisms are based on the simulation model with the base year of 2010.

[20] The net positions are shown in the Additional Tables in chapter 9.

by a GCM compared to the status quo; Austria, in contrast, would face considerably higher contributions compared to the status quo as well as the situation without any abatement. This may be explained by the fact that it would be the only beneficiary of today's abatements which would not benefit from a GCM at a threshold of 0.35%, due to its lower net contributions.

However, in order to achieve a higher compensation for the UK and the Netherlands and in order to abolish the fiscal debasement for Austria caused by a GCM, either a decrease in the threshold or an increase in the refund rate would be needed as well as an increase in the maximum refundable volume of € 7.5 billion which would be exceeded at a threshold of lower than 0.27%. In Fig. 27, the effects of a decrease of the threshold to values of 0.25% and 0.2% are shown.

Fig. 27. Distributive consequences of GCM with reduced threshold

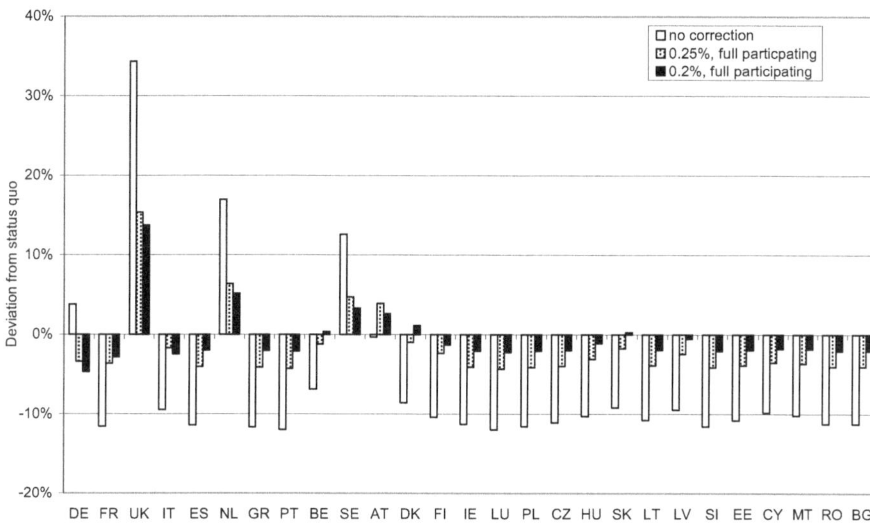

Simulation results for % change of total own resources payments in 2010.

Source: own calculations.

It can be seen that a further decrease of the threshold to 0.2% converges most of the non-beneficiaries of a GCM to their payments in the status quo while causing no major declines in the gross contributions of the UK and the Netherlands. This is caused by the fact that at this threshold 3 further countries (Denmark, France and Italy) would profit from a generalised correction mechanism and absorb part of the increase in refund volume.

Hence, an increase in reimbursements only for the countries benefiting from today's abatements would only be feasible with an increase in the refund rate a at a relatively high threshold z. In Fig. 28, the effects of an increase of the refund rate up to its most extreme level of 100% are displayed for the case of a threshold of 0.25% and full participation in financing.[21]

The figure shows that the choice of the most extreme parameter for the refund rate (100%) displaces the increase of the gross contributions for the UK under 10%. The gross payments of most other member states stay close to the status quo. However, the choice of these parameters generates one big winner, Germany, which would undergo the highest decline in gross contributions compared to the status quo. By contrast, Austria would suffer substantial losses because it would undergo increasing gross contributions with increasing refund rate.

Fig. 28. Distributive consequences of GCM with increased refund rate

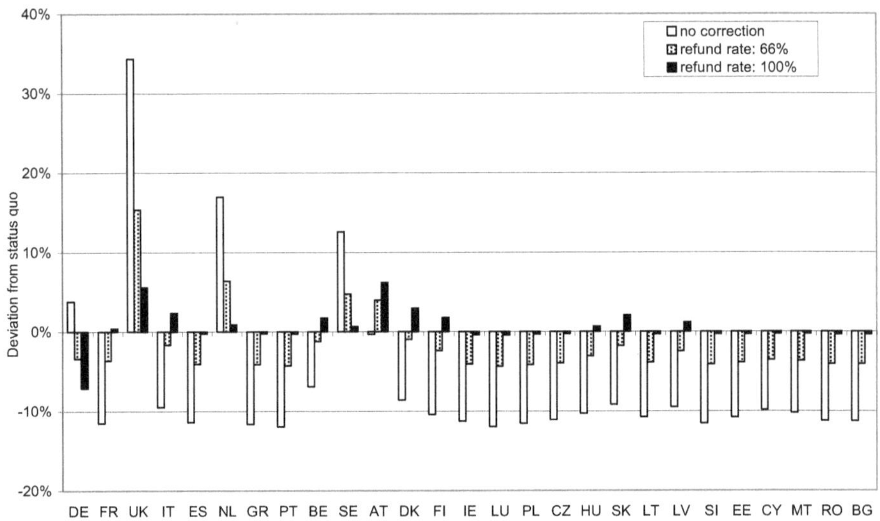

Note: Simulation results for % change of total own resources payments in 2010.

Source: own calculations.

All in all, this quantitative analysis shows that depending on the choice of the parameters there is a multiplicity of different patterns of distribution of the contributions. This reflects the capability of a GCM to compensate countries which would face highly increasing gross contributions in the case of the abolishment of the UK rebate and other abatements.

Creating a Predefined Net Position

The intention of the "equity safeguard mechanism" proposed by the Padoa-Schioppa report (1987) consists in not only correcting for excessive negative net positions through reimbursements but also in correcting for highly positive net po-

[21] Similar parameters were proposed by the German Minister of the Interior, Rudolf Seiters in 1997 (for details, see Euler, 2005, and Lefebvre, 2005).

sitions by making the affected countries pay higher contributions. In comparison to the proposals above, the GDP per head is added as a further parameter.

Similar to the original design, a progressive system is assumed; the "acceptable" net transfer to the EU budget shows a non-linear rise with increasing GDP per head. It is emphasised that the quantitative design of the parameters depends on political decisions. For example, it is proposed to set an acceptable net transfer of 3% of GDP for countries with a GDP per head of up to 50% of the EU average, a balanced net position at 100% and a negative net position of -1% at 130% of the EU average.[22] A fluctuation margin is set around these levels which determines the area in which the net contributions of the countries may move without leading to a correction. Beyond this band, corrections will be paid from the EU budget if the national net transfer to the budget is higher or the net payments from the budget are lower than indicated by the margin. If a country pays too little or receives too much, a correction payment to the EU budget is established. Furthermore, it is stated that countries below a certain GDP per capita threshold should not have to pay for the correction.

In Fig. 29, the functioning of the Padoa-Schioppa mechanism is indicated. Therein, the net positions are displayed – without any of the existing rebates – which were estimated for 2010 with our simulation model as well as the most recent indication of national GDP per head (in PPS) relative to the average of the EU-15 (estimated for 2008 by Eurostat).

Several qualitative consequences can be derived from the application of the Padoa-Schioppa mechanism compared to a generalised correction mechanism as presented before. Firstly, focussing on the national GDP per head, in addition to the national net position, would extend the number of countries asking for correction reimbursements due to an excessive net burden. This group of countries comprises Italy with a negative net position which is, however, below the usual thresholds of a generalised correction mechanism but above the net burden regarded as acceptable for a country of that wealth. Several net receivers (Cyprus, Malta and Portugal) could complain about a budgetary disadvantage compared to countries of similar wealth. Secondly, especially Ireland would face high correction payments due to its positive budgetary net position[23] but also some Eastern European member states have favourable net positions compared to other countries of similar wealth.

A further proposal, similar to the one from the Padoa-Schippa report, goes back to de la Fuente and Doménech (2001). They propose a multi-stage procedure in the budgeting process. First, it is necessary for the national representatives to agree on the expenditure level and, most importantly, on the desired level of redistribution. From this agreement, indicative net balances for every country are derived which have to be inversely correlated to the income levels. Second, resources will be allocated to specific expenditure programmes without regarding

22 Due to the Eastern enlargement, these values would not satisfy today's demands to an acceptable redistribution.

23 The status of Belgium is dominated by its high share of administration expenditure which should not be taken into account in a correction mechanism.

national net positions. Finally, a correction mechanism comes into play, which assures (by structural spending, compensatory payments or rebates) that the agreed distribution will realise.

Fig. 29. Padoa-Schioppa mechanism

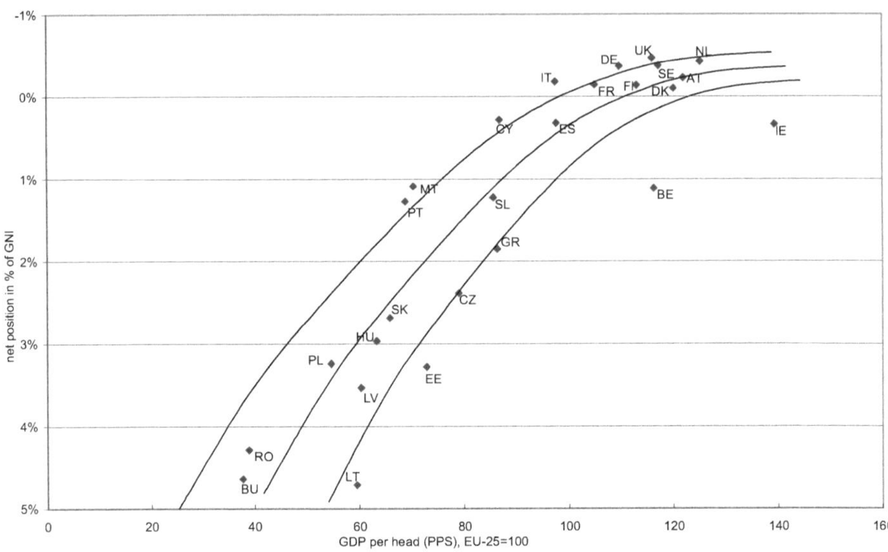

Source: Eurostat; own calculations.

Both proposals have in common that the intended degree of progressiveness of the overall EU budget is fixed by transparent and observable national characteristics like GDP per head and not by the result of diverging treatments of member states on the expenditure side. The fact that these concepts play a minor role in the current discussion about the system of own resources might be due to the fact that they overshoot the mark. Although it is undoubtedly true that the EU budget already has a redistributive function, such a system would codify an explicit European system of equalisation payments. It is unlikely that the governments of the net payer states would agree to this at the current level of integration.

It might also be countered that one main target of a reform, namely the reduction of political struggles, would not be reached. Discussing the redistribution of resources directly is likely to result in further conflicts as all national politicians would be exclusively judged by their voters according to their success in acquiring money.

5.4.5 Merits and Problems of a Generalised Correction Mechanism

The principle idea of a generalised correction mechanism is very often met with skepticism. A frequent point of criticism is that the replacement of the UK rebate by such a system would legitimise the "juste retour" thinking of the member states (e.g., Becker, 2005a). A similar opinion is held by the report of the rapporteur of the EP Committee on Budgets, where it is stated that a generalised correction mechanism "would only strengthen the anti-communitarian character of the system and cement the short-sighted approach of a quantifiable 'juste retour'" (Lamassoure, 2007: 11).

Although we share the general undesirability of the "juste retour" thinking with these critics, it should be pointed out that they neglect the fact that the "juste retour" thinking is a fact of political life as it could be observed in detail during the negotiations on the Financial Perspective whether it is legitimate or not. However, in our opinion, the reasons for the complaints about excessive burdens can be predominantly found on the expenditure side, which is responsible for the majority of the redistribution between the EU member states that is contested by the net payers, mainly in the agricultural area. Consequently, as discussed in section 5.1, the first best solution would be to reform the expenditure side in such a way that an unwished redistribution is reduced to the effect that the basis for "juste retour" thinking is narrowed.

Assuming that no major reforms on the expenditure side occur, a second best solution has to be found. Therefore, two main merits of a generalised correction mechanism can be found: Firstly, a generalised correction mechanism, once introduced, might be able to reduce the tensions which currently exist between the national governments because of the net positions and an unequal treatment in the correction of excessive net burdens. Secondly, visibly reducing the high burden of single countries might be an instrument to increase the acceptance of the EU in these countries (e.g., the German "Zahlmeister" discussion). In contrast to the current situation with unilateral exemptions, such a mechanism would make a correction more comprehensible to the citizens. Nevertheless, some methodological weaknesses of a generalised correction mechanism of the form proposed by the European Commission (2004a) exist, which will be presented in the following.

Budgetary Balance

All the concepts presented above focus on the net balance, i.e. the difference between the gross contributions and the attributable backflows that a country receives from the EU budget. This concept is generally criticised by the European Commission as well as by scientists (see Lefebvre, 2005) as it does not sufficiently reflect the true advantages a country receives through its membership in the Union. For example, the European Commission (2005) states that regional policy does not only have a positive effect on the benefited country as it also entails imports from other member states.[24] Moreover, positive effects from economic integration which differ between member countries are totally neglected.

---

24 Ciprani and Pisani (2004) show that due to national differences in industrial structures, the interrelations through trade lead to very different net positions than budgetary flows alone.

Nevertheless, the importance of the concept for the member states is self-evident as it is usually consulted to judge the immediate budgetary advantages and disadvantages of the membership in the EU. This is also reflected by the governments' strong focus on the national net positions usually inducing the top net contributors to complain about their heavy financial burden. But the formalisation of the concept of the net balance, which would be the prerequisite for the introduction of a generalised correction mechanism, would not be unambiguous. As the European Commission (1998, Annex 3) declares, "no fewer than 30 to 40 perfectly defensible definitions of budgetary balances" can be found. According to the Commission (2005), assumptions have to be made about 4 main issues in order to define the net position:

- the items to be included in the calculation of EU revenues;
- the items to be included in the calculation of attributable expenditures;
- the use of cash versus accrual data;
- the possibility of adjusting the resulting set of budgetary balances so that they sum up to zero.

While many of these issues only have a limited quantitative effect on the national budgetary balances, some have major impacts causing problems that need to be solved when introducing a generalised correction mechanism based on budgetary balances (Coussens, 2004).

Traditional Own Resources (TOR)

The amount of revenues collected by the member states on behalf of the EU is not incorporated into the net position underlying the UK correction. Nevertheless, it is often incorporated by authorities in the member states at the calculation of their net position, which is called "accounting net balance" by the European Commission (2005). This has a significant quantitative impact as, for instance the Antwerp-Rotterdam effects accounts for higher TOR payments of several countries due to major harbours mainly (the Netherlands and Belgium). This accounts for higher negative net balances for those countries which would make them demand its inclusion into a generalised correction mechanism leading to higher reimbursements for them. But it may be argued against it by objecting that it would not be justified to completely attribute these revenues to the respective member states as the burden for the duties is very often borne in other countries and the revenues are the result of the common policies.[25]

Administration Expenditure

Another change from the current calculation underlying the UK correction might be the omission of the administration expenditure, which is currently included. Administrative expenditure is almost completely assigned to Belgium and Lux-

25 Gelauff, Stolwijk and Veenendaal (2006) estimate that about 70% of the tariffs collected in the Netherlands are actually paid by foreign customers.

embourg, the two countries with the headquarters of most EU institutions, which leads to a major improvement of their net positions. Although this high concentration of institutions increases the purchasing power in the two countries, much of the payment is disbursed to politicians or bureaucrats from other countries. This may lead to the claim on its omission by Belgium and Luxembourg, which would significantly worsen their budgetary balance and, thus, might increase their reimbursements from a generalised correction mechanism.

Undesirable Correction of Cohesion Payments

One negative feature of a generalised correction mechanism as it was proposed by the European Commission (2004a) consists of the redistribution of cohesion funds which counteracts the purpose of this field of policy. As this is intended to reduce the regional and national economic disparities within the EU, it necessarily causes a certain degree of redistribution from the richer countries of the Union to the poorer ones.

Due to the fact that this redistribution inevitably worsens the budgetary balance of the net payers, the introduction of a generalised correction mechanism with the aim to reduce the burden of the net payers would lead to a partial diversion of the payments. It would even lead to the inconsistent effect that an increase of cohesion payments would only at a small share be paid by the richer countries. Instead, it would mainly be borne by the poorer countries themselves as the worsening of the net positions of the net contributors would have to be financed by them.

Summed up, there are good arguments to exclude policies with a clear redistributive function, such as cohesion funds, from a generalised correction mechanism. A reallocation of redistributive payments does not only contrast the purpose of these policies but also reduces the transparency of the EU budget. In order to ensure transparency it would be better to agree on the desirable degree of redistribution on the expenditure side (through cohesion funds) and that this decision would not be distorted by a correction on the revenue side.

Incentive Effects

A possible effect of a generalised correction mechanism on the behaviour of the nation states is widely ignored, described by Cuthbert and Cuthbert (2006) as a "perverse incentive effect". These authors hold the view that the current UK rebate reduced the country's incentive to engage in EU programmes in the past even if these exclusively favoured the UK. Generally, a national government evaluating the introduction of a certain EU programme would compare the fraction of extra EU expenditure attributable to the country with the share of the resources it has to contribute to finance it. They calculate that at best, in which case a programme only benefits the UK, and in the absence of any correction mechanism, the EU would contribute 42% giving the country a high incentive to demand such a programme. But in the situation with the current UK correction on operation, further costs appear for the UK: As any additional return from the EU improves the overall net position of the country, the payments in the course of the UK rebate are cut by 66% of the amount of the received payments. As a result, the UK finally has to contribute 86% of the costs of the new programme, thereby, significantly reducing the incentives to pursue such a programme. The authors conclude that this may explain the low take-up of discretionary programmes by the UK as well as their indifference towards policy proposals with a more dispersed group of recipients.

Obviously, similar effects to the ones observed in the UK can be expected in the net payer countries which benefit from a generalised correction mechanism. Their incentive to attract attributable payments would decline due to the fact that these payments would reduce the reimbursements from the correction mechanism almost to the same amount.

We do not pursue Cuthbert and Cuthbert (2006) who interpret this incentive effect purely in a negative light. It must be stressed that from the perspective of the common pool problem (see section 3.5.2), this consequence of a generalised correction mechanism can also pose an advantage: Member countries would benefit less from directing special spending programmes towards their countries since the correction mechanism would automatically neutralise some of the net effects. As a consequence, national representatives may view the composition of the EU budget from a different perspective so that European public good type expenditures are considered more attractive.

However, there may be also negative effects resulting from such a system. If national governments lose the interest in cooperating with the EU, this will lead to a substitution of European projects supported by the EU with purely national projects, which may become a threat for the further integration process of the EU. Thus, it has to be closely examined in which policy areas a declining national incentive to attract payments may be regarded as desirable and in which areas as harmful

6 A Reform Proposal

6.1 Starting Point

The preceding analyses have resulted in a plethora of insights. These serve as a basis for our reform proposal and can be summarised in the following manner:

EU Tax

It was shown that some of the prominent reform proposals may not be as convincing as their proponents suggest. As one of the strengths of the status quo, the successful capping of the budget through the own resources ceiling and the national budgetary self-interest of Council members in an economical use of EU resources should be pointed out. Like any other federal level the EU level is not immune to inefficient spending pressure resulting from the common pool problem or centralisation interests so that incentives for fiscal discipline must be ensured. The fact that the current own resources system establishes a direct budgetary link between national budgets and the EU budget is an important element of fiscal discipline since this explains the reliable interest of the Council in budgetary discipline at the EU level. An EU tax would not only tend to cut that helpful link. A further major disadvantage of any conceivable tax has been demonstrated through the calculation of the substantive redistributive effects of any of the discussed tax bases (see section 5.2.4). Instead of neutralising the "juste retour" debate, any of the debated taxes would rather intensify disputes on correction needs.

GNI Resource

In contrast to any conceivable EU tax, the distribution resulting from the GNI resource is less controversial. It should be underlined that the GNI resource has implicitly experienced overwhelming support in the literature and in the political debate in the sense that this instrument as such is hardly ever criticised. Therefore, the conclusion is justified that this revenue source is widely accepted with regard to both its distributive consequences and its operative functioning including its administrative cost-effectiveness. This favourable assessment justifies the continuous use of the GNI resource as the central financing instrument in the future.

VAT Resource

Among the existing types of own resources the VAT resource has the poorest justification. Not only due to all the reforms in recent years, which have resulted in an ever declining relative importance of this source of finance, is the time ripe for a complete abolition which also could contribute to higher administrative cost efficiency.

Principle Justification for a Correction Mechanism

In principle, a transparent and simple revenue system without any correction mechanism is desirable. However, as long as the spending focus on the expenditure side produces distribution patterns only loosely related to relative country wealth, some correction mechanisms are indispensable to safeguard political acceptance of the system. An abolition of any rebate system would run the risk of an even more distribution-oriented fine tuning of the expenditure side. In this sense a correction mechanism can be interpreted as a valve taking away some of the redistribution pressure from expenditure allocation decisions.

Major Shortcomings of Current Rebate System

However, even if – in the absence of an expenditure side "revolution" – correction mechanisms remain necessary, the current rebate will have a number of obvious shortcomings related, amongst others, to its selective focus, its degree of complexity and the fact that even desirable distributive effects (e.g., related to the regional convergence objective) are partially reversed.

6.2 Reform Proposal

6.2.1 Elements of the Reform Proposal

Although the definition of feasible reform proposals is limited by many political and economic restrictions, there is room for manoeuvring EU finances towards a more efficient and integration compatible system. Our proposal is based on the following three key elements:

- Complete phasing-out of the VAT resource,
- Accepting the GNI resource as the dominant and permanent source of finance,
- Establishing a generalised but limited correction mechanism (GLCM).

While the first and second elements are self-evident given the arguments summarised above, the GLCM requires a thorough explanation.

First of all, the advantage of a generalised correction mechanism compared to the selective one of the status quo is obvious: If there is a need to correct burden sharing in the Community, the extent and structure of correction payments will be identifiable on the basis of objective and measurable country data. Any such generalised approach will clearly outperform the current UK rebate with regard to the system's perceived fairness. Privileging one or several countries within the correction formula – even if this may have been justified in the historical situation of the rebate's establishment – must undermine the system's credibility from the citizens' perspective.

In the definition of a generalised mechanism, different decisions have to be taken including the applied formula and the covered policy areas whose distributive effects are to be partially corrected. With regard to the latter dimension, a far-reaching correction mechanism reverting distributive effects of the complete spending side as specified in the Commission proposal from 2004 has several weaknesses (see the extensive discussion in section 5.4.5): It treats distributive outcomes on the same footing irrespective of the fact that they are regarded as fair and in line, for example, with the principle of EU solidarity or whether they are regarded to be unfair, for example, because they do not mirror relative country wealth. From this a further disadvantage emerges immediately: In the course of time such a generalised mechanism would not react to a shift in spending from policies with problematic distributive consequences towards policies with politically accepted distribution results. Hence, a generalised mechanism covering the complete expenditure side would tend to be perpetual no matter which progress could be reached with regard to the future spending focus.

These problems can be addressed by the concept of a generalised limited correction mechanism (GLCM) whose "limitation" refers to the inclusion of policy areas into the base to be corrected. Similar ideas have been mentioned in the literature a few times. In 1987, the Commission presented a proposal (European Commission, 1987) which called for a reform of the UK correction by reducing the correction base to agricultural spending only. This early proposal was renewed in the discussion of a generalised but limited correction mechanism by Coussens (2004) which shares the feature of the general applicability to all net contributors with the generalised correction mechanism. The author argues that it is not appropriate to include several kinds of solidarity spending, for example, for cohesion, into the correction mechanism as this spending is intended for redistribution purposes. We believe that these ideas deserve far more attention since they point to the solution for a rational revenue system beyond the year 2013.

In our view, the future correction mechanism should be of the GLCM type correcting only a subset of spending policies. Hence, two baskets have to be defined:

- *Basket 1* includes those policies whose distributive effects are either not measurable or are politically accepted. The financing of basket 1 would be based on GNI resources (in addition to TOR).
- *Basket 2* includes those policies whose distributive effects are not regarded as acceptable. While the first step financing is based on GNI resources, a correction mechanism corrects the resulting distribution profile associated with these basket 2 policies.

It should be stressed that this separation merely serves to calculate own resources payments from member countries and would have no consequences for the budgetary process. In particular, the unity of the budget would not be affected or endangered.

6.2.2 Principles of Allocating Policies to Distinct Baskets

The decision to assign policies to basket 1 or basket 2 will ultimately be a political decision. Given the current constitutional set-up there is no alternative to deciding this assignment under unanimity. Realistically this implies that the resulting distributive patterns should not be too different from the status quo at the moment of regime change. Below (section 6.2.4) we will demonstrate how different specifications could come close to that condition.

Nevertheless, some guiding principles can be developed which may be helpful for the identification of both types of policies. In our view, clear favourites for basket 1 policies are:

- Policies where spending cannot be allocated to individual countries due to the nature of payments (example: external policies).
- Policies where payment flows into individual countries may be identifiable but this payment structure is no sensible proxy for the share of country benefits from that policy, for example, because of substantive European public good properties[26] (example: environmental spending). This would hold, in particular, for policies where EU member states agree on the existence of a substantial "European value added".
- Policies where payment flows into individual countries are identifiable and also indicate the countries' relative benefits from an EU policy but where the distributive effects are accepted or even the very objective of the respective policy (example: regional convergence).

In contrast, favourites for basket 2 policies are:

- Policies which are deemed to be desirable from a political point of view but which produce substantial distributive effects as a by-product which are politically inacceptable, for example, since these effects are only loosely related to relative country wealth. Without a doubt, the CAP is the clearest candidate for basket 2 since its distributive consequences are largely responsible for the unequal budgetary positions of different member states with similar GNI (see section 3.6.3). Moreover, this may also affect other policy areas with unsystematic distribution patterns, for instance, in the structural policy (example: 'Competitiveness and Employment' regions).

[26] For an attempt to identify EU policies with the character of European public goods, see Alesina, Angeloni and Schuhknecht (2005). We are sceptical that any such differentiation on an objective basis is possible.

6.2.3 Key Advantages of the Two Basket Approach

As explained in the motivation of the GLCM approach, this solution would overcome the shortcomings associated with a generalised correction mechanism. In particular, the necessary complexities and intransparencies of any correction mechanism would be confined to those policy areas where undeniable distributive problems exist.

Furthermore, for those policies included in basket 2, the common pool problem and the national engagement for larger benefits from these policies could be contained. Since the mechanism corrects a country's excessive benefits from basket 2 policies, it reduces incentives of countries to fight for an expansion of these policies. Therefore, including policies into basket 2 would also set limits to inefficient spending pressure by making pork barrel policies less rewarding (see section 3.5.2).

Furthermore, an evolution of the spending side with a constant relative diminution of CAP would automatically diminish the correction mechanism's relevance. Hence, the introduction of a GLCM would set the system on a path where – without further necessary discretionary change – the correction mechanism would be phased out continuously. Hence, this reform option would overcome the status quo bias associated with the current system (and also associated with any unlimited correction mechanism).

6.2.4 Parametric Specification and Simulation

The general usefulness of a GLCM does not depend on the specific choice of parameters. In principle, the idea of a GLCM can be combined with any of the models included in our survey in section 5.4.4. In the following, we present a couple of simulations in order to demonstrate which distributive patterns could be achieved and to show that these patterns can be brought close to the status quo which is a precondition for our proposal's political chances.

The formula applied for the determination of the correction payments of a GLCM closely corresponds to the GCM formula presented in 5.4.4. However, it differs insofar as not the overall net position of the country is regarded but only the net position with respect to the policy areas which are included in the GLCM. Hence, the formula can be defined as follows:

$$\text{Reimbursement of country } i = \begin{cases} 0, if \left(\frac{OR_i}{\sum_{j=1}^{27} OR_j} - \frac{AP_i}{\sum_{j=1}^{27} AP_j} \right) \times \sum_{j=1}^{27} AP_j - zY_i \leq 0 \\ a \times \left[\left(\frac{OR_i}{\sum_{j=1}^{27} OR_j} - \frac{AP_i}{\sum_{j=1}^{27} AP_j} \right) \times \sum_{j=1}^{27} AP_j - zY_i \right], else \end{cases}$$

with OR_i = own resources payments of country i (excluding traditional own resources); AP_i = payments attributable to country i; Y_i = GNI of country i.

Equivalently to the GCM, the parameters of the threshold z and the reimbursement rate a are to be freely determined. Moreover, a further parameter enters the formula, which is the choice of the policy areas which are included in the attributable expenditures AP_i. The net position of a country for a given policy area is, hence, calculated as the difference between the amount it pays for it under GNI proportionality, which corresponds to the overall expenditures of this policy area multiplied by the GNI share, and the amount it actually receives as attributable expenditures from the respective policy area. In the following, different sets of policy areas are included in the attributable expenditures to reveal the distributive effects which can be generated by different choices of these parameters.

A first straightforward approach would be the sole inclusion of direct agricultural payments in the attributable expenditures as proposed by Coussens (2004). As it has been discussed above, this policy area is usually regarded as the source of undesirable distributive effects of the budget (see section 3.6.3). In Fig. 30, the effects of the application of a GLCM which only corrects CAP expenditures are shown for a threshold set at $z = 0.1\%$ of GNI. Two extreme cases are compared to the complete elimination of any corrections as discussed in section 5.4.2, (1) a refund rate of 66% and full participation of the beneficiaries in the financing, and (2) a refund rate of 100% and no participation of the beneficiaries.

We observe that a GLCM applied to CAP expenditures with a threshold of 0.1% of GNI has effects which are qualitatively similar to those of the GCM discussed in section 5.4.4 as the countries which benefit from abatements today are partially disburdened compared to the situation where all corrections are abolished without substitution. However, these corrections differ in size as they are much lower than the maximum effects generated by a GCM. Moreover, three further countries would become eligible for reimbursements, Cyprus, Luxembourg and Malta.

A further relief of the countries which are negatively affected by the phasing out of all corrections may be achieved by setting the threshold at a level of 0.0% of GNI (see Fig. 31). As can be seen, the choice of a threshold of 0.0% leads to major distributive effects, especially when a refund rate of 100% and no participation of the beneficiaries is regarded as the extreme case. While disburdening the current beneficiaries of abatements much more than at a higher threshold, many other countries become eligible for corrections, namely Belgium, Finland, Italy and Slovenia. However, this high number of countries eligible for correction payments is reflected in increasingly high burdens for the countries financing the corrections.

Fig. 30. Distributive consequences of GLCM applied to CAP payments, threshold: 0.1% of GNI

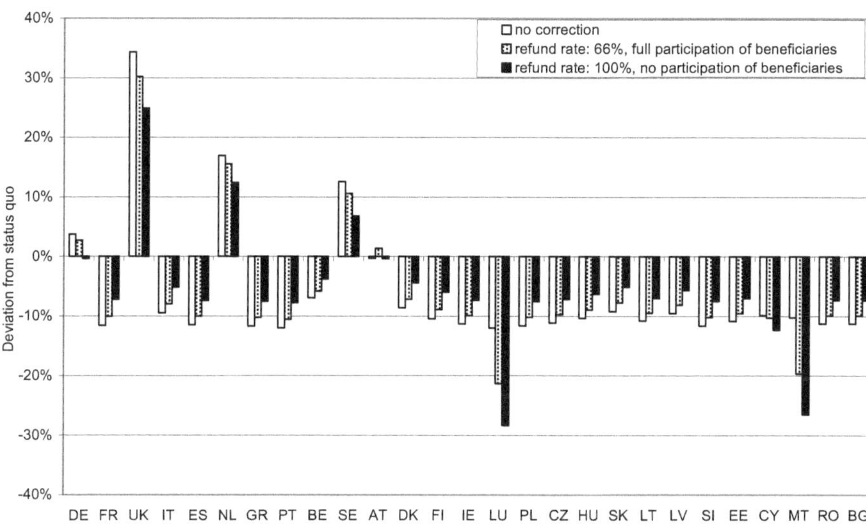

Note: Simulation results for % change of total own resources payments in 2010.

Source: ZEW calculations.

As an alternative to the sole consideration of direct agricultural spending, a wider definition of CAP may be applied which also includes the budgetary headings of rural development and fisheries. In Fig. 32, the effects of this definition are compared to the sole application of direct CAP expenditures as shown above exemplarily for the choice of a threshold of 0.1% of GNI, a reimbursement rate of 66% and full participation of the beneficiaries in the financing.

Compared to the sole inclusion of direct CAP payments, the gross contributions, in particular those of the United Kingdom and the Netherlands, are significantly reduced by the inclusion of rural development and fisheries. However, Austria and Sweden tend to lose from the application of this broader definition of agricultural spending.

Further relief for the member states which suffer today from an excessive net position due to low returns from the budget may be achieved by the inclusion of further policy areas into the amount of attributable expenditures. The most extreme case is shown in Fig. 33, which shows the effect of the inclusion of all attributable expenditures which would be included in a GCM excluding the expenditures with the most indisputable redistributive purpose, i.e. 'Cohesion' and 'Regional Convergence' funds. This is visualised in the setting of the threshold at 0.1% of GNI, a reimbursement rate of 66% and the full participation of all beneficiaries in the financing.

Fig. 31. Distributive consequences of GLCM applied to CAP payments, threshold: 0.0% of GNI

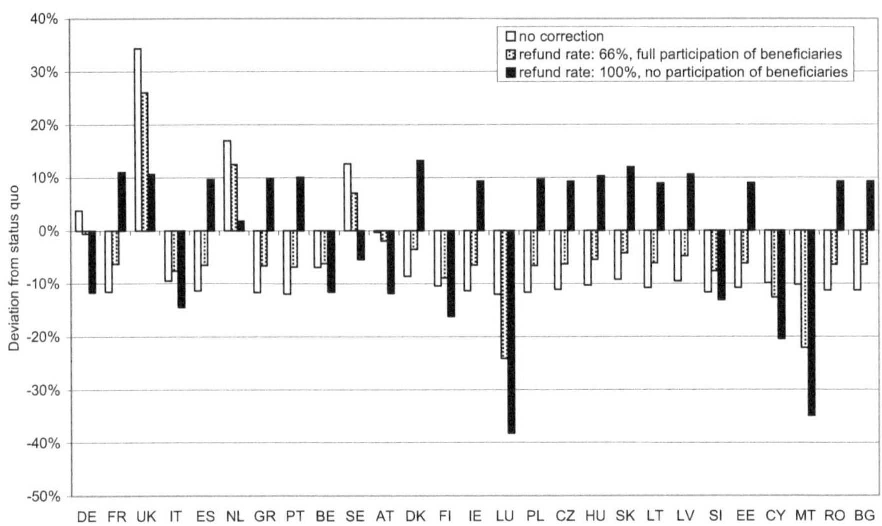

Note: Simulation results for % change of total own resources payments in 2010.

Source: ZEW calculations.

We observe that the application of this widest definition of attributable expenditures for the GLCM leads to a further massive relief for the UK and the Netherlands. Further reductions might even be generated through a lower threshold than 0.1%, a higher refund rate or a lower participation of these countries in the financing. Similar to the GCM, this allows for a variety of allocations of the contributions and enables to limit the increase in gross contributions of the UK and the Netherlands to about 10%.

For all imaginable specifications of a GLCM we can state that it is possible to compensate those countries which would, at least partially, lose due to the abolishment of today's corrections. With regard to the quantity of these compensations it is decisive which policy areas are included in the mechanism. The sole inclusion of agricultural spending reflects the underlying reasons for the unequal treatment of member states on the expenditure side best which justifies the introduction of a GLCM. However, major reimbursements can only be generated by choosing more severe parameters than under a GCM; explicitly a threshold of 0.1% or even lower is necessary to generate significant corrections. However, the inclusion of further policy areas in the attributable expenditures enables the generation of corrections similar to a GCM and the freedom to generate the intended distribution of the contributions.

Fig. 32. Distributive consequences of GLCM applied to a wider definition of agricultural spending

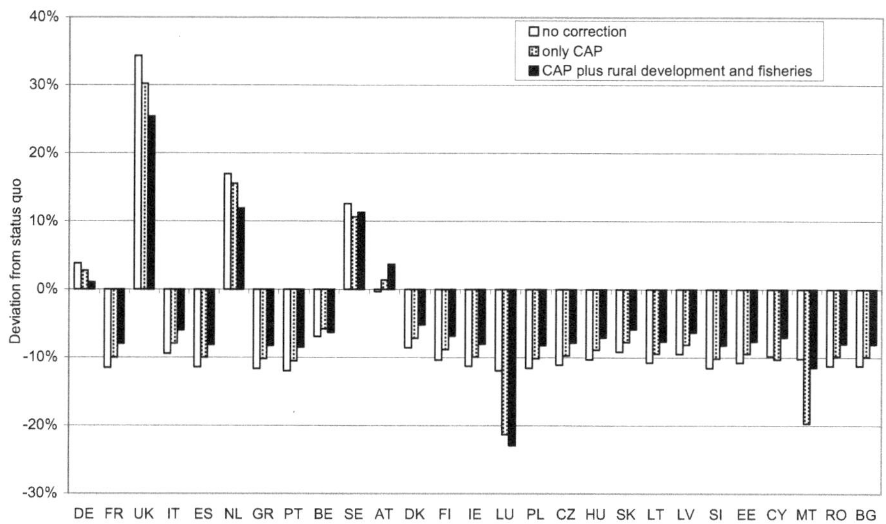

Note: Simulation results for % change of total own resources payments in 2010.

Source: ZEW calculations.

In Fig. 34, the net positions of the four current main beneficiaries of the UK rebate and other abatements (the UK, the Netherlands, Sweden and Germany) are compared to the net positions of two further large countries, France and Italy; the countries are plotted with decreasing GDP per head (in purchasing power standards, data estimated for the year 2008) from the left to the right. The net positions are shown for two budgetary outcomes, (1) the status quo, and (2) a GLCM which comprises spending for CAP, fisheries and rural development.

As the figure indicates the phasing out of today's corrections and the introduction of a GLCM worsen the net positions of the current beneficiaries of abatements with the exception of Germany with a nearly unchanged net position. However, this shifts the countries' net positions more in line with their relative wealth. Under the status quo, the Netherlands, the UK and Sweden show a net position which is more favourable than the German one and brings them in a position similar to France and Italy although the wealth of the former three countries (measured in GDP in PPS per head) is considerably higher. In applying the GLCM, these three countries show a net position which is slightly more negative than that of Germany, and in contrast, Italy and France are disburdened. Consequently, the application of the GLCM reflects the relatively lower wealth of Germany, France and Italy in the relation of the net positions more effectively than the status quo.

Fig. 33. Consequences of GLCM applied to all policy areas excluding Cohesion and Regional Convergence

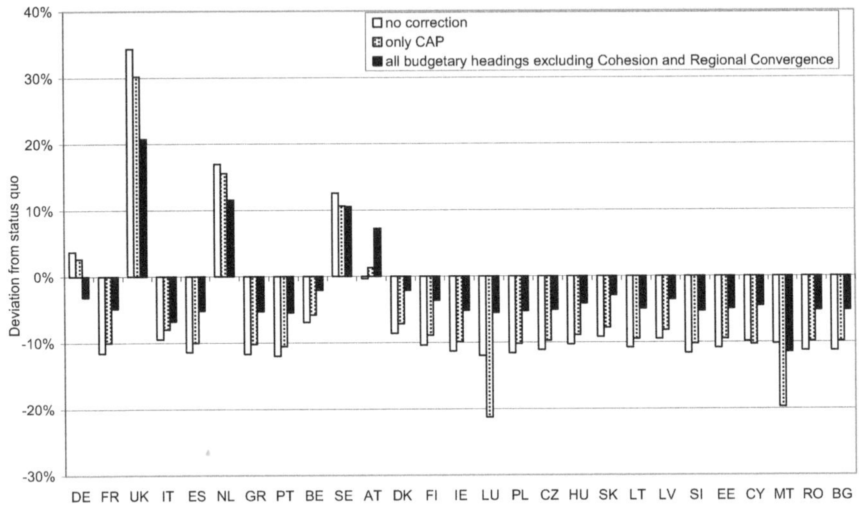

Note: Simulation results for % change of total own resources payments in 2010.

Source: ZEW calculations.

Fig. 34. National net positions of status quo and GLCM

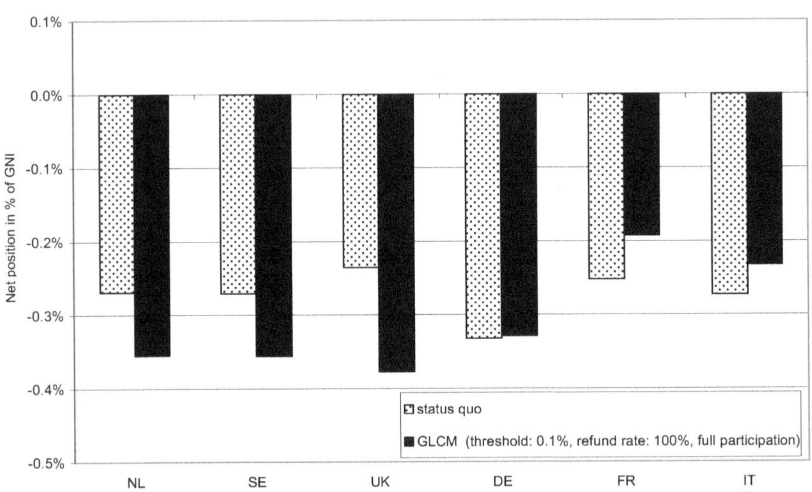

Note: Subscript: GDP per head (PPS) estimated for 2008 by Eurostat, average of EU-15 = 100. Simulation results for the year 2010.

Source: ZEW calculations.

In summary, the simulation study underlines the merits of our reform proposal in the following respects:

- The inclusion of policies with particularly controversial distributive consequences into the correction mechanism is sufficient to establish a clear link between relative wealth and budgetary burden sharing in the Community.
- Depending on the choice of parameters, specific distributive outcomes that largely vary can be achieved. This demonstrates the flexibility of this approach which is important from the political perspective.
- In particular, results can be achieved which do not diverge too far from the status quo albeit with one qualification: A higher burden for the UK, privileged under the current system, is to a certain extent a necessary characteristic of any approach based on a generalisation of the correction principle. However, it must be stressed that the GCLM addresses precisely those distributive characteristics of the status quo which are heavily criticised by the British side and regularly used to defend the UK rebate, namely the distributive consequences of agricultural policies. Taking these British concerns seriously, a GCLM compensating for the CAP's distribution effect should, therefore, be acceptable for the UK.
- If some of the limited distributive effects are politically unacceptable for certain countries due to losses compared to the status quo, temporary side payments will prepare a smoother transition. In any case, we would expect this new system to lead to a decreasing demand for special provisions in the medium term. As shown extensively in section 3.6, a large part of the complexity of the status quo including the increased number of special provisions is closely related to the distributive effects corrected by our GLCM.
- Compared to the current rebate system, the GLCM is based on a far simpler formula, thus, contributing towards making the system more comprehensible. Nevertheless, the simple formula presented is a favourable starting point for refinements, for example, along the lines of the Padoa-Schioppa approach with its wealth dependent differentiation of acceptable upper limits for net contributions (see section 5.4.4). From the point of view of transparency we would not recommend such a move, but it is important to underline that our reform model offers degrees of freedom which can be used if there is a political consensus, for example, to establish a more progressive revenue system.

6.3 The Sub-National Dimension

In section 3.5.3 we analysed the intra-national sharing of the EU own resources payments burden in Belgium, Denmark, France, Italy, Germany, Poland, the Netherlands, Spain and the United Kingdom. Our expert interviews showed that in all EU member states with the exception of Austria, the EU contributions are exclusively paid by the national level. As a consequence, in most member countries the federal states and the municipalities do not contribute to the funding of the European Union whereas in Austria, the total EU contributions are shared amongst the national government (totalling 76.8% in 2005), the federal states (19.6%) and the municipalities (3.6%).

We used these findings to discuss the relevance of the common pool problem by distinguishing between the financial sharing of EU contributions in Austria (the "Austrian model") with that of the rest of the EU members. In brief, the central message of the common pool problem is that a high degree of asymmetry between costs and benefits would bias the budgetary efficiency. The main reason for this is that the actors involved in the budgetary process do not fully internalise the costs resulting from an EU-financed project since they only bear a (marginal) share of the costs.

In the case of the current funding of the EU budget it becomes clear that the incentives of the regional level are not always identical to those of the national level. In that respect, the national governments, especially those of the net payers, have a strong incentive to limit the EU budget because any additional money saved at the EU level will be (at least partially) available for the national governments. By contrast, the cost-benefit calculus of the regions differs in that they are an important recipient of transfers through cohesion policy and the rural development part of the Common Agricultural Policy. Hence, those federal states which do not have to contribute to the funding of the EU budget, as the whole share of the contributions is borne by the national level, have a strong interest in EU policies without internalising any costs. However, those federal states which do have to contribute to the EU funding internalise the costs at least partially. Consequently, this set-up strongly influences the degree of distortion of the cost-benefit calculus.

Although regional political representatives do not have direct budgetary responsibility at the EU level, their preferences can be expected to reach the EU level through different channels: Members of the European Parliament directly responsible for regional constituencies will be influenced by regional preferences; in federal countries with a politically influential parliamentary chamber of regional representatives, the regions have a strong political influence on national politics. Finally, regional representatives influence a country's political opinion and are present in Brussels in the form of the Committee of the Regions. Looking at all these channels combined, a distorted regional view on EU spending must be regarded as a relevant disadvantage of the status quo.

By applying these insights to the current intra-national sharing of the EU funding, we can conclude that under the Austrian model the federal states have a more balanced view on EU spending while in the other EU member countries the common pool problem is highly virulent at the regional level.

Against this background one can conclude that it is possible to increase the budgetary efficiency of the European Union by including the regional level in the financing of the EU budget. Thus, the distorted cost-benefit calculus of the regions would improve by taking the arising costs of the EU spending into account. In that respect the German Laender would internalise the resulting costs of the EU spending and would drive back their claims for EU spending.

Obviously, the European Union is not permitted to set up regulations on how to share the financial burden intra-nationally as the member states are still mainly responsible for the EU funding. However, the net payers of the EU at least might have an interest in integrating the regional level so that the regions also internalise the existing costs. This could reduce exorbitant claims for EU spending by the regional level.

Even though this would increase the budgetary efficiency, this proposal also contains a drawback. If the regional level were to be involved in financing the EU budget, it could also demand to be involved in the negotiation process of the Financial Perspectives and/or in the annual budget procedure. This would increase the number of participants in the budgetary framework and complicate the negotiation process. Nevertheless, we would recommend reassessing the possibility of a regional contribution to EU own resources payments in order to ensure that regions are aware of the financial burden of EU spending.

6.4 Changing the Wording in EU Budgetary Policy

A final recommendation for reform concerns a seemingly unimportant side aspect related to terminology. It is an established practice since "Delors I", the first multi-annual financial framework for the years 1988-1994, to define the size of the budget in percent of GDP. In addition, a corresponding table of commitments of appropriation is agreed upon, which is defined in real terms, i.e. for constant prices of a basis year. This practice fundamentally differs from budgetary practices in most member countries where budgetary planning refers to the nominal size of the budget.

From the perspective of a rational and fully informed homo oeconomicus, this framing issue should not make a difference. Under full rationality, the preferred size and growth of a budget should not be influenced by the metrics used. However, a growing literature based on the insights of behavioural economics indicates that framing issues can matter substantially (Tversky & Kahneman, 1986). For example, with regard to the perceived fairness of a tax system, the metrics involved make a significant difference: Experiment participants express a preference for larger progressivity of tax systems when the framing is based on percent compared to a use of absolute amounts of money (McCaffery & Baron, 2005). This "metric effect" shows that completely synonymous expressions merely differing in the used units of measurement can lead to different perceptions.

We would strongly argue that a similar metric effect is given with regard to the financial framework's practice of looking at the EU budget either in terms of percent of GNI (with regard to the own resources ceiling) or in terms of real Euro (with regard to the amounts allocated to different expenditure categories). Compared to a framing in terms of nominal Euro, this specific European framing leads to a dampened perception of budgetary growth at the European level.

This presumption is backed by the fact that the different framings have different consequences for the definition of budgetary "growth": With a metric in percent of GNI, a "constant" budget is given if a budget expands in nominal terms by the sum of real growth and the rate of inflation. With a metric in real Euro, a "constant" budget still allows for a budget nominally expanding in line with the rate of inflation. The most rigid metric is, of course, the nominal view dominating at the national level, where a "constant" budget can even imply a real decline of the budget (and an even faster decline relative to GNI). Hence, the different units of measurement lead to different perceptions of the budgetary development at the national level on the one hand and the European level on the other hand. The term "constant budget" at the national level usually refers to nominal constancy, in the European context the same term is rather understood as constancy relative to GNI.

This varying use of terminology constitutes a relevant difference in negotiations on the size of the budget. Negotiations are typically restricted by natural reference points. The natural reference point in budgetary negotiations is the size of the last budget. The well-established status quo bias (Samuelson & Zeckhauser, 1988) explains that the negotiation result will be heavily influenced by this reference point. Due to the different metrics, however, the status quo bias in negotiations on the European budget has a different impact compared to the national situation where a nominal view prevails. These differences in framing can be expected to bias the budgetary outcomes towards an expansion of the European budget compared to the national level.

These presumptions are supported by observations from negotiations on the financial framework. The nominal implications of the debated frameworks are hardly ever stated. Instead, the point of reference for the Financial Framework 2007-2013 has been either an amount of real Euro or the GNI ratio. The net payers' position to limit the budget at 1% of GNI has regularly been criticised as overly restrictive although it implies a comfortable budgetary expansion in line with the nominal growth of EU GNI – a growth rate which cannot be taken for granted for many national or sub-national public budgets.

Apart from a bias towards overexpansion, the European budgetary framing has an additional problematic consequence. The definition of the financial framework in terms of real Euro implies that the EU budget will be fully compensated for whatever level of inflation materialises. Given the fact that budgetary authorities at the EU level, thus, act on the basis of a fully indexed budget, they do not have a self-interest in containing inflation.

Clearly, there are also advantages linked to the GNI and real Euro metrics: Growth disappointments or changing inflation rates automatically translate into an adjustment of the own resources ceiling and expenditure levels. Since the Financial Framework is binding over a period of seven years, this automatism is more important compared to the national level where budgetary authorities are usually free to annually react to a changing inflation and growth environment. These aspects are strong counterarguments against fully abandoning any link of nominal ceiling to growth or inflation.

Taking account of this ambivalence, we would recommend the following compromise: Future negotiations should be framed in terms of nominal Euro amounts, both with regard to the own resources ceiling and to the single expenditure items. However, the resulting nominal table could be supplemented by an adjustment clause that would trigger automatic upward or downward adjustments to these nominal amounts whenever inflation or real growth would leave predefined bands. In order to guarantee a self-interest of budgetary authorities with regard to low inflation rates, the trigger clause should be asymmetrically designed with respect to inflation: While a downward adjustment as a consequence of lower than expected inflation is desirable, an upward adjustment for a higher than expected inflation rate should be absent.

7 Final Remarks

Our reform proposal would imply changes far from a revolutionary upheaval of the system. We have clarified that well-established and functioning elements of the status quo should be retained, such as the contribution-based link between national budgets and the European budget. This feature is particularly helpful in setting up the right incentives to foster fiscal discipline and in constituting a certain counterweight to the common pool problem which is also virulent at the EU level.

With our appeal in favour of a consequential GNI resource-based finance in combination with a generalised correction mechanism and the clear rejection of any new tax-based own resource, our reform proposal appears to be close to the status quo. From the point of view of political acceptability, this is no disadvantage. Nevertheless, the suggested changes would address the main weaknesses of the status quo in that they deal with the distribution issue in a more transparent and explicit way than in the current system. Whereas under the status quo an inflation of special provisions has been necessary to create a politically acceptable burden sharing, our model could reach this objective in a far simpler and more transparent way.

Box 5 summarises, in the light of our four assessment criteria, the progress achievable through our reform proposal. A fundamental difference between our proposal and many other far-reaching visions in the literature is most certainly that we accept the distribution issue as an undeniable fact of life in European budgetary politics. Hence, we do not define it away but offer mechanisms to cope with it as efficiently and transparently as possible. We also believe that a GLCM can be readily presented as a fair system which is important in gaining acceptance from the voters' perspective. This improved fairness perception would also reduce political pressure on governments of member countries governments to fight for higher spending shares in expenditure negotiations. Hence, collective European goods will have better chances to prevail over transfer policies once the system change has occurred. Therefore, we would claim that our reform proposal is not only politically realistic because it is related to prevalent fairness criteria, but it would also boost budgetary efficiency at the EU level.

Box 5. Major improvements associated with our reform proposal

Fostering efficient public goods provision

Achievement:

- "Juste retour" issue is not negated but addressed in a transparent and focussed way
- This reduces political pressure to fight for higher national spending shares
- Better cost-benefit analysis on regional level through regional contribution to own resources payments

Constraining narrow self-interest and creating budgetary discipline

Achievement:

- Link between EU budget and national budgets remains in place which is important for fiscal discipline
- Nominal metrics conducive for budgetary balance

Integration compatibility

Achievement:

- Simplification
- Generalised but limited correction mechanism offers a transparent mechanism to cope with politically necessary correction issue
- Flexibility of two basket structure creates sufficient space for compromises

General principles of taxation

Achievement:

- GNI resource with its favourable characteristics becomes the corner stone of the system
- VAT resource problems solved

8 Appendix

8.1 Assessment Criteria

8.1.1 Introduction – Criteria in the Literature

For the normative evaluation of the current system of own resources as well as discussed proposals for the reform of the system, the literature offers a wide range of assessment criteria. Some attempts have been made so far to offer a comprehensive set of criteria, for example, European Commission (1998; 2004a), Caesar (1990), Cattoir (2004), Begg and Grimwade (1998), Walthes (1996), Henke (1997) and Heinemann (2003).

Apart from these often resembling sets of criteria, we have developed our own view as summarised in chapter 2. This is necessary as many of the existing approaches share the weakness that the choice of these criteria seems to be biased according to the author's view, either in favour of or against giving more financial autonomy to the EU, for example, by introducing an EU tax. Another weak point of many sets of criteria is their rather ad hoc construction due to a lacking link to economic theory.[27]

Therefore, these links will be highlighted in the following to ensure a high degree of transparency and unbiasedness of the choice of the criteria. The set of criteria used is derived from 4 different approaches:

- First, the theory of *fiscal federalism* is introduced aiming at the optimal distribution of responsibilities between the different tiers of government within a federation.
- Secondly, criteria are derived from the *public choice theory*, which is characterised by its focus on the role of self-interested public agents.
- Thirdly, some criteria are introduced which shall account for EU-specific questions regarding the issue of *political integration of the Union*.
- Fourth, ideas from *general tax theory* provide widely accepted guidelines for an efficient tax system.

---

[27] One notable exception is Begg and Grimwade (1998).

Especially the set of criteria offered by the European Commission (2004a) has been widely noticed in the literature. Due to its prominent role in the discussion on potential reforms of the system of own resources, the main differences to our choice of criteria will be emphasised and discussed in more detail in the following. One main difference is the non-inclusion of the criterion "financial autonomy" which was included by the European Commission. We hold the view that this is not a criterion per se but rather an instrument which might contribute to the achievement of certain goals, like budgetary discipline or fiscal efficiency.

8.1.2 Fiscal Federalism

A first line of argumentation results from the theory of fiscal federalism. This theory originates from the seminal works by Oates (1972).[28] It deals with the optimal assignment of public good provision and the power to tax to different tiers of government within a federation. As it is often argued, the European Union at its current stage of integration can certainly not be regarded as a federation in the political sense. But the existing redistribution via the EU budget as well as the current discussion on giving greater financial autonomy to the EU level reflect the importance of fiscal federal structures in the Union. This shows the development towards a construct which is more similar to a fiscal federation than a "club good", as which the financing of international organisations is usually characterised.

The assignment of tasks according to the theory of fiscal federalism should mainly be done according to the following trade-off: On the one hand, the decentralisation of certain tasks may be favoured as smaller regions imply both a smaller heterogeneity of preferences and a higher closeness of decision makers to the people. Moreover, a diversified public supply offers the citizens the possibility of choice, either by migration or by opposition (Oates' decentralisation theorem, Oates, 1972). Furthermore, for public services with a regionally defined user group the decentralised provision fulfils the principle of fiscal equivalence (Olson, 1969) which demands the identity of users and payers in order to guarantee an undistorted decision on the level of provision. The idea of subsidiarity as a guideline of European politics is also based on the decentralisation theorem implying that any decision shall be made at the lowest tier of government which can do this efficiently. On the other hand, a high degree of decentralisation may also reduce efficiency. This is the case when public goods provision or taxation may allow economies of scale or give rise to externalities and spill-over effects. Then, a higher level government would be able to internalise such effects leading to a more efficient outcome.

While the optimal provision of public goods and, thus, the expenditure side of the EU budget is beyond the scope of this work, the basic theory of fiscal federalism can give us some useful guidelines regarding the optimal assignment of funds on the revenue side. But it is important to keep in mind that the institutions of the European Union, constituting the highest tier, do not fit to the original picture of

28 For an overview, see Oates (1999).

fiscal federalism that the literature usually implies. This view assumes a strong highest level of government as it is the case in national federations like the United States or Germany. Thus, this theory cannot be applied one-to-one to the conditions in Europe with a share of EU expenditures of only around 1% of GDP. For example, the application of the theory of fiscal federalism would demand the assignment of the redistribution function at the most centralised level of government. This would avoid the migration of poor citizens to areas with high benefits which would make a decentralised system unsustainable. But the centralisation of the redistribution function is far from being supported by citizens or politicians in the EU. Similarly, the stabilisation function should also be assigned to the highest tier of government but this would be incompatible with the current low level of EU spending.

A further difference of the EU fiscal activities from standard fiscal federalism assumptions is that the expenditures financed can hardly be overwhelmingly characterised as European public goods. Structural spending, for example, by definition has more the character of a regional (or national) public good. The financing of public goods with a nationally or even regionally defined group of benefiting citizens contradicts the principle of fiscal equivalence since users and payers are not identical. This problem has an immediate relevance for the challenges of the revenue side: The case for financing the EU budget out of a common EU revenue pool is the weaker the lower the share of true European public goods in the budget is. Instruments like national or regional co-financing constitute valuable approaches to correct resulting inefficiencies and distortions of budgetary incentives.

Allowance of National Preferences and Properties

As the theory of fiscal federalism argues, one main reason for decentralisation of tax levy should be the allowance of regionally differing preferences of the people. As Cnossen (1990: 473) argues with reference to the EU,

> tax diversity takes account of differences in preferences for one tax over another in the various member states which reflect differences in economic and social structures, different perceptions on the role of taxation, differences in the acceptability and feasibility of various taxes and, perhaps more fundamentally, differences in preferences for public sector size among the member states.

Derived from this argumentation it is required that the system of own resources must not excessively interfere into the composition of the national tax systems. Instead, its design should allow for diverging preferences and minimise the distortion due to differences in national preferences.

Externalities and Spill-Overs

One main argument in favour of assigning taxes to a higher tier is the aspect of externalities and spill-overs. This may be relevant if a centralised tax would be able to account for positive externalities which are not fully internalised in the taxation on a lower tier level, for example, an environmental tax. In that case assigning the task to the highest tier would significantly increase the welfare of citizens. Related to the EU, this criterion implies that the allocation of the power of taxation to the highest level would be mainly efficient if externalities exist which are not internalised at the taxation by the national states.

Another aspect concerns the so-called fiscal externalities. This refers to the case when an increase of the tax on a mobile base in one country has a positive effect on the base in another country due to tax evasion. The effect is, therefore, closely related to the negative aspects of tax competition as discussed below. The main criterion for the assignment of different revenue sources to the vertical tiers of government in this sense is the degree of mobility of the tax base. According to this, revenues with a highly mobile tax base should be assigned to the highest tier of government because a decentralised allocation might lead to a distorting evasion of the tax bases. Consequently, lower tiers of government should be endowed with taxes with rather immobile bases or fees (Oates, 1999).

Regional Arbitrariness

A further aspect pointing to a more centralised assignment of a revenue source is the existence of so-called regional arbitrariness. This term implies cases where it is impossible to assign the revenues from a specific source to lower tiers because the tax base is not identifiable at all or only at high administrative costs (Cattoir, 2004). Related to the EU, this would mainly be applicable when the source of revenues is a common EU policy as it is the case, for example, with custom duties. Then there is a clear case in favour of assigning the revenues to the EU level.

Avoidance of Interference of National Fiscal Federalism

One further aspect regarding federalism affects the interference with national federal structures. In some countries of the EU, for example, Germany and Spain, the national tax system is characterised by a national fiscal federalism which has evolved over time. An interference of this system would occur if national financial equalisation mechanisms (like the *Länderfinanzausgleich* in Germany) were disturbed or if a revenue source, such as a tax base, which is originally also taxed by lower national tiers, was assigned to the EU. This would lead to the reduction of sovereignty of lower national tiers which is problematic as it would contradict national preferences reflected by national federal structures. Thus, EU revenues should avoid the disturbance of equilibria regarding the assignment of national sovereignties (Caesar, 1990).

Tax Competition

Another important aspect derived from the theory of fiscal federalism is the matter of tax competition. Today competition exists in the EU between the member states as the overwhelming majority of taxes has not been harmonised yet (see section 4.2). This competition might be interfered by the introduction of a common tax.

Thereby, it is not undisputed whether to assume a positive or a negative effect of tax competition (for an overview, see Wilson, 1999).

The opponents of tax competition will warn against too much pressure on the level of the national budgets if the countries' tax systems compete for mobile factors. If each country was able to attract the mobile factor from other states by cutting its taxes, a vicious circle would start making other countries lowering their rates as well. This might finally result in too low tax revenues and, hence, a suboptimal low provision of public goods. Thus, it is often demanded to assign the taxation of labour and capital income to the highest level of government, in this case to the EU level.

The proponents of more decentralised taxation stress the positive effect of competition as a constraint of the politicians' and bureaucrats' tendency to overtaxation (see section 8.1.3). The possibility of evasion or the reference to other countries (exit and voice in the sense of Hirschman, 1970) will consequently lead to increasing pressure on the public authorities and, thus, to a more efficient public sector.

8.1.3 Political Economy

The public choice theory represents another line of literature which has, in contrast to the view of the welfare-maximising governments underlying the theory of fiscal federalism, a much less idealistic attitude towards the driving motivations of political and bureaucratic agents. This view can be expressed by the famous picture of the "Leviathan" introduced by Brennan and Buchanan (1980). This depicts politicians and bureaucrats which tend to maximise their utility by increasing public revenues even at the expenses of excessive taxation of the citizens. If these motivations were relevant for EU fiscal agents as well, the system of own resources of the EU would have to be designed in a restrictive fashion in order to protect tax-paying citizens.

Bureaucratic Self-Interest

A challenge resulting from the political-economic approach for the system of own resources is that it is able to cope with the self-interest of bureaucrats. As shown, one main aspect of public choice theory is the assumption that rent-seeking bureaucrats strive for increasing their power and prestige implying a tendency towards an expansion of the budget. Similar to this approach, Popitz already 80 years ago called attention to the "attraction of the central budget", known as Popitz' Law (Popitz, 1927). This implies that it is also in the interest of rent-seeking politicians to support the expansion of the budget on the highest tier as at the EU level.

Therefore, it has to be guaranteed that the abilities and the incentives of EU authorities to increase their budget or the revenue have to be restricted. As long as any increase of the EU budget mainly serves redistributive purposes and not the welfare-increasing provision of public goods, this may be interpreted in the sense of public choice theory as the satisfaction of centralisation interests by the EU authorities.

Similar to the argumentation above, a possible reform of the revenue side also has to be designed in the way that the overall burden of the citizens is not increased. As national authorities also show bureaucratic self-interests, they may have an incentive to use a reform of the revenue system as pretext to increase their own budget. This may happen if the national contributions were reduced in return for an increase of tax autonomy to the EU and if these reductions were not passed on to the citizens so that their overall tax burden and the national budget would be increased. Such behaviour would be harmful as it allows governments to pass the buck of the tax increase to the EU, which might damage their reputation among the citizens.

Approach to the Common Pool Problem

The common pool problem is a general problem for the efficiency of budgetary decision-making. The "common pool" term generally refers to the over-utilisation of a common resource by various demanders when the individuals have to contribute only to a small amount to their demanded good while benefiting to a relative large extent. This problem may be applied to the EU budget as analysed in detail in section 3.5.3. As argued there the common pool view is of even particular relevance at the European level and, therefore, must not be ignored in the foundation of reform options.

8.1.4 Integration Compatibility

One further political feature the system of own resources has to fulfil is that it has to be compatible with European integration. This request has two aspects: First, on the level of politics, the financing of the EU shall not be the reason for further political struggle between member states or European institutions. The recent negotiations on the Financial Perspective 2007-2013 showed how such disputes can poison the relationships between member states. Secondly, the design of the system of own resources must not have a negative impact on the people's attitudes towards European integration but should rather help to encourage the participation of the citizens in the political process.

Avoidance of Political Struggles

In the past, the process of European integration has very often been accompanied by struggles regarding the EU budget. On the one hand, there were disputes between member states mainly driven by the desire to improve their own net budgetary position, which is also known as the "juste retour" problem. On the other hand, struggles between European institutions and member sates regarding their relative power emerged. The system of own resources has, therefore, to be designed in such a way to avoid such disputes driven by national or individual interests which might hurt the process of integration in the future.

Visibility

One demand usually made to revenue systems is to fulfil certain requirements of visibility by the tax payers. While visibility may also be regarded as a general requirement to any tax system, in the context of EU finances it is mainly put forward for political reasons. Many proponents of EU taxation regard the lack of visibility and comprehensibility of the EU revenues as a main factor for the low public support and participation of the citizens. In their view, higher transparency would automatically create a direct link between the citizens and the EU and, hence, help to increase the participation of citizens and their support regarding European integration (Begg & Grimwade, 1998).

Thus, a high visibility of EU finances is important as it enables the people to compare the advantages and disadvantages of EU actions, especially regarding the use of their financial resources. It would increase the accountability of EU authorities for their budget and might finally lead to more public involvement and more control of the EU politicians. This would help to put pressure towards a more efficient budget which better serves the preferences of EU citizens regarding integration.

Tangibility

The criterion of tangibility of EU revenues was demanded by an earlier report of the European Commission in 1995 (see Kraff, 1998). Tangibility means that the burden of EU payments should not be borne by a small group of people in the countries or in a hidden way but that the payments are tangible for every tax payer. This criterion cannot be derived from tax theories as an efficient tax system does not exclude the use of specific taxes on small groups of people as long as the general aims like equity and fairness are fulfilled. Thus, it is mainly a political demand which is connected to the idea of visibility as it is intended to make all people participate in the financing of the European Union. This shall equally distribute the costs and make the people sensitive to their individual contributions, hence, giving the citizens an impression of the actual costs of the European Union.

Equity

Similar to the general claims of tax theory, vertical as well as horizontal equity of EU financing is desirable. The idea of vertical equity is similar to its principle on the national level meaning that the individual contribution should increase with the ability to pay. This is not necessarily a precondition for the system of EU own resources. The European Commission (2004a), for instance, does not consider it in its set of criteria. This is obvious as a regressive European tax would not necessarily have a strong impact on the progressiveness of the national tax systems due to its small amount and as it is counteracted by other progressive taxes on the national level. But several authors (e.g., Cattoir, 2004: 11) hold the view that vertical equity might be, nevertheless, a favourable political feature of a European revenue system. Applying this, he argues that "acceptance of an EU tax for the European citizens would probably require it to involve some degree of income redistribution". This seems reasonable as it can be assumed that the financing of the EU with a highly regressive effect at the individual level would decrease the support for the EU as it would be regarded as highly unfair by the citizens.

The principle of horizontal equity generally prohibits imposing unequal fiscal burdens on comparable people within a country, for example, the discrimination of regions or specific groups of individuals. This gets an additional international dimension considering European revenues. Any revenue system which leads to diverging contributions of comparable citizens in different European countries would be taken as injustice and unfairness and would not support the acceptance of integration either.

Further problems may arise from differences in tax moral or the quality of the tax administration within a fiscal federation (Milbrandt, 2001). If the efficiency of tax systems differs between regions, the revenues between them will differ as well. This makes comparable citizens in different regions contribute to a different amount consequently leading to undesirable distributional effects even when the design of the revenue source is identical in the whole federation. In this case, the use of the affected revenue source would not be appropriate.

Flexibility of Progressiveness

Very often the commonly accepted ability to pay principle, which is also demanded by the solidarity in the EU as defined by Art. 158 TEC (2 TEC), is translated one-to-one into the EU budget financing. The European Commission (2004a: 12), for example, demands "equity in gross contributions", which means in their view that "the burden should be fairly shared among member states as well as citizens". This idea of fairness between countries is derived from the ability-to-pay principle, which means that more capable citizens should contribute more than those less capable. While the application of this principle to European countries is undisputed in order to reduce the disparities in national welfare and to increase cohesion, we hold the view that it is wrong to have an isolated view on the revenue side. Instead, the often cited criterion of "fairness" can only be applied to the overall distributional effects of the EU budget. As a consequence, it does not have to be unconditionally fulfilled by the system of own resources.

At the moment, the spending side is dominated by a high degree of redistribution, thus, reducing the need for a highly progressive revenue side to ensure fairness. But with changing tasks of the EU, for example, a higher amount of spending on public goods and less redistributive spending or changing attitudes of the citizens towards redistribution, fairness might demand a more or less progressive revenue side. For this purpose, the system of own resources should be designed flexible enough in its degree of progressiveness that it could easily be adjusted with changing demand for redistribution on the expenditure side to ensure fairness in the long term.

8.1.5 Further Conventional Principles of Taxation

Tax theory offers a number of widely accepted requirements which have to be fulfilled by any efficient tax system as well as by public funding in general. As a prominent example, Stiglitz (1994) demands the following criteria: efficiency, simplicity, flexibility, transparency and equity. Another desirable feature which is usually stated is a certain degree of progressiveness according to the ability-to-pay principle. But it is important that these criteria cannot be applied to each revenue source solely, like a potential EU tax. They rather have to be fulfilled by the system as a whole (Caesar, 1990). For example, one regressive indirect tax will not have to contradict the wish for a progressive tax system if it is counteracted by progressive direct taxes.

For the derivation of criteria for the analysis of EU-specific questions, one has to keep in mind that EU contributions only constitute a small part of the revenues levied by the national tax systems of the member states. This means that the violation of some criteria does not mean a lack of efficiency of the national systems if measures of the EU are equalised by other national measures. This mainly concerns widely accepted attributes like equity and the ability-to-pay principle.

Nevertheless, tax theory also allows us to derive some criteria which have to be fulfilled by any single revenue source considered for the financing of the EU which will be presented in the following.

Low Compliance Costs

Like in every tax system, any component of the system of own resources of the EU has to fulfil the general request of low compliance costs. This means that the costs linked with the levy of funds, like administration costs, should be relatively low compared to the revenues for the taxpayers as well as for the administration.

In the case of systematic reforms of the current system of own resources, one further aspect regarding the compliance costs has to receive attention. In addition to administration costs which also accrue for any taxation on the national level, the introduction of a new revenue source may also demand the harmonisation of national tax bases. In addition to the delayed introduction of such a revenue source, this would also be connected with harmonisation costs for tax authorities as well as for tax payers.

Neutrality

Public interventions into the market usually cause distortions as they have an effect on decisions in the production process or the choice of consumers and, therefore, change relative prices. This effect is normally not desirable and reduces the efficiency of an economy. An efficient allocation of resources usually requires neutrality, which implies relatively low distortions caused by raising levies. This implies for the choice of revenue sources for the EU that a further distorting effect on the behaviour of people in the member states, which adds up to the effects of existing taxes, shall be reduced. Therefore, the discrimination of certain economic activities caused by EU financing has to be avoided as far as possible.

But there are also potential cases where it is intended to change the behaviour of the individuals with the help of administrative payments. This happens in order to correct for imperfections of the market which may be the case if negative externalities exist, for example, in the environment field. If in these cases public finances are intended to correct for the imperfections, the theory of fiscal federalism has to be consulted for the efficient allocation of the public action within a federation (see section 8.1.2).

Sufficiency

Any revenue system shall endow its recipient with the amount of funds it needs to fulfil its tasks. In the EU, the level of the budget is fixed within multi-annual Financial Perspectives (see section 3.2).

The EU expenditure has to be completely financed by the system of own resources without running the risk of insufficient revenues. Sufficiency also implies that any further increases (or decreases) of the budget in the long run, agreed in forthcoming Financial Perspectives, for example, due to further enlargement or changing tasks of the Union, should also be financially feasible without need for radical modifications of the system of own resources. On the one hand, this implies that any financial resource which declines over time is not appropriate for the EU (Cattoir, 2004). On the other hand, it demands a certain degree of flexibility, which makes the adjustment to a changed demand of funding possible.

Obviously, the "sufficiency" principle must not be interpreted too superficially. It cannot be desirable that any federal level is confronted with a soft budget constraint and with the lacking awareness about the scarcity of tax resources (for this ambiguous interpretation of "sufficiency", see chapter 2). Hence, the key question behind that principle is whether the "necessary level of expenditures" is correctly defined, i.e. for example, without distortions from budget-maximising agents or from pork-barrel oriented politicians. If budgetary institutions led to an excessive demand for funds, insufficient own resources could even be an advantage because they may offer a helpful corrective cap on inefficient budget expansion.

Stability

Usually it is claimed that the revenues from the system of own resources have to be stable to guarantee the sufficient endowment of the European Union, which means that the revenues should not react too sensitive to the business cycle or the price of a specific commodity which is taxed (Cattoir, 2004). This view is contrary to the stabilisation view towards taxation usually assumed at the national level, which explicitly demands a built-in flexibility in order to increase revenue at booms to flatten the business cycle.

The demand for stability is of major importance for the EU than for national states since it lacks the ability to lend money if the revenues will not be high enough due to temporary effects, for example, during a recession. Even if the revenues were counterbalanced by excessive revenues during the following upswing leading to a sufficient endowment on average, these cyclical deficits would not be manageable in the short-run without the right to borrow.

Enforceability

A final trivial criterion is the enforceability of the levy of the different components of the system of own resources. This has practical and legal implications. Practically, sources of revenue have to be designed in such a way to minimise the susceptibility to fraud or evasion. For European purposes, the legal dimension also has important implications. Hence, any EU-wide measure has to be in accordance with national laws as well as with European law.

8.1.6 Conclusion

Summing up, it can be stated that the set of assessment criteria for a rational revenue system developed above shares many similarities with existing ones. Additionally, it puts forth several new ideas and focusses on some uncommon issues. In comparison with the criteria proposed by the European Commission (2004a), differences arise rather in detail such as we argue that visibility of the financing also implies its tangibility. Moreover, we point out a different meaning for the criteria of fairness suggesting that fairness between member states does not require fairness regarding the gross contributions. Instead, the spending side of the budget has to be considered implying that flexibility has to be a criterion for the system of own resources.

As mentioned above, we do not incorporate the claim for financial autonomy into our set of criteria. Instead, several diverging criteria have been developed. These can be mainly attributed to the complex "political economy", which is neglected in the Commissions' work. Moreover, we highlight that by assigning revenue sources to the European level, national conditions (like national federal structures or differing national preferences) have to be respected.

8.2 History of the System of Own Resources

The following historical survey based on the extensive surveys in Raddatz (2005), Euler (2005) and the European Commission (2002) shows how the different components of the current system have emerged.

8.2.1 Initial Situation

Even before the foundation of the European Economic Community (EEC) with the Treaty of Rome in 1957, the European Coal and Steel Community (ECSC) had been already empowered to finance its expenditures (mainly administration costs) through a system of own resources. Its head, the High Authority, was granted the right to impose levies on the production of coal and steel by the member states. It had free choice of the tax base and rate (only an increase of the rate over 1% needed to be approved by the Council of Ministers), it had its own tax administration, and it was to a certain extent even endowed with the right to borrow. Therefore, Peffekoven (1994) refers to this as "quasi-taxation". However, such far-reaching autonomy has never been reached again by any further financial instrument conceded to the European level.

8.2.2 Treaty of Rome, 1958-1970

Challenge

The foundation of the EEC in 1957 demanded the establishment of a budget for the new institutions. Political considerations ruled out unequal and, therefore, redistributive contributions of the member states.

Outcome

The Treaty of Rome determined the financing of the EEC with national contributions. The quota was fixed according to a political allocation formula, which reflected the relative size of the countries but imposed equal contributions to the groups of countries with similar sizes: Germany, France and Italy each contributed 28%, Belgium and the Netherlands 7.9%, Luxembourg 0.2% (with a different scale for the social fund). Moreover, it was explicitly stated that this arrangement was only intended for a transitional period. Art. 201 of the treaty demanded the review of the introduction of a system of own resources at a later date, especially of the revenues from the common customs tariffs which were introduced with the foundation of the EEC.

8.2.3 First Own Resources Decision, 1971-1985

Challenge

The proceeding integration of the European Community (EC) and the request to reduce the dependency from the member states put pressure on the enforcement of Art. 201 from the Treaty of Rome. Especially the French President Georges Pompidou demanded the introduction of a financial constitution in return to the approval of the accession of the UK to the Community (Lindenthal, 2000). Therefore, it was decided that own resources should be assigned to the Community to cover all their expenditure.

Outcome

The first own resources decision of April 1970 established a system of own resources comprising three sources which was planned to come into effect in 1971. The first two resources were considered as "traditional" own resources (TOR). These revenues, which were the result of the common policies, comprised agricultural levies and customs duties. They should flow completely into the EC budget apart from 10% of the revenues which were refunded as collection costs to the respective member state. While agricultural levies were completely paid to the EC from 1971 on, customs duties were assigned to the EC gradually from 1971-1974; since 1975 they were completely paid to the Community.

In addition to that, a third pillar was introduced. This resource was based on a uniform harmonised assessment base of VAT revenue. The justification for this resource is given by Menéndez (1999: 9) assuming that "consumption could be regarded as a decent proxy for the actual benefit individuals derived from the Communities at that time". It should cover the difference between the revenues from traditional own resources and the overall expenditures, therefore, its rate had to vary every year (it was fixed at the annual budgetary procedure). The maximum rate was initially limited to 1% of the harmonised VAT base. The VAT resource was gradually applied as progress was made in harmonising the VAT base. The payment of the resource was intended to start in 1975 but due to problems regarding the harmonisation of the base in many countries, the actual start had to be postponed to 1980. In the transitional period until 1979, member states paid contributions according to their GDP to balance the EC budget whereby shares were based on the mean of GDP of the past three years. This transformation rule was also applied to new members so that Greece and Portugal paid contributions instead of VAT until 1986 and 1988, respectively.

8.2.4 Second Own Resources Decision, 1986-1988

Challenge

Because of a seemingly unfair fiscal burden compared to its share of the Community GNP, the United Kingdom had repeatedly demanded for a reduction of its net contributions since 1974. As a reason for this, the relatively low agricultural production in the UK was stated, which led to high payments of agricultural levies and a low return from the agricultural funds. Earlier attempts to correct for this had failed; a first generalised correction mechanism which was enforced from 1976 to 1980 had never been triggered, and a second one provided compensation for the UK on the expenditure side in the form of specific measures.

Furthermore, a financial crisis due to the depreciation of the U.S. dollar and the increase of the spending for the Common Agricultural Policy demanded an increase of the Community revenues. Because of a number of free-trade agreements with non-member countries (e.g., in the context of GATT), the TOR revenues had even declined. Thus, the maximum VAT rate of 1% was not sufficient anymore for financing the EU. As a consequence, the member states had to pay extra funds in 1985 and 1986. This made the Commission demand an increase of the VAT ceiling to 2%.

Outcome

The 1984 Fontainebleau Council decided the introduction of a correction for the UK. For 1985, a flat-rate reduction of 1 billion ECU in UK's VAT contributions was agreed. From 1986 on, a rebate equivalent to 0.66% of the UK's net balance was granted, which was refunded via a reduction of the VAT base. The costs of this correction mechanism were shared between the other member states according to their VAT shares with the exception of Germany, whose share was reduced by a third. In order to overcome the financial crisis, the maximum VAT rate was increased from 1.0% to 1.4% starting in 1986.

8.2.5 Third Own Resources Decision (Delors I), 1988-1994

Challenge

Changes in the system of own resources were again claimed because of insufficient revenues. The TOR revenues continued to decline, and the VAT resource did not grow as fast as the economic activity because of a reduction of the share of consumption in GNP. Moreover, the further increase in spending for agricultural policy and the enlargement of the Community (Spain and Portugal entered in 1986) led to an increase in the expenditures which had to be equalised. Thus, the Commission demanded the increase of the overall funds to a level of 1.4% of overall GNP.

Finally, the existing system with its lion's share of VAT resources on the funding was criticised by some new member states for its regressive character. According to its critics the VAT resource disproportionally affected the poorer countries with their higher consumption/GDP ratio. Especially Spain proposed a capping arguing that the high inflow of foreign tourists increased the Spanish VAT revenue above proportion (Wissenschaftlicher Beirat, 1998).

Outcome

In 1988, the Council decided to meet the financial requirements with the introduction of a fourth resource. This resource was based on the GNP share of the member states. It was intended to replace the VAT resource as residual because the other three resources had already been completely exploited. In contrast to the system before, no ceiling for maximum GNP resources was introduced. Instead, a maximum ceiling for the total amount of expenditures of 1.15% of the Union's GNP was agreed for 1988, which meant a significant increase of the revenue as this was equivalent to a VAT rate of around 2%. The maximum ceiling of GNP should later rise to 1.2% in 1992.

In return to this, the VAT-based own resources was adjusted to allow for disparities in economic structures. The maximum rate to uniform VAT base was maintained at 1.4% but it was agreed that the VAT base may not exceed 55% of the national GNP in countries with a GNP per capita of less than 90% of the average. The correction mechanism for the UK was retained so that it did not benefit or get penalised by the changes of the own resources system.

Finally, a more technical change allowed the member states to retain 10% of the TOR which they collected to cover their collection costs instead of the previous refunding via the expenditure side.

8.2.6 Fourth Own Resources Decision (Delors II), 1995-2002

Challenge

At least from the perspective of the Commission, the further integration of the Community called for another increase in the funds, which was quantified at 1.37% of GNP. Furthermore, the criticism of the poorer member states against the redistributive effects of the VAT resource again demanded a revision of this instrument. Therefore, the Commission requested in its proposals more fairness and the abolishment of the regressive VAT resource.

Outcome

In order to meet the still rising funding requirements, the 1992 Edinburgh Council decided to gradually increase the own resources ceiling from 1.20% to 1.27% in 1999. Furthermore, a margin for unseen expenditures of 0.01% was introduced.

Additionally, the VAT resource lost again in importance at the benefit of the GNP resource. The maximum rate applicable to the VAT base was reduced from 1.4% to 1.0% in equal steps over the period of 1995-1999. In addition to that, for four poorer countries (Greece, Ireland, Portugal and Spain) the base cap was reduced from 55% to 50% from 1995 on; for other countries it was reduced to 50% in equal steps over the period from 1995 to 1999.

8.2.7 Fifth Own Resources Decision (Agenda 2000), 2002-2006

Challenges

The continuous reduction of the budgetary share of agricultural spending let the initially unfair fiscal burden of the UK diminish. This made other net contributors, especially Germany, eager to demand a generalised correction mechanism. By contrast, some poorer member states (mainly Spain and Portugal) even demanded a more progressive design of the own resources system (European Commission, 1998: Annex 7).

The foreseeable accession of several CEE countries made further reforms necessary. But the Commission expected the revenue ceiling to be sufficient for an enlarged Union and did not propose an increase of the budget.

Outcome

The 2000 Berlin Council decided some reductions of the burden of the traditional net contributors. The payments to finance the UK rebate of Germany, the Netherlands, Austria and Sweden were reduced to only one quarter of the normal share; the remaining three quarters had to be financed by the other states. Moreover, technical adjustments were made to the UK rebate to offset windfall effects due to the Eastern enlargement arising from an increase in collection costs and pre-accession expenditure. Another relief was entitled to the countries with large ports (especially the Netherlands) by raising the allowance for collection of TOR from 10% to 25%.

The importance of the GNP resource was again increased with the reduction of the maximum call-in rate of VAT to 0.75% in 2002 and 2003 and finally to 0.5% in 2004. With the new Financial Perspective, this was finally reduced to 0.3% in 2007. Thus, the overall level of the budget stayed constant, the ceiling remained at its 1999 level of 1.27% of GNP, which was expressed for statistical reasons as 1.24% of GNI.

9 Additional Tables

Table 12. Distributive effects of special regulations on expenditure side

Country	Sum of allocated expenditure (2007-2013), in Euro	Change in net position (in %)
Germany	345,802,473	-0.01
France	527,158,905	-0.01
United Kingdom	141,199,653	-0.01
Italy	1,404,914,488	0.00
Spain	2,579,117,224	0.03
Netherlands	0	-0.01
Greece	15,983,389	-0.01
Portugal	464,212,102	0.03
Belgium	0	-0.01
Sweden	365,223,649	0.01
Austria	199,820,673	0.00
Denmark	0	-0.01
Finland	642,932,572	0.04
Ireland	58,300,347	-0.01
Luxembourg	0	-0.01
Poland	918,565,444	0.04
Czech Republic	266,903,698	0.03
Hungary	170,115,182	0.01
Slovakia	17,065,458	-0.01
Lithuania	121,111,466	0.06
Latvia	81,646,376	0.06
Slovenia	18,786,169	0.00
Estonia	47,522,895	0.04
Cyprus	361,895,758	0.31
Malta	0	-0.01
Romania	0	-0.01
Bulgaria	0	-0.01

Source: European Council (2005); own calculations.

Table 13. Net positions resulting from different reform options I

	Status quo (see section 3.6)		No correction (see section 5.4.2)		GCM, threshold: 0.35%, refund rate: 66%, full participation (see section 5.4.4)	
	Gross contributions in EUR million	Net position in % of GNI	Gross contributions in EUR million	Net position in % of GNI	Gross contributions in EUR million	Net position in % of GNI
DE	21,296	-0.33	22,102	-0.37	21,427	-0.34
FR	18,227	-0.25	16,123	-0.14	16,997	-0.19
UK	13,970	-0.24	18,768	-0.47	16,823	-0.37
IT	14,838	-0.27	13,432	-0.18	14,134	-0.23
ES	10,141	0.21	8,983	0.32	9,436	0.28
NL	5,195	-0.27	6,077	-0.43	5,721	-0.36
GR	2,004	1.73	1,770	1.85	1,861	1.80
PT	1,535	1.16	1,351	1.28	1,423	1.23
BE	4,363	1.02	4,062	1.11	4,213	1.06
SE	2,637	-0.27	2,969	-0.37	2,876	-0.34
AT	2,246	-0.23	2,239	-0.23	2,360	-0.27
DK	2,261	-0.18	2,067	-0.10	2,171	-0.14
FI	1,697	-0.24	1,520	-0.14	1,603	-0.18
IE	1,773	0.22	1,573	0.34	1,650	0.29
LU	289	4.17	254	4.29	268	4.24
PL	2,547	3.13	2,252	3.24	2,366	3.20
CZ	1,125	2.27	1,000	2.38	1,049	2.34
HU	992	2.86	890	2.97	933	2.92
SK	458	2.59	416	2.69	436	2.64
LT	273	4.60	243	4.72	255	4.67
LV	179	3.44	162	3.54	170	3.49
SI	329	1.11	291	1.23	306	1.18
EE	147	3.17	131	3.28	138	3.24
CY	188	0.17	169	0.28	177	0.24
MT	60	0.97	54	1.09	56	1.04
RO	844	4.17	749	4.29	786	4.24
BG	283	4.53	251	4.65	264	4.60

Table 14. Net positions resulting from different reform options II

	GCM, threshold: 0.35%, refund rate: 66%, no participation (see section 5.4.4)		GCM, threshold: 0.25%, refund rate: 66%, full participation (see section 5.4.4)		GCM, threshold: 0.20%, refund rate: 66%, full participation (see section 5.4.4)	
	Gross contributions in EUR million	Net position in % of GNI	Gross contributions in EUR million	Net position in % of GNI	Gross contributions in EUR million	Net position in % of GNI
DE	20,292	-0.29	20,569	-0.30	20,293	-0.29
FR	17,769	-0.23	17,561	-0.22	17,705	-0.22
UK	15,885	-0.33	16,114	-0.34	15,886	-0.33
IT	14,755	-0.27	14,587	-0.26	14,468	-0.25
ES	9,836	0.24	9,729	0.25	9,936	0.23
NL	5,462	-0.32	5,525	-0.33	5,462	-0.32
GR	1,942	1.76	1,920	1.77	1,962	1.75
PT	1,486	1.19	1,469	1.20	1,502	1.18
BE	4,346	1.02	4,310	1.03	4,379	1.01
SE	2,724	-0.30	2,761	-0.31	2,724	-0.30
AT	2,239	-0.23	2,334	-0.26	2,305	-0.25
DK	2,264	-0.18	2,239	-0.17	2,287	-0.19
FI	1,676	-0.22	1,656	-0.21	1,675	-0.22
IE	1,719	0.25	1,700	0.26	1,736	0.24
LU	279	4.21	276	4.22	282	4.20
PL	2,468	3.16	2,441	3.17	2,493	3.15
CZ	1,092	2.30	1,080	2.31	1,103	2.29
HU	972	2.88	961	2.89	981	2.87
SK	454	2.60	449	2.61	459	2.59
LT	265	4.63	262	4.64	267	4.62
LV	177	3.45	175	3.46	178	3.44
SI	319	1.14	315	1.15	322	1.13
EE	143	3.20	141	3.21	144	3.19
CY	183	0.20	181	0.21	185	0.19
MT	58	1.00	57	1.01	58	0.99
RO	819	4.20	810	4.21	827	4.19
BG	275	4.56	272	4.57	277	4.55

Table 15. Net positions resulting from different reform options III

	GCM, threshold: 0.25%, refund rate: 80%, full participation (see section 5.4.4)		GCM, threshold: 0.25%, refund rate: 100%, full participation (see section 5.4.4)		GLCM (only CAP), threshold: 0.10%, refund rate: 66%, full participation (see section 6.2.4)	
	Gross contributions in EUR million	Net position in % of GNI	Gross contributions in EUR million	Net position in % of GNI	Gross contributions in EUR million	Net position in % of GNI
DE	20,244	-0.29	19,779	-0.27	21,878	-0.36
FR	17,866	-0.23	18,302	-0.26	16,399	-0.16
UK	15,551	-0.31	14,747	-0.27	18,191	-0.44
IT	14,832	-0.27	15,182	-0.30	13,654	-0.20
ES	9,887	0.23	10,112	0.21	9,126	0.31
NL	5,408	-0.31	5,241	-0.28	6,003	-0.41
GR	1,952	1.76	1,998	1.74	1,799	1.84
PT	1,494	1.18	1,530	1.16	1,373	1.26
BE	4,363	1.02	4,438	1.00	4,109	1.10
SE	2,717	-0.30	2,654	-0.28	2,916	-0.36
AT	2,355	-0.27	2,384	-0.28	2,276	-0.24
DK	2,275	-0.19	2,328	-0.21	2,100	-0.11
FI	1,685	-0.23	1,727	-0.25	1,546	-0.15
IE	1,727	0.25	1,766	0.23	1,597	0.32
LU	281	4.20	288	4.18	227	4.38
PL	2,481	3.15	2,538	3.13	2,288	3.23
CZ	1,097	2.29	1,122	2.27	1,016	2.37
HU	976	2.88	998	2.86	903	2.95
SK	457	2.60	467	2.57	422	2.67
LT	266	4.63	272	4.60	247	4.70
LV	177	3.45	181	3.42	165	3.52
SI	320	1.14	328	1.11	295	1.21
EE	144	3.19	147	3.17	133	3.27
CY	184	0.19	187	0.17	169	0.29
MT	58	1.00	59	0.98	48	1.20
RO	823	4.20	841	4.18	761	4.27
BG	276	4.56	282	4.53	255	4.63

Table 16. Net positions resulting from different reform options IV

	GLCM (only CAP), threshold: 0.10%, refund rate: 100%, no participation (see section 6.2.4)		GLCM (only CAP), threshold: 0.00%, refund rate: 66%, full participation (see section 6.2.4)		GLCM (only CAP), threshold: 0.00%, refund rate: 100%, no participation (see section 6.2.4)	
	Gross contributions in EUR million	Net position in % of GNI	Gross contributions in EUR million	Net position in % of GNI	Gross contributions in EUR million	Net position in % of GNI
DE	21,219	-0.33	21,181	-0.33	18,806	-0.23
FR	16,917	-0.18	17,088	-0.19	20,237	-0.36
UK	17,446	-0.41	17,616	-0.41	15,454	-0.31
IT	14,069	-0.22	13,718	-0.20	12,691	-0.13
ES	9,394	0.28	9,483	0.27	11,115	0.11
NL	5,841	-0.38	5,844	-0.38	5,289	-0.29
GR	1,853	1.81	1,871	1.80	2,201	1.63
PT	1,416	1.23	1,430	1.23	1,689	1.06
BE	4,199	1.07	4,093	1.10	3,856	1.17
SE	2,817	-0.33	2,823	-0.33	2,494	-0.23
AT	2,238	-0.23	2,202	-0.21	1,980	-0.13
DK	2,162	-0.14	2,182	-0.15	2,559	-0.31
FI	1,595	-0.18	1,547	-0.15	1,422	-0.08
IE	1,643	0.30	1,658	0.29	1,937	0.13
LU	207	4.45	219	4.41	179	4.54
PL	2,356	3.20	2,378	3.19	2,792	3.03
CZ	1,044	2.34	1,054	2.33	1,229	2.17
HU	929	2.93	938	2.92	1,094	2.76
SK	434	2.65	438	2.64	512	2.48
LT	254	4.68	256	4.67	297	4.51
LV	169	3.50	171	3.49	198	3.32
SI	304	1.19	304	1.19	286	1.24
EE	137	3.24	138	3.23	160	3.07
CY	165	0.31	164	0.32	149	0.41
MT	44	1.27	46	1.22	39	1.37
RO	783	4.25	790	4.24	922	4.08
BG	263	4.60	265	4.60	310	4.44

Table 17. Net positions resulting from different reform options V

	GLCM (CAP, fisheries and rural development), threshold: 0.10%, refund rate: 66%, full participation (see section 6.2.4)		GLCM (ex Cohesion and Regional Convergence), threshold: 0.10%, refund rate: 66%, full participation (see section 6.2.4)	
	Gross contributions in EUR million	Net position in % of GNI	Gross contributions in EUR million	Net position in % of GNI
DE	21,513	-0.34	20,632	-0.31
FR	16,769	-0.18	17,344	-0.21
UK	17,516	-0.41	16,867	-0.38
IT	13,951	-0.21	13,834	-0.21
ES	9,318	0.29	9,616	0.26
NL	5,814	-0.38	5,796	-0.38
GR	1,837	1.82	1,898	1.79
PT	1,404	1.24	1,451	1.21
BE	4,087	1.10	4,273	1.05
SE	2,934	-0.36	2,915	-0.36
AT	2,329	-0.26	2,408	-0.29
DK	2,144	-0.13	2,213	-0.16
FI	1,581	-0.17	1,636	-0.20
IE	1,630	0.30	1,681	0.28
LU	223	4.39	273	4.23
PL	2,336	3.21	2,412	3.18
CZ	1,036	2.35	1,068	2.32
HU	922	2.94	950	2.91
SK	431	2.65	444	2.62
LT	252	4.68	259	4.65
LV	168	3.50	173	3.47
SI	302	1.19	311	1.16
EE	136	3.25	140	3.22
CY	175	0.25	179	0.22
MT	53	1.10	53	1.10
RO	777	4.25	801	4.23
BG	261	4.61	269	4.58

List of Figures

List of Tables

List of Boxes

References

Alesina, A., I. Angeloni and L. Schuknecht (2005), What Does the European Union Do?, *Public Choice* 123 (3-4), 275-319.

Balassa, B. (1964), The Purchasing Power Parity Doctrine: A Reappraisal, *Journal of Political Economy* 72 (6), 584–696.

Becker, P. (2000), Die Reformbereitschaft der Europäischen Union auf dem Prüfstand – Die Agenda 2000, in: Lippert, B. (Ed.), *Osterweiterung der Europäischen Union – Die doppelte Reifeprüfung*, Bonn, 61-104.

Becker, P. (2005a), *Der EU-Finanzrahmen – Auf dem Weg zu einer europäischen Finanzverfassung oder Fortsetzung der nationalen Nettosaldopolitik?*, SWP-Studie 2005/S36, Stiftung Wissenschaft und Politik – Deutsches Institut für Internationale Politik und Sicherheit, Berlin.

Becker, P. (2005b), *Die EU-Finanzverhandlungen Agenda 2007 vor der dritten Phase. Die Rolle des Europäischen Parlaments*, Diskussionspapier der FG 1, Stiftung Wissenschaft und Politik – Deutsches Institut für Internationale Politik und Sicherheit, Berlin.

Becker, P. (2006), Mehr Geld für Europa. Die Verständigung auf einen neuen EU-Finanzrahmen 2007-2013, *SWP Aktuell* 4, 1-8.

Becker, P. (2007), *EU-Reform frühzeitig gestalten! Optionen der deutschen Europapolitik bei der Revision der europäischen Finanzverfassung 2008/09*, SWP-Studie 2007/S2, Stiftung Wissenschaft und Politik – Deutsches Institut für Internationale Politik und Sicherheit, Berlin.

Begg, I. (2004), Future Fiscal Arrangements of the European Union, *Common Market Law Review* 41 (3), 775-794.

Begg, I. (2007), The 2008/2009 Review of the EU Budget: Real or Cosmetic?, *CESifo Forum* 8 (1), 45-50.

Begg, I. and N. Grimwade (1998), *Paying for Europe*, Sheffield.

Begg, I. and F. Heinemann (2006), New Budget, Old Dilemmas, Centre for European Reform briefing note, February 2006.

Belafi, M. (2006), *Eine Steuer für Europa? Konzepte steuerbasierter Direktfinanzierung der Europäischen Union*, CAP Aktuell No.2/2006, Bertelsmann Forschungsgruppe Politik, Munich.

Biehl, D. (1996), Braucht die Europäische Union eine eigene Steuerhoheit?, in: Gick, W. (Ed.), *Die zukünftige Ausgestaltung der Regionalpolitik in der EU*, Munich, 29-54.

BIS (2005), *Triennial Central Bank Survey of Foreign Exchange 2004*, Bank for International Settlement, Basel.

Bortz, J. (2004), *Statistik für Human- und Sozialwissenschaftler*, 6th ed., Heidelberg.

Brennan, G. and J.M. Buchanan (1980), *The Power to Tax*, Cambridge.

Busch, B. (1998), *Zur künftigen Finanzierung der Europäischen Union*, Beiträge zur Wirtschafts- und Sozialpolitik 242, Institut der deutschen Wirtschaft, Cologne.

Caesar, R. (1990), Neue Steuern für die Europäische Gemeinschaft? – Kriterien und Vorschläge, in: Biehl, D. and G. Pfennig (Eds.), *Zur Reform der EG-Finanzverfassung*, Bonn, 57-105.

Caesar, R. (1996), Zur Reform des Einnahmensystems der Europäischen Union, in: Zolnhöfer, W. (Ed.), *Europa auf dem Wege zur politischen Union?*, Berlin, 145-173.

Caesar, R. (2001), An EU Tax? – Not a Good Idea, *Intereconomics* 36 (5), 231-233.

Cattoir P. (2004), *Tax-Based EU Own Resources: An Assessment*, European Commission Taxation Papers Working Paper No. 1/2004, Brussels.

Cipriani, G. and S. Pisani (2004), The European Budget: An Alternative to Budgetary Balances to Assess Benefits for the Member States, paper presented at the XVI Conferenza della Società Italiana di Economis Pubblica, Università di Pavia, October 7-8.

Cnossen, S. (1990), The Case for Tax Diversity in the European Community, *European Economic Review* 34 (2-3), 471-479.

Cnossen, S. (2001), Tax Policy in the European Union: A Review of Issues and Options, *FinanzArchiv* 58 (4), 466-558.

Cnossen, S. (2006), *Alcohol Taxation and Regulation in the European Union*, CESifo Working Paper No. 1821, Munich.

Coussens, W. (2004), *A Fair Solution to the UK Rebate Conundrum,* Ideas Factory Europe, Idea 3, European Policy Centre, Brussels.

Cuthbert J. and M. Cuthbert (2006), *The Wrong Sort of Rebate – The Need to Reform the UK Budget Adjustment*, CEPS Working Document No. 236, Centre for European Policy Studies, Brussels.

de la Fuente, A. and R. Doménech (2001), The Redistributive Effects of the EU Budget: An Analysis and Proposal for Reform, *Journal of Common Market Studies* 39 (2), 307-330.

Deutsche Bundesbank (2007), *Annual Report 2006*, Frankfurt/M.

Duverger, M. (1954), *Political Parties: Their Organization and Activity in the Modern State*, London.

Elschner, C. and M. Overesch (2007), Trends of Corporate Tax Levels in Europe, *Intereconomics* 42 (3), 127-132.

Enderlein, H., J. Lindner, O. Calvo-Gonzalez and R. Ritter (2005), *The EU Budget: How Much Scope for Institutional Reform?*, ECB Occasional paper series No. 27, Frankfurt/M.

Euler, M. (2005), *Ansatzpunkte für eine Reform des Finanzierungssystems der Europäischen Union*, Frankfurt/M.

Eurobarometer (2006), The Future of Europe, Special Eurobarometer 251/Wave 65.1, Survey requested and coordinated by Directorate General Press and Communication (European Commission), Brussels.

European Commission (1987), Report on the Financing of the Community Budget, COM(87) 101, Brussels.

European Commission (1998), Financing the European Union, Commission report on the operation of the own resources system, DG XIX, Brussels.

European Commission (2002), *European Union Public Finance*, Office for Official Publications of the European Communities, Luxembourg.

European Commission (2004a), Financing the European Union, Commission report on the operation of the own resources system, DG XIX, Brussels.

European Commission (2004b), Underlying Assumptions Concerning Economic Growth Till 2013 – Economic Growth Rates by Member State, Multiannual Financial Framework 2007-2013, Fiche No. 1b, April 16, Brussels.

European Commission (2004c), Payment Schedules by Expenditure Heading, Multiannual Financial Framework 2007-2013, Fiche No. 2a, March 29, Brussels.

European Commission (2004d), Proposal for Renewal of the Inter-Institutional Agreement on Budgetary Discipline and Improvement of the Budgetary Procedure, COM(2004) 498 final, July 14, Brussels.

European Commission (2005), Calculating Member States' Net Budgetary Balances, Working Document of the Commission Services, Multiannual Financial Framework 2007-2013 Fiche No. 83 rev1, February 24, Brussels.

European Commission (2006a), Financial Report 2005, Office for Official Publications of the European Communities, Luxembourg.

European Commission (2006b), Fifth Report from the Commission on the Operation of the Inspection Arrangements for Traditional Own Resources (2003-2005), COM(2006) 874 final, Brussels.

European Commission (2006c), Economic Forecasts Autumn 2006, *European Economy No. 5/2006,* Directorate-General for Economic and Financial Affairs, Brussels.

European Commission (2006d), Indicative Breakdown of Expenditure Within Individual Headings and Sub-Headings, after the trialogue of 4 April 2006 (COM, Fiche No. 94 rev1), Brussels.

European Commission (2007), *VAT Rates Applied in the Member States of the European Community*, Brussels.

European Council (2002), Copenhagen European Council 12 and 13 December 2002 Presidency Conclusions, POLGEN 84, 15917/02, January 29, 2003, Brussels.

European Council (2005), Final Comprehensive Proposal from the Presidency on the Financial Perspective 2007-2013, CADREFIN 268, 15915/05, December 19, Brussels.

European Council (2007), Presidency Conclusions of the Brussels European Council 21/22 June 2007, CONCL 2, June 23, Brussels.

European Court of Auditors (1998), Special Report No. 6/98 Concerning the Court's Assessment of the System of Resources Based on VAT and GNP Together with the Commission's Replies (98/C 241/02), Luxembourg.

European Court of Auditors (2000), Special Report No. 17/2000 on the Commission's Control of the Reliability and Comparability of the Member States' GNP Data Together with the Commission's Replies (2000/C 336/01), Luxembourg.

European Parliament (1999), Report on the Proposal for a Council Decision on the System of the European Union's Own Resources (COM (1999) 333 – C5-0092/1999 – 1999/0139(CNS)), Strasbourg.

European Parliament (2001), Report on the Situation Concerning the European Union's Own Resources in 2001, Committee on Budgets (2001/2019(INI)), Brussels.

European Parliament (2004), Final Adoption of Amending Budget No. 9 of the European Union for the Financial Year 2004 (2004/888/EC, Euratom), December 28, Brussels.

European Parliament (2005), Report on Policy Challenges and Budgetary Means of the Enlarged Union 2007-2013 (2004/2209(INI)), Temporary Committee on Policy Challenges and Budgetary Means of the Enlarged Union 2007-2013, Rapporteur: Reimer Böge, Final A6-0153/2005, May 19, Brussels.

European Parliament (2006a), Final Adoption of Amending Budget No. 4 of the European Union for the Financial Year 2006 (2006/869/EC, Euratom), December 15, Strasbourg.

European Parliament (2006b), Final Adoption of Amending Budget No. 8 of the European Union for the Financial Year 2005 (2006/5/EC, Euratom), January 13, Strasbourg.

European Parliament (2006c), Final Adoption of Amending Budget No. 6 of the European Union for the Financial Year 2006 (2006/995/EC, Euratom), December 30, Strasbourg.

European Parliament, European Council and European Commission (2006), *Inter-Institutional Agreement Between the European Parliament, the Council and the Commission on Budgetary Discipline and Sound Financial Management*, Official Journal of the European Union C 139 of 14/06/2006, 1-17.

European Values Study Foundation and World Values Survey Association (2006), European and World Values Surveys Four-Wave Integrated Data File, 1981-2004, v.20060423.

Fehr, H. (2001), Der Haushalt der Europäischen Union – Aktuelle Entwicklungstendenzen und Reformoptionen, *Zeitschrift für Wirtschaftspolitik* 50 (1), 36-48.

Gelauff, G., H. Stolwijk and P. Veenendaal (2006), *Europe's Financial Perspectives in Perspective*, ENEPRI Working Paper No. 46, Brussels.

Goulard, S. and M. Nava (2002), *A More Democratic System for Financing the EU Budget: A Challenge for the European Convention*, European Commission, Brussels, mimeo.

Gros, D. and S. Micossi (2005), *A Better Budget for the European Union – More Value for Money, More Money for Value*, CEPS Policy Brief No. 66, Centre for European Policy Studies, Brussels.

Hallerberg, M. and J. von Hagen (1999), Electoral Institutions, Cabinet Negotiations, and Budget Deficits Within the European Union, in: Poterba, J. and J. von Hagen (Eds.), *Fiscal Institutions and Fiscal Performance*, Chicago, 209-232.

Haug, J. (2001), More Fairness, Democracy and Transparency!, *Intereconomics* 36 (5), 226-228.

Heinemann, F. (2003), Perspektiven einer zukünftigen EU-Finanzverfassung, *Integration* 26 (3), 228-243.

Heinemann, F. (2006), Das common pool-Problem in der EU-Finanzverfassung, *Zeitschrift für Staats- und Europawissenschaften/Journal for Comparative Government and European Policy* 4 (2), 188-213.

Henke, K.-D. (1997), Die Finanzierung der EU, *Wirtschaftsdienst* 77 (1), 45-49.

Hirschman, A. (1970), *Exit, Voice and Loyalty: Responses to Declines in Firms, Organisations and States*, Cambridge.

Hix, S. (2005), *The Political System of the European Union*, New York.

Hix, S. and A.G. Noury (2007), After Enlargement. Voting Patterns in the Sixth European Parliament, research paper draft 3, London.

Huber, B. (2001), Zur Finanzierung der Europäischen Union, *Zeitschrift für Wirtschaftspolitik* 50 (1), 49-58.

IBFD (2006), *European Tax Handbook*, Amsterdam.

IEA (2006), Key World Economic Statistics, Paris.

Kauppi, H. and M. Widgrén (2004), What Determines EU Decision Making? Needs, Power or Both?, *Economic Policy* 19 (39), 221-266.

Kovács, L. (2006), Kommissar treibt EU-Steuer voran, *Financial Times Deutschland* 3.3.2006.

Kraff, M. (1998), *Der Finanzausgleich in der Europäischen Union*, Bonn.

Lamassoure, A. (2007), Draft Report on the Future of the European Union's Own Resources (2006/2205(INI)), European Parliament Committee on Budgets, Brussels.

Le Cacheux, J. (2007), *Funding the EU Budget with a Genuine Own Resource: The Case for a European Tax*, Notre Europe Studies No. 57, Paris.

Lefebvre, M. (2005), The European Budget at the Test of Enlargement, in: Lefebvre, M. (Ed.), *What Kind of European Budget for 2013*, Paris, 13-45.

Lindenthal, D. (2000), *Die Finanzierung der EU: Ein Beitrag zur europäischen Integration*, Stuttgart.

Lindner, J. (2003), Institutional Stability and Change: Two Sides of the Same Coin, *Journal of European Public Policy* 10 (6), 912-935.

Lijphart, A. (1984), *Democracies: Majoritarian and Consensus Patterns of Government in Twenty-One Countries*, New Haven.

Lijphart, A. (1994), *Electoral Systems and Party Systems: A Study of Twenty-Seven Democracies 1945-1990*, New York.

Lührmann, A., G. Schick and R. Steenblock (2006), *Grüne Vorschläge zur Reform der EU-Finanzierung*, Diskussionspapier Bündnis 90/Die Grünen Bundestagsfraktion, Berlin.

Mackay, J., M. Eriksen and O. Shafey (2006), *The Tobacco Atlas*, Brighton.

Marks, G. (1993), Structural Policy and Multilevel Governance in the EC, in: Cafruny, A.W. and G.G. Rosenthal (Eds.), *The State of the European Community*, London, 391-410.

McCaffery, E. and J. Baron (2005), *The Political Psychology of Redistribution*, USC CLEO Research Paper Series C05, Los Angeles.

Meermagen, B. (2002), *Beitrags- und Eigenmittelsystem. Die Finanzierung inter- und supranationaler Organisationen, insbesondere der Europäischen Gemeinschaften*, Munich.

Menéndez, A.J. (1999), Taxing Europe – Two Cases for a European Power to Tax (with Some Comparative Observations), *Columbia Journal of European Law* 10 (2), 1-41.

Milbrandt, B. (2001), *Die Finanzierung der Europäischen Union – Perspektiven für eine Osterweiterung*, Baden-Baden.

Monar, J. (1994), Inter-Institutional Agreements: The Phenomenon and Its New Dynamics After Maastricht, *Common Market Law Review* 31 (4), 693-719.

Mueller, D. (2003), *Public Choice III*, 3rd ed., Cambridge.

Müller, C. (2006), Eine Steuer für Europa? Das Argument des vertikalen Steuerwettbewerbs, in: Bertholt, N. (Ed.), *Wirtschaftspolitik im Systemwettbewerb*, Berlin, 70-91.

Musso, A. and F. Westermann (2005), *Assessing Potential Output Growth in the Euro Area – A Growth Accounting Perspective*, ECB Occasional Paper No. 22, Frankfurt/M.

Mutén, L. (2001), The Case for an EU Tax Is Not Convincing, *Intereconomics* 36 (5), 228-230.

Nam, C.W., R. Parsche and B. Schaden (2001), *Measurement of Value Added Tax Evasion in Selected EU Countries on the Basis of National Accounts Data*, CESifo Working Paper No. 431, Munich.

Norris, P. and M.N. Franklin (1997), Social Representation, *European Journal of Political Research* 32 (6), 185-210.

Noury, A.G. (2002), Ideology, Nationality and Euro-Parlamentarians, *European Union Politics* 3 (1), 33-58.

Oates, W.E. (1972), *Fiscal Federalism*, New York.

Oates, W.E. (1999), An Essay on Fiscal Federalism, *Journal of Economic Literature* 37 (3), 1120-1149.

OECD (2007), *Taxing Wages*, Paris.

Olson, M. (1969), The Principle of "Fiscal Equivalence": The Division of Responsibilities Among Different Levels of Government, *American Economic Review* 59 (2), 479-487.

Overesch, M. (2005), The Effective Tax Burden of Companies in Europe, *CESifo DICE Report* 4/2005, 56-63.

Padoa-Schioppa, T. (1987), *Efficiency, Stability and Equity – A Strategy for the Evolution of the Economic System of the European Community*, Oxford.

Peffekoven, R. (1981), Verteilung internationaler Finanzierungslasten, *List-Forum* 11 (1), 14-30.

Peffekoven, R. (1994), *Die Finanzen der Europäischen Union*, Mannheim.

Pollack, M.A. (1997), Delegation, Agency and Agenda Setting in the European Community, *International Organisation* 51 (1), 99-134.

Popitz, J. (1927), Finanzwirtschaft der öffentlichen Körperschaften, in: Gerloff, W. and F. Meisel (Eds.), *Handbuch der Finanzwissenschaft Bd. 2*, Tübingen, 338-375.

Raddatz, G.K. (2005), *Das Eigenmittelsystem der Europäischen Union*, Frankfurt/M.

Raddatz, G.K. and G. Schick (2003*), Wege zur europäischen Verfassung III – Braucht Europa eine Steuer?*, Argumente zu Marktwirtschaft und Politik No. 77, Stiftung Marktwirtschaft, Berlin.

Rodden, J. (2002), The Dilemma of Fiscal Federalism: Grants and Fiscal Performance Around the World, *American Journal of Political Science* 46 (3), 670-687.

Rösl, G. (2002), *Seigniorage in der EWU: Eine Analyse der Notenbankgewinnentstehung und -verwendung des Eurosystems*, Frankfurt/M.

Samuelson, W. and R. Zeckhauser (1988), Status Quo Bias in Decision Making, *Journal of Risk and Uncertainty* 1 (1), 7-59.

Sachverständigenkommission zur Vorklärung finanzverfassungsrechtlicher Fragen für künftige Neufestlegungen der Umsatzsteueranteile (1981), *Maßstäbe und Verfahren zur Verteilung der Umsatzsteuer nach Art. 106 Abs. 3 und Abs. 4 Satz 1 GG*, Bonn.

Sapir, A. (2004), *An Agenda for a Growing Europe: The Sapir Report*, Oxford.

Schick, G. and J. Märkt (2002), Braucht die EU eine eigene Steuer?, *Deutsche Steuer-Zeitung* 90 (1-2), 27-35.

Schratzenstaller, M. and B. Berghuber (2006), Finanzierungsalternativen zum EU Budget, *Wifo Monatsberichte* 12/2006, 893-910.

Schreyer, M. (2001), The Own Resources System Needs Rethinking, *Intereconomics* 36 (5), 223-225.

Schüssel, W. (2006), Presentation of the Austrian Presidency's Programme, Speech by the President of the European Council, Federal Chancellor Wolfgang Schüssel, January 18, Brussels.

Schwartz, T. (1994), Representation as Agency and the Pork Barrel Paradox, *Public Choice* 78 (1), 3-21.

SEP (2005), Own Resources: Evolution of the System in a EU of 25, Study for the European Parliament, Study Group for European Policies, Brussels.

Shackleton, M. (1990), *Financing the European Community*, London.

Shepsle, K.A. and B.R. Weingast (1982), Political Preferences for the Pork Barrel, A Generalization, *American Journal of Political Science* 25 (1), 96-111.

Sinn, H.-W. and H. Feist (1997), Eurowinners and Eurolosers: The Distribution of Seigniorage Wealth in EMU, *European Journal of Political Economy* 13 (4), 665-689.

Stark, J. (1996), Die künftige Finanzierung des EU-Haushaltes und der Beitrag der Bundesrepublik Deutschland, *Integration* 19 (3), 159-163.

Stiglitz, J.E. (1994), *Finanzwissenschaft*, Munich.

Strauss-Kahn, D. (2004), *Building a Political Europe. 50 Proposals for Tomorrow's Europe*, 1st ed., Brussels.

Turnovec, F., J.W. Mercik and M. Mazurkiewicz (2007), Duality of Power in the European Parliament, Paper presented at the First World Meeting of the Public Choice Society, Amsterdam, March 29-April 1.

Tversky, A. and D. Kahneman (1986), Rational Choice and the Framing of Decisions, *Journal of Business* 59 (4), 251-278.

United Kingdom Presidency of the EU (2005), European Union Financial Perspectives 2007-13 – United Kingdom Presidency Proposal, December 5, Brussels.

von Hagen, J. (1992), Budgeting Procedures and Fiscal Performance in the European Community, *European Economy. Reports and Studies* 3, 315-418.

von Hagen, J. (2005), *Political Economy of Fiscal Institutions*, GESY Discussion Paper 149, Bonn.

Walthes, F. (1996), *Europäischer Finanzausgleich*, Berlin.

Wigger, B. U. and U. Wartha (2003), How to Allocate the Power to Tax in Europe?, in: Holler, M.J. (Ed.), *European Governance*, Tübingen, 173-196.

Wilson, J.D. (1999), Theories of Tax Competition, *National Tax Journal* 52 (2), 269-304.

Winner, H. (2005), Has Tax Competition Emerged in OECD Countries? Evidence from Panel Data, *International Tax and Public Finance* 12 (5), 667-687.

Wissenschaftlicher Beirat (1998), Neuordnung des Finanzierungssystems der Europäischen Gemeinschaft, Wissenschaftlicher Beirat beim Bundesministerium für Wirtschaft und Technologie, statement, Bonn.

SPRINGER NATURE

GPSR Compliance

The European Union's (EU) General Product Safety Regulation (GPSR) is a set of rules that requires consumer products to be safe and our obligations to ensure this.

If you have any concerns about our products, you can contact us on ProductSafety@springernature.com

In case Publisher is established outside the EU, the EU authorized representative is:

Springer Nature Customer Service Center GmbH
Europaplatz 3
69115 Heidelberg, Germany

FSC
www.fsc.org
MIX
Papier | Fördert gute Waldnutzung
FSC® C083411

Kolibri 360 GmbH
Ferdinand-Jühlke-Straße 7
99095 Erfurt, Deutschland
produktsicherheit@kolibri360.de